Stirring It

Feminist Perspectives on The Past and Present
Advisory Editorial Board

Lisa Adkins, *University of The West of England, UK*
Harriet Bradley, *University of Sunderland, UK*
Barbara Caine, *University of Sydney, Australia*
Sara Delamont, *University of Wales College of Cardiff, UK*
Mary Evans, *University of Kent at Canterbury, UK*
Gabriele Griffin, *Nene College, UK*
Jalna Hanmer, *University of Bradford, UK*
Maggie Humm, *University of East London, UK*
Sue Lees, *University of North London, UK*
Diana Leonard, *University of London, UK*
Terry Lovell, *University of Warwick, UK*
Maureen McNeil, *University of Birmingham, UK*
Ann Phoenix, *University of London, UK*
Caroline Ramazanoglu, *University of London, UK*
Sue Scott, *University of Manchester, UK*
Janet Siltanen, *University of Edinburgh, UK*
Dale Spender, *Australia*
Penny Summerfield, *University of Lancaster, UK*
Martha Vicinus, *University of Michigan, USA*
Claire Wallace, *University of Lancaster, UK*
Christine Zmroczek, *Roehampton Institute of Higher Education, UK*

Stirring It:
Challenges for Feminism

Edited by
Gabriele Griffin, Marianne Hester, Shirin Rai
and Sasha Roseneil

UK	Taylor & Francis Ltd, 4 John St., London WC1N 2ET
USA	Taylor & Francis Inc., 1900 Frost Road, Suite 101, Bristol, PA 19007

© Selection and editorial material copyright Gabriele Griffin, Marianne Hester, Shirin Rai and Sasha Roseneil, 1994

All rights reserved. No part of this publication may be reproduced, stored in a retrieval system, or transmitted, in any form or by any means, electronic, mechanical, photocopying, recording, or otherwise, without permission in writing from the Publisher.

First published 1994

A Catalogue Record for this book is available from the British Library

ISBN 0 7484 0213 6
ISBN 0 7484 0214 4 pbk

Library of Congress Cataloging-in-Publication Data are available on request

Series cover design by Amanda Barragry.

Typeset in 11/13pt Times
by Franklin Graphics, Southport

Printed in Great Britain by Burgess Science Press, Basingstoke on paper which has a specified pH value on final paper manufacture of not less than 7.5 and is therefore 'acid free'.

Contents

Introduction	Stirring It: Challenges for Feminism *Gabriele Griffin, Marianne Hester, Shirin Rai and Sasha Roseneil*	1
Section I	**Feminist Politics in Action**	9
Introduction		11
Chapter 1	Paying Our Disrespects to the Bloody States We're In: Women, Violence, Culture and the State *Ailbhe Smyth*	13
Chapter 2	History of Women's Liberation Movements in Britain: A Reflective Personal History *Jill Radford*	40
Chapter 3	Nondecision-Making. . . A Management Guide to Keeping Women's Interest Issues Off the Political Agenda *Jennifer Marchbank*	59
Section II	**Disrupting Sexual and Gender Identities?**	71
Introduction		73
Chapter 4	Dire Straights? Contemporary Rehabilitations of Heterosexuality *Sue Wilkinson and Celia Kitzinger*	75

v

Contents

Chapter 5	Flaunting the Body: Gender and Identity in American Feminist Performance *Angelika Czekay*	92
Chapter 6	Anti-Monogamy: A Radical Challenge to Compulsory Heterosexuality? *Becky Rosa*	107
Section III	**Imaging and Imagining**	121
Introduction		123
Chapter 7	Angry Young Women? Sex and Class in Nell Dunn's *Up the Junction* *Kim Clancy*	127
Chapter 8	'Not Happy but Hopeful': Readers of Catherine Cookson in the North-East of England *Sue Thornham, Elaine Brown and Angela Werndly*	142
Chapter 9	Splitting the Difference: Adventures in the Anatomy and Embodiment of Women *Margrit Shildrick and Janet Price*	156
Section IV	**Women's Studies and Feminist Practice**	181
Introduction		183
Chapter 10	Interventions in Hostile Territory *Lynda Birke*	185
Chapter 11	Eastern European Women with Western Eyes *Nora Jung*	195
Chapter 12	Relations among Women: Using the Group to Unite Theory and Experience *Wendy Hollway*	211
Notes on Contributors		223
Index		227

Introduction

Stirring It: Challenges for Feminism

Gabriele Griffin, Marianne Hester, Shirin Rai and Sasha Roseneil

The title of this book — *Stirring It: Challenges for Feminism* - suggests that the articles appearing herein not only deal with troublesome issues but also intend to make trouble. Challenging orthodoxies, questioning the taken for granted — stirring it — is the business of feminists, and we are at a historical moment where feminist dynamism is much needed.

We are writing this introduction at the end of a year — 1993 — which has seen women and feminism under fire around the world. In the territories of the former Yugoslavia women's bodies have become the battleground for men conducting ethnic warfare. In Britain a wave of moral outrage and condemnation has been directed at lone mothers, who have been held responsible for everything from juvenile crime to the decline of Western civilization, and at feminists, who have been accused of sowing the seeds for the collapse of the family. Amongst the chattering classes and in the academic world, in Britain and the US, 'political correctness' is now established as public enemy number one, represented as the supposed tyranny of feminists and minorities over free speech and common sense. Whether we label these developments 'backlash' (Faludi, 1992; Walby, 1993) or see them as part of a project of 'patriarchal reconstruction' (Smart, 1989), they all represent serious challenges for feminists and feminism.

Deeds and discourses of misogyny and anti-feminism need to be understood within a theoretical framework which recognizes women's agency, the power and significance of women's pro-actions and women's re-actions and resistances. The widespread, systematic raping of women in the former Yugoslavia has called forth a vigorous feminist response. Feminists in Serbia and Croatia are protesting against the war and its sexual violence, and are establishing support services for women who have been raped. Feminists from outside the former Yugoslavia have offered assistance, and have taken the issue of rape in war to the United Nations Conference on Human Rights, placing it firmly on the international agenda.

Meanwhile discourses which blame unmarried women and feminists for every social problem afflicting present-day Britain, and which identify the ideological hold of feminism within the academy as stronger than that of the men of the Enlightenment, must be understood as a response to the very real challenge that feminism has posed to male domination in the family and in intellectual production (Roseneil, 1993). These women-blaming discourses operate by a process of reversal (McNeil, 1991). They invert dominant power relations, constructing single mothers as the oppressors of 'properly' constituted families (e.g., Murray, 1990) and tax-payers, and presenting feminist writers and thinkers as the group which rules universities and publishing, and which censors and suppresses the work of good men, dead and alive. Whilst these discourses serve to mystify women's ongoing oppressions, they have arisen in response to feminism's success and influence.

One of the most important examples of the success of feminism in recent years is the growth of Women's Studies. With the spread of undergraduate and postgraduate courses in Women's Studies throughout British education, with the explosion of feminist research and writing that has accompanied this and the strengthening of networks of feminist researchers, new problems and challenges have come to the fore. These include the challenge of understanding women's agency and its relationship to the material and discursive structuring of women's lives by patriarchy, the challenge of theorizing differences among women, and the diversity and fluidity of our experiences and identities.

Women's Studies grew out of, and was informed by, the practice and debates of feminists during the 1970s and 1980s. One of its central preoccupations was, and in many respects continues to be, the relationship between feminist theory and feminist practice. An unfortunate development has been the tendency to represent this as a split between the then (when we practised) and now (when we theorize), and as a split between women in academe (the theorizers) and women outside academe (the practitioners), thus losing sight of the crucial links between feminist theorizing and practice, whereby practice informs theory, theory informs practice, in an ongoing spiral.

Feminist practice is predominantly considered in one of two ways: it is either nostalgically and historically located as something that happened during the period of the Women's Liberation Movement (apparently no longer in existence), when every woman, at least within the movement, seemed to do it. Alternatively, it is regarded as something that is now done by those newly disenfranchised within feminism, women working in women's refuges, health promotion campaigns, anti-war activities etc. Where the former, historically inflected position fails to do justice to current feminist campaigning and activism, the latter reinforces the notion that theorizing is not feminist work and is in some way unrelated to practice.

We need to give more regard to the divisiveness of this model of feminism, with its replication of centre/margin dichotomies which are depressingly familiar from malestream thinking, and its mirroring of hierarchies of value which maintain that there is something worthier in the word than in the deed — or is it the other way round? Whichever way value is attributed, it is the hierarchy that should be worrying us. We need to ask ourselves what investment we as feminists can possibly have in such hierarchization and whose interests are served by supporting it.

We should further be alerted to the question of women's agency because we may be doing ourselves a gross disservice by aligning the idea of agency simply with a narrow interpretation of feminist practice or activism as exemplified by the campaigns of the Women's Liberation Movement in the 1960s and 1970s. Feminist activism is not a phenomenon of the past. Fighting for our rights — if that is how we read 'activism' — is of utmost and continued importance at a time when, for example, legislative interventions seek to re-regulate women's lives and control over our bodies by exploding the boundaries of the minimum wage and changing the laws governing such issues as access to housing, reproductive intervention, child benefit, and the pensionable age, all of which potentially affect many women. Battles about these issues cannot be regarded as fought and won. We must not consider links to the Women's Liberation Movement of the late 1960s and the 1970s as historical and now severed: we need to work at keeping the past alive in our consciousness — not least because, in many respects, it is a feminist success story. We also need to clarify the developments that have taken (and need to) take place in order to enhance and secure women's position, and to change a society which continues to exploit the gender and other differences it constructs.

Students new to Women's Studies and to feminism in the 1990s need both information about the history of feminist struggles and an understanding that the direction of historical change is fought over. In terms of the history of women's movements, it is important to see knowledge and action as located in relation to context; the opportunities available to and the limitations imposed upon women vary across time and space (Hester, 1992; Griffin, 1993). This is made evident in the first section of this volume in which each chapter addresses the issue of feminist action in terms of its locatedness within particular social, institutional and political contexts. The essays also highlight how feminist agendas have changed over time, in dialogue with general historical developments. Thus where Jill Radford's chapter, about the 1970s and 1980s, offers an account of feminist activism which focuses on the personal and on issues of feminist campaigns in the British context, Ailbhe Smyth's chapter reflects on the problematic of nationalisms and how women feature within this. Jennifer Marchbank's essay, on the other hand, addresses women's marginalization and strategies within specific institutions in which, by now, we are supposed to have arrived.

Women's Studies is an obvious arena for dissemination and discussion of such knowledge. It is not the only one, but it is a crucial one in a world where fragmentation and general economic malaise have led to many women feeling timid about the possibilities of effecting change. It is important, therefore, to recognize Women's Studies as a form of feminist activism which encourages women to look at our situation in society, to consider how historically it has been shaped (by women as well as by patriarchy), and how we can mobilize for change. Some women who wish to make changes in their lives may find education a good entry point. Women should not be made to feel uncomfortable because that is the path they have chosen. They will have enough battles on their hands, being made to justify to the world 'outside' why they are doing Women's Studies. Additionally, we should not assume that because someone does Women's Studies in the academy, she is therefore not also active (and note the 'also') in other forms of feminist endeavour. It is an insult to women working in women's refuges and crisis centres, women's health promotion campaigns, helplines etc. who also do Women's Studies to suggest by implication or directly that they are in some way less 'worthy' in one role than another.

Feminist battles are about fighting women's continued oppressions in a variety of contexts. In present-day Britain they are about understanding and resisting a period of restrictiveness, a period of long-term Conservative government and backlash against the gains we have made. The current backdrop for feminist action is one of the reaffirmation of 'traditional family values' (an ideal/l, never a reality), of cuts in benefit and other measures used to promote this insitutionalization of heterosexuality, by scaring women back to the hearth, as well as the presentation of the perpetual threat of violence against women promoted by the media. Set against this is women's activism, politically and culturally, in seeking to understand how we are regulated through, for example, the control of our bodies and our sexualities.

This is what the second section of *Stirring It* addresses. The women who have fronted this kind of activism have been women whose very understanding of their differences from a heteropatriarchal norm has enabled them to resist and reject the imperatives of that norm. Sue Wilkinson and Celia Kitzinger's and Becky Rosa's chapters offer lesbian feminist critiques of heterosexuality and monogamy and their validation/s, while Angelika Czekay's chapter suggests how women may be able to reclaim the ownership of our bodies and sexuality through performance art. This section offers one example of how an understanding of difference can be used constructively to critique circumscriptions of women's roles in heteropatriarchy and to promote women's rights to ourselves.

The remaining sections of the book continue to look at troublesome issues for contemporary feminism — women's agency in cultural production and questions of difference. The understanding of the importance of women's cultural figuration which informs Czekay's chapter also forms the basis for the third section in this volume which considers the imaging and imagining of women and the ideological implications of these. The chapter by Clancy, Thornham *et al.* and Shildrick and Price all ask questions about how the presentation of women and the female body has served to express anxieties about female strength and female power: the strength to flaunt sexual desire, to bear and cope, to procreate. These chapters not only demonstrate female agency within the academy but also suggest the continual interplay of patriarchal demands and female resistance which underlie feminist action.

Feminist action is also crucial in the context of issues which concern differences between women. Race, nationality, ethnicity, as well as sexuality and dis/ability, are all terms which delineate boundaries intimately constructed and sustained through images and imaging of women. Here women's selves are inscribed both as definers and authenticators of cultures, of values. Women's silences and voices are both expropriated for the purpose of authenticating discourses that engage in creating, disputing, defending boundaries. Violence, and the threat of violence — that is part of the state and the civil (*sic*) society — sustains silences, and prevents women from speaking and from fighting back.

A shift is starting to manifest itself amongst feminists which honours our diversity but also seeks to use difference constructively. While a recognition of difference remained the prioritized agenda through the 1980s, in the 1990s we see the debate moving on to the process of 'coalition-building' (Liddle and Rai, 1993; Yuval-Davis, 1993). We still lurch from celebrating difference that those being celebrated do not wish for, to disengagement because it is too difficult to engage with the 'other' on terms that are not necessarily our own. For instance, black critiques of the dominant white feminism(s) have brought to light the problems of a friendship that is not informed by sensitivity or understanding.

The question of confronting difference is one fraught with dangers for women. There is a sense in which despite our celebration of difference we still shy away from confrontation. Who is to speak and how? Can only those who experience particular oppressions speak out against them? How do we confront issues of difference within Women's Studies? This is what the fourth section of *Stirring It* examines.

While both Birke and Jung address the problem of territories and boundaries — national, cultural, sexual and those that are inscribed on the feminist intellectual terrain — Hollway makes us aware of how comforting it is not to confront these boundaries while never being able to forget that they exist. 'Sister/outsider' is a theme that makes us all feel uncomfortable. This is also the reason why the question of boundaries and negotiating them is so important. Birke speaks of being an outsider-scientist in Women's Studies gatherings, as well as remaining always a woman/lesbian-outsider in her laboratory. For Jung, meanwhile, the 'Western Eye' view of Eastern Europe represents not only the dynamics of international power but also problems of representation. Hollway's research brings together the themes of difference and that of building bridges in her study of a support group in which mature women students on a university course learn from each other to confront and negotiate difference. Ultimately, stirring the sediment of sisterly dis/harmonies in this way becomes a part of discovering new paths of development for feminism.

References

FALUDI, SUSAN (1992) *Backlash: The Undeclared War Against Women,* London, Chatto and Windus.
GRIFFIN, GABRIELE (1993) *Heavenly Love? Lesbian Images in 20th Century Women's Writing,* Manchester, Manchester University Press.
HESTER, MARIANNE (1992) *Lewd Women and Wicked Witches: A Study of the Dynamics of Male Domination,* London, Routledge.
LIDDLE, JOANNA and RAI, SHIRIN (1993) 'Between Feminism and Orientalism', in KENNEDY, MARY, LUBELSKA, CATHY and WALSH, VAL (Eds) *Making Connections: Women's Studies, Women's Movements, Women's Lives,* London, Taylor and Francis.
McNEIL, MAUREEN (1991) 'Making and Not Making the Difference: The Gender Politics of Thatcherism', in FRANKLIN, SARAH, LURY, CELIA and STACY, JACKIE (Eds) *Off-Centre,* London, HarperCollins.
MURRAY, CHARLES (1990) *The Emerging British Underclass,* Choice in Welfare Series no. 2, London, Health and Welfare Unit, Institute of Economic Affairs.

ROSENEIL, SASHA (1993) 'The Coming of Age of Feminist Sociology: Some Issues of Practice and Theory for the Next Twenty Years', paper presented to the British Sociological Association Annual Conference, University of Essex.

SMART, CAROL (1989) 'Power and the Politics of Child Custody', in SMART, CAROL and SEVENHUIJSEN, SELMA (Eds) *Child Custody and the Politics of Gender,* London, Routledge.

WALBY, SYLVIA (1993) ' "Backlash" in Historical Context', in KENNEDY, MARY, LUBELSKA, CATHY and WALSH, VAL (Eds) *Making Connections: Women's Studies, Women's Movements, Women's Lives,* London, Taylor and Francis.

YUVAL-DAVIS, NIRA (1993) 'Beyond Difference: Women and Coalition Politics', in KENNEDY, MARY, LUBELSKA, CATHY and WALSH, VAL (Eds) *Making Connections: Women's Studies, Women's Movements, Women's Lives,* London, Taylor and Francis.

Section I

Feminist Politics in Action

Introduction

The three chapters in this section provide very different examples of both feminist and *anti*-feminist politics in action, reminding us that the study of feminist praxis is (or should be) central to Women's Studies. Ailbhe Smyth talks about feminist action in the context of war, colonialism and nationalism (in Ireland and elsewhere); Jill Radford documents her own involvement in and the activities of feminist groups and campaigns during the 1970s and 1980s (in England); while Jennifer Marchbank takes a look at specifically anti-feminist strategies in local government (in Scotland). The chapters outline some of the many different concerns of women from different backgrounds of race/ethnicity, class, sexuality and location; yet they also show the incredible similarities in the dynamics and processes of their oppression as women.

A common theme is the need for feminism – as ideas, politics, and action – to be visible and upfront. Feminist campaigns have made, and do make, a positive impact on wider political agendas and public policy as well as on the individual and collective lives of women. Ailbhe Smyth describes how feminist activity has been of central importance to the resetting of political agendas in Ireland: how feminism 'has launched the most enduring, widespread and resonant challenge to the ideology and politics of our nation-state'. By voicing feminist criticisms and concerns, 'women ... refusing to pay their respects to the state they are in', a redefinition of nationalism and national identity is taking place. Jill Radford talks, as one of her examples, about the changes brought about through the local activities of feminists in Winchester. The women who made up Winchester Women's Liberation Group in the late 1970s were very diverse (as was the case with many women's liberation groups at that time). Linking the personal with the political, the group explored

Gabriele Griffin, Marianne Hester, Shirin Rai, Sasha Roseneil

differences and experiences, creating individual change and empowerment, as well as developing a number of successful local campaigns and actions.

Jennifer Marchbank's very different example of anti-feminist activity within local government shows how feminism, clearly seen as a force for change, is perceived as a direct threat to most of the local authority employees concerned to maintain the (male) status quo. She describes the strategies used by the latter to ensure that feminist politics were discredited and eradicated from the local authority's childcare agenda. Another of the anti-feminist strategies she describes, that of 'issue suppression', highlights the importance of making visible feminist activity. Potential gains for women can easily be undermined by the process of actively ignoring, not identifying or not 'naming' the ideas and actions of feminists. But this problem is not confined merely to determined anti-feminists; it can also apply within the feminist community and to Women's Studies courses.

Ailbhe Smyth, for instance, talks about the problems that arise from the silence surrounding the concerns of Irish and Northern Irish women in the debates about difference in Britain. Jill Radford discusses how the history of feminist activity is being re-presented on some Women's Studies courses in ways that falsify and negate the crucial links between feminist theory and action. She argues for more obvious links to be made between Women's Studies and feminist politics, and for Women's Studies to become part of the development of the 'next wave' of a feminist movement with a global vision.

Chapter 1

Paying Our Disrespects to the Bloody States We're In: Women, Violence, Culture and the State

Ailbhe Smyth

1 Global Question:

What Violence?
Whose Culture?
Which State?
And undergirding and overarching:
Which Women?

Each one of these themes is both an entirety in itself and inextricably linked with the others. Each one is freighted and fraught, burdened and bent under a weight of intricately inflected meanings, all complex, often contradictory, and crucial for all of us, diverse though we be, as feminists.

I could say that each is crucial to feminist *discourse*, which is another way of saying not quite the same thing, but I won't, because it's not enough: feminist practice (in which I include feminist thinking) needs real live heart and body and head and soul feminists to challenge and protest and take up the issues and do something about them. BRING BACK POLITICS, and the material, messy world of the everyday, because that's where it hurts, in women's bodies and hearts and heads and souls. And that's what we need to be talking and thinking and doing something about.

You think that's too concrete for Women's Studies? Well, some days I wake up and read the paper, like today or almost any day, and I think that Women's Studies is too abstract for feminist politics. Discourse — I'm picking on it because we're all doing it — is no protection against the violations of spirit and flesh. The terrain of discourse is a safe place, but a little inaccessible when you're out there in the battle zone, on your own homefront.

I am daunted by the vastness, the complexity and the immediacy of these themes and the questions they force us to confront: what are the relations between them, and how is feminism, how are feminists, to change the (bloody) state(s) women are in?

I am a middle-class, middle-aged white European feminist,
I know how to say where I'm coming from.
Whatever I may do,
I have learnt how not to say
the words that keep other women there.
I have a job, a house, a pension,
principles (for what they're worth),
and the privileges and guarantees
accruing to a woman like me
from all the above.

But still.

I live in a state of confusion and disbelief
I live in a state of anger and outrage.
If you don't believe me, look into my heart
while I try to find the words
to stiffen my own backbone
to reach beyond my fear
of thickening violence
and what it does
to all of us, in cruel solidarity.

Words in my head and on my tongue
flimsy shapes and sounds
insubstantial instruments
ambiguous respite, false refuge.
too precise or too subtle
to stop brutality in its tracks.

Mass rape devastates each woman separately and individually; policies of collective control are lived as acts of individual annihilation, in genocidal/gynocidal wars. But each woman bears the mark, and the hurt, in her body, in her head, in her soul, in her sense of herself.[1]

Women are dying of hunger or thirst or heat or cold or curable

Women, Violence, Culture and the State

disease or the myriad ills consequent on stupid Eurocentric 'development' policies and wicked multi-national spoliation; half-living (i.e., half-dying) in poverty and indigence because the North/the West is so fat, lazy and crassly indifferent, because powerful nations put neither their backs nor their hearts into the enforcement of the 'Universal' Declaration of Human Rights.[2] Murdered, mutilated, assaulted, abused, used, bought, sold and bartered, silenced, beaten, kicked, punched, physically and psychically devastated at home, at school, at the market, at work, at play, in republics, kingdoms, colonies, protectorates (oh irony), in every state. All these are fact, all documented[3] (French, 1992).

Don't take it personally, they say. But I do. How else am I to take it? Women, wherever and whoever, are not abstractions. If I don't take it personally, I might as well surrender my feminism. Without the personal, the passionate, the particular, why would I give it more than a passing thought? But the swamp of overwrought emotionalism is as much a trap as the clichéd desert of academicism.

The very seriousness of these themes, their urgency and strong affective undertow make me reticent. Trying to make sense of the lethal twists and turns of patriarchal sadism, at war or at peace (but when is it ever not at war?), from place to place and time to time, in all its ordinary and hideous forms is a necessary task, but not in itself a protection. Without knowledge there can be no resistance, but bare knowledge is not a shield.

> As I was saying learning, thinking, living in the beginning of being men and women often has in it very little of real being. (Stein, 1989, p. 53).

Can sense be made of such violence and can sense put a halt to it? Stories and poems, analyses and theories are such frail defence against the relentless battering of women by men.

> When she fled
> with the children
> she left the house
> in such a state
>
> with the bread
> gone green mould
> and the tea
> half drunk in cups.

Ailbhe Smyth

> Kids' clothes
> sour memories
> and echoes of voices loud,
>
> and that smell
> of something rotting
> decay it was, decay.
>
> That cobwebby smell
> that walked up to you
> in the hall and said,
>
> 'The Woman who lived here
> pissed fear'...
>
> (Rita Ann Higgins: 'The Woman Who Lived Here', 1990, p. 90)

You cannot live, in any real meaning of the word, in such a state of fear. Some days, like now as I'm writing, I fear it cannot be stopped, for the prevailing definition of masculinity in so many of its states depends upon the availability of bodies for its cause. And the bodies of those who are denied economic, social and political power are always and ever available and expendable.

Women's sexuality is used as a pawn in men's power games, and classically so in struggles over 'ownership' of national territory. Trojan women, constantly re-constructed. Symbols, functions and instruments of the nation, guarantors of its 'legitimacy', reproducers of its destiny, targets and prizes for its enemies. Women's bodies are national property, common currency, boundary between 'us' and 'them', there for the taking and the invading and the expending (Anthias and Yuval-Davies, 1989; Enloe, 1988, 1989; Hélie-Lucas, 1991; Jayawardena, 1986; Kandiyoti, 1991).

Whatever the official story — so often glossed over, justified as 'legitimate' defence or just plain lost — the truth is that so many of our states have been founded and are maintained by and through coercion, bloody struggle and the redemptive glorification of violence:

> We must accustom ourselves to the thought of arms, to the sight of arms, to the use of arms. We may make mistakes in the beginning and shoot the wrong people; but bloodshed is a cleansing and sanctifying thing, and the nation which regards it

as the final horror has lost its manhood. (Padraig Pearse (1916), Irish Independence Leader, in Moran, 1991, p. 17)

The constitutive elements of Irish nationhood and its relation with the state combine in historically and culturally specific ways.[4] For all that, there is nothing unique or distinctive about the strategies it has used to construct itself (Goldring, 1993) — which does nothing to lessen my fear. Between homes and wars, private and public, local and global, nations and multi-nations, there are too many connections, even though I cannot always see them clearly.

2a Irish Question: So What's the Question?

There are approximately two and half million women in Ireland, give or take a few hundred, as they do, relentlessly or indifferently, every year.[5]
What is the state of women in that state which is not one, but two?

> I was trapped in the wrong house
>   the wrong dream
> and soldiers kept on banging
>   at that unknown door
>
>   (Catherine Byron: 'Night Flight to Belfast', 1985, p. 41)

The Irish Situation
The Irish Problem
The Irish Question

Always skewed, because the form of the question shapes the nature of the answer. We make jokes, to blunt pain as well as puzzlement: 'As soon as the Brits find an answer, the Irish change the question'. We make jokes to mask indifference: 'Well, nobody is dead [as a result of the explosion]. At the end of this opera, everybody is dead'.[6]
So many euphemisms, elisions and evasions: the 'Ancient Quarrel', the 'Troubles': those words mean war, whatever the sound they make:

> Killing Enniskillen, killing
> Enniskillen will not linger

Ailbhe Smyth

> on front page news
> On front page news they're only Irish
> and of course it happens there
> all the time
>
> (Smyth, 1991, p. 136)

War as in maiming and death: 3,000 people killed and countless thousands injured in the North of Ireland in the past twenty-three years: as I am writing this, I hear the news that paramilitaries carried out thirty-five shootings, eleven bomb attacks and sixty-three hijackings during the weekend (Loyalists this time, as it happened; next time, retaliation time, the IRA will take its killing turn; and the troops will turn on both, for this civil war has three sides);[7] war as in weapons, bullets, bombs, the arms industry; war as in armed forces: occupying troops ('our boys'), and paramilitaries (someone else's boys); war as in Internment, imprisonment, the Prevention of Terrorism Act, detention without trial, trial without jury; war as in the 'humiliating and degrading treatment of strip searching' of women as of men (McWilliams, 1991); war as in flight and exile and emigration; war as in poverty, unemployment, and a stagnant economy; war as in homelessness and the destruction of family life; war as in intimidation and victimization;[8] war as in increased vandalism and anarchy (Leonard, 1992); war as in the everyday price paid by women:

> For many Northern Irish families, especially those in working-class areas, violence has become part of daily living. Under these circumstances, it is often the woman, in her role as wife or mother, who has the heavy responsibility of trying to bring up a family in a situation similar to a war environment.
>
> (Edgerton, 1986, p. 77)

War as in women's fear of men trained and equipped to fight and hurt and kill, schooled to prove their manhood through militaristic violence (Enloe, 1989):

> Women in Northern Ireland live in what can only be described as an armed patriarchy. . . . The point is simply that the power gained outside the home may be deployed within it, adding an extra dimension to all of the means men normally have for oppressing women and engendering fear. (Evason, 1982, cited in Edgerton, 1986, p. 79)

The 'extra dimension' has now been the norm in Northern Ireland, with repercussions in the Republic and in Britain, for almost a quarter of a century. Is that prolonged duration one of the reasons why the 'situation' is so rarely referred to as war?[9] Because none of us (I mean all of us, in Ireland and in Britain) knows how to end the war, we call it something else so as to deny its ever-present reality.[10] Distance, whether of language or geography, makes the heart grow cooler. And distant drums have a less than urgent beat. There is a war being waged in the North of Ireland, and calling it by any other name will neither sweeten it nor bring it to a quick and tidy end.

Yet this 'war that no one can win' (Ward, 1988) spills bloodily over and beyond the war zone, wherever that is:[11]

> In the seventh zone
> stands the gate to the no-go area
> Go, God help you, there you're on your own.
>
> (Paula Meehan, 'No Go Area', 1991, p. 31)

Women are indeed on their own, unshielded, in the no-go/no-holds-barred area of anything goes in war. 'Information' and 'security' as these words figure in Irish and British political rhetoric about Northern Ireland *never* refer to the 'no-go area' of men's violence against women in 'interpersonal relations'.[12] That is privately-owned territory, outside the jurisdiction, a personal matter, beyond 'politics' and the affairs of the state.

We (I mean in Ireland and Britain) know remarkably little about the links between militarism/paramilitarism and violence against women as a consequence of the continuing war in Northern Ireland (Leonard, 1993; McLaughlin, forthcoming). Why is this so? Such gaping holes in our knowledge cannot be accidental. Whose powerful interests are being protected by such deep wells of silence?

Monica McWilliams records that when Derry Women's Aid raised the issue of 'domestic' violence in the 1970s, the paramilitaries became angry because the women were refusing to distinguish between the violence involved in 'political punishments' (i.e., as carried out by the paramilitaries), the violence inflicted by state forces and the violence inflicted on women by their husbands.[13] She observes that during Internment, in the 1970s, while women in Northern Ireland protested strenuously against the violence of the British troops, they were actually 'less likely to protest against the violence of their male partners in their own homes' (McWilliams, 1991, p. 84).

Women are coerced and intimidated into silence — in itself a serious violation of human freedom — in many ways, not least of which is the primacy attributed to 'The Cause', always male, on whichever side. The Cause must never be betrayed, must never be represented as anything but wholly good and legitimate, even when, especially when, it is founded on the silent acquiescence of women and the smell of their fear.

It is 'widely known' that the circulation of pornographic publications and videos is an element in the paramilitary business empire. Paramilitary operations need money to buy guns to 'take' territory: women's bodies are one of the means. It is 'widely known' that the military forces are being sexually 'serviced': women's functions in war extend far beyond the stoking of the homes fires (see Enloe, 1988, 1989). All this is widely but not *specifically* known, as in investigated, researched, studied.[14]

Why not?
Wells of silence drowning floods of violence

More men than women or children have been killed in Northern Ireland. But gender and number of the dead are not the only measure of the impact and seriousness of war. The war damages people in gender-specific and class-specific ways: physically, psychologically and emotionally and in terms of their personal, social, economic and political experiences and possibilities. Catholic *and* Protestant women in certain urban working-class areas, and on the border, suffer more than middle-class women, for this is a war fought on working-class terrain.[15]

One of the direct consequences of the war is the complex impact it has had on the political mobilization of women. It is abundantly clear that Northern Irish women are politically active. Their perseverance and effectiveness in campaigning on social and economic issues is remarkable in extremely adverse political circumstances. The prevailing ideology is deeply conservative, whether orange, unionist and Protestant, or green, nationalist and Catholic. But the political and democratic processes in the North have been truncated through the institution of Direct Rule, with the result that actual *opportunities* for participation in policy-making are severely limited. Further, the religious conservatism (on both sides of the sectarian divide) and the 'inward-looking nature of the society' (Davies and McLaughlin, 1991) are a major brake on women's formal participation in the public sphere (Edgerton, 1986; Shannon, 1992; Ward and McMinn, 1985).

Most importantly, the development of the women's movement was severely restricted by the fact of war (Evason, 1991). Social movements do not flourish in times of turmoil when the hatches of change are firmly battened down. In situations of national conflict, women's demands and concerns get pushed right to the end, if not right off, the political agenda (Ridd, 1986). Women in Sinn Fein, for example, invested years of energy before the party agreed to incorporate a policy on abortion in its agenda. Monica McWilliams recounts how a campaigning group of Protestant and Catholic women 'took the Liverpool boat-and-train to London where they lobbied their MPs to oppose the Social Security Bill which was going through Parliament at that time. They were appalled to find that their own political representatives were more interested in opposing the Anglo-Irish Agreement . . . and hence refused to meet them on the grounds that they were too busy' (McWilliams, 1991, p. 91).

While Northern Irish women have actively protested against both military and paramilitary violence, they have mobilized principally 'as the guardians of family life and in the interests of the community rather than as fighters for women's benefits alone' (Roulston, 1989, p. 222).[16] Their individual interests — and even the admission that such interests have a material base — have had to be subordinated to their mobilization in the name of the collective interest of nation and family (Roulston, 1989). The status quo becomes all the more ferociously static and repressive when under threat:

> I believe that the husband is the head of the wife and the home. I believe that the father should be prophet, priest and king in his home. As king, he should exercise rulership. (Rev. Ian Paisley, In Fairweather *et al.*, 1984).

Of course, the time is never 'right' for women's challenge to the patriarchy and its operations: the affairs of the state, threatened or not, take automatic precedence. Women must remain subject to the interests of the prophet, priest and king, and if they do not, they are wiped out.

The annihilating violence of total silence

Silencing is most stiflingly experienced by lesbians: there is no published material on the situation or experiences of lesbians in Northern Ireland.[17]

In so far as sexuality has been studied at all, the focus of even feminist research and analysis has been on heterosexual women, although it is hardly the case that lesbians are protected by a special defence mechanism from the effects of poverty, war and violence. Lesbians have been centrally active in the most important campaigns of the women's movement, yet we know only in scattered, impressionistic and subjective ways what it signifies to be a lesbian or how the construction of homo/heterosexuality occurs in such a traditional, religious and strife-ridden culture. Geraldine Bradley, in a study of feminism in locally-based Belfast women's groups, found that while self-identification as feminist was problematic and highly volatile for almost all the groups she talked with, 'one of the most prevalent concerns seemed to be a worry about being mistaken for lesbians'. As one woman in the study commented: '[T]hey called us "a pack of lesbians" and the shock that I got was something unbelievable' (Bradley, 1992). Just last year, an International Women's Day event in Belfast City Hall went ahead despite a City Council ban on inviting lesbians. Lesbians are still not written in to the history of the movement because sexuality is not an upfront public feminist issue. Briege Gilhooly argues that this is 'part of the Irish feminist refusal to engage seriously with the politics of exclusion which operates not only within patriarchal institutions but within its own ranks' (Gilhooly, 1993). This politics of exclusion is immeasurably strengthened by the homogenizing ideologies of nationalism, whether republican or unionist, which depend for their mobilizing myths upon the acquiescence and availability of 'real' women, conveniently tethered to heterosexuality for more direct rule.

Carmel Roulston argues that 'the greatest success of the women's movement [in Northern Ireland] is perhaps that it continues to exist' (1989, p. 235). But it does so against the odds, riven with the divisive tensions generated by the war situation and at the cost of significant exclusions: the conflict over alignment with republicanism versus autonomous structures and strategies has been the major polarizing, and fragmenting, factor in the women's movement — which should be no surprise to anyone. There is nothing like a national emergency to keep women occupied, in their place and out of the women's movement.

> Sleepwalking woman,
> You shuttlecocked
> From jail to jail
> On dutiful visits,
> Your eyes were old
> They did not match

The bright hair
That made men watch you
Avidly.

(Linda Anderson, 'Gang-Bang Ulster Style', 1988, p. 144)

2b Irish Question: So Who's Asking?

This is not a manifesto (READ MY LIPS), but to make some — any — sense of women's state and the state, first state (the nature of) your state — unless we're bent on the wrong question.

The Irish Question
The National Question

I actually find it very hard to talk about our bloody state, I mean Ireland, when I'm in Britain. Even among feminists. It's not that British women don't listen, you do. You seem interested, curious, respectful almost (I'm taking it personally, you understand, because I don't live my life in a state of objectivity and because I couldn't keep the emotions in some separate place, even if I tried). I think you are *too* respectful and that is part of my difficulty (not all of it), because it signals (to me) that you believe I know more about it than you do; that I, as an Irish woman, must have information, views, a *position* which you cannot, really, be expected to have.

I want to know why YOU never ask the question? It seems to me that it's not even thought of as a question for British feminism. It's not on the agenda now and it hasn't been since the early 1970s, as perusal of recent histories of feminism in Britain amply demonstrates (Rossiter, 1992). Apart from *Spare Rib*, which took a consistently republican stance, I can think of *no* fairly recent publication in which *British* women address the issue of Ireland. This is all the more disturbing given the greater emphasis within the women's movement in Britain, since the 1980s, on issues of race, ethnicity, minorities and citizenship as these intersect with gender, and the centrality of the problematic — problem? — of 'difference' within feminist theory (Lovenduski and Randall, 1993).

Of course perspectives differ with 'nationality', but Irish women are not so very much more homogeneous as a group than British women, even though *some* of our differences are different. As a Southern middle-class, academic feminist, you can be sure that my understanding of what it means to be a woman in Ireland is every bit as different as yours from that of a working-class Northern Irish woman living in the war zone. You have become more sensitive to differences among women in your own country, but it is just as crucial to recognize that the story I tell is not the same as that of some other Irish woman whose social and political situation differs from mine. But representing the 'Other' as always one and the same is one of the principal mechanisms of all oppressive systems. In theory, in feminism, we know all about that. In practice, it needs to be applied to the non-homogeneous 'Otherness' of Irish women.

The Irish National Question remains the preserve of Irish women in Ireland and of Irish women in Britain. Why should this be so? I can't speak *for* you and you can't speak *for* me, but that need not prevent you, or me, from speaking about relations *between* us and about the socioeconomic and political systems which we resist and challenge in so many similar ways. In truth, I think the preserving is done by women on both sides of the water which separates us as patriarchal history, politics and economics, paradoxically, have not done.

Of course, Irish women are hyper-suspicious of anything whiffing even remotely of imperialist appropriation: doubly objectified, by colonialist and nationalist patriarchalism, it has taken a long time to get to the point of articulating a sense of ourselves as historical subjects, for 'we are human history, not natural history' (Boland, 1990, p. 38). In the light of a long and difficult colonial past, and the continuing divisiveness of Partition, there is a reluctance to simply hand over the hard-won gain of subjectivity on a plate.

'What's yours is mine and what's mine's my own', women to men, black to white, Irish to British: it takes a long time to heal the pain of having been owned, to believe that it is over, to know that you will not be (mis)represented as a freak show.

British colonial discourse produced the Irish as wild, emotional, charming but feckless: 'The Celtic genius (*sic*), sentiment as its main basis, with the love of beauty, charm, spirituality for its excellence, [had] ineffectualness and self-will for its deficit' (Matthew Arnold, 1962, quoted in Cairns and Richards, 1988, p. 48). The self-appointed task of the British was thus to rule the unruly Irish, and explain them to themselves, for their own benefit and for the greater glory of Britain. To be sure, the construction of the Irish as essentially inferior and subordinate, equally incapable of either coherent thought or self-government, greatly facilitated the goals of British expansionist imperialism.

Women, Violence, Culture and the State

It is banal to observe that racist and imperialist constructions do not disappear of themselves, from one day to the next, simply because an ex-colony claims or gains its independence. Those constructions continue to mark ex-colonizers and colonized discursively and materially. They continue to shape the way we think or choose not to think about one another, and to structure our economic relations, typically in ways which constrain the freedom and development of the new state (see Mohanty, 1991). Ex-colonizers do not readily relinquish their long-ingrained sense of superiority and go on 'blaming' the ex-colonized, with a remarkable absence of logic, for a perceived 'backwardness' they themselves have constructed. And the colonizers leave behind them a legacy of interiorized inferiority which is extraordinarily difficult to shake off — a sense of inferiority translated, at least in the case of Ireland, into a fiercely protective, often ludicrously misplaced and overly-compensatory pride in all things Irish — qualities, achievements, people.[18]

Racial Pride
It must be admitted
that our ancestors' blood was shed
that they were drowned
in the waves of their own blood
that they cried out
as they were sinking
that their cry echoed
echoed
echoed
and echoes still
in our veins.

And though that cry
is tearing us apart
we keep it alive
lest anyone believe
that our ancestors' labour
was not worthwhile.

(Aine Ni Ghlinn: 'Racial Pride', trans. from the Irish 'Mortas Cine', by Gabriel Fitzmaurice, Ni Ghlinn, 1993, p. 189)

Yet years of conditioning have done their work. In Britain, I feel compelled to demonstrate that I am at once Irish and radical, Irish and a-religious, Irish and pro-abortion, Irish and sophisticated, Irish and competent, Irish and sober (some of which I am by no means always *chez moi*). The knowledge that the compulsion is in my head lessens it not one whit: it's the negative effect of residual shame at coming from where I do come from. I get angry each and every time I am 'complimented' for displaying some stereotypically 'Irish' quality: I instantly want to be rude, not 'charming'; cerebral, not 'emotional'; ponderous, not loquacious; some other pigmentation entirely, not red-haired and freckled.

I am deeply, if not very rationally, irritated by the fact that I know, because I have to know, far more about you than you do about me; that I must be both Other and the same. I am exhausted trying to clarify the complexities of Irish referenda and judgments on abortion to women who are perfectly capable of reading the small print on very complicated legislation on all kinds of things in Britain. I am driven mad explaining that just because we speak, roughly, the same language, just because we both have Marks and Spencers and Principles, watch BBC and ITV and read more or less the same books from the same chains (I also get to watch Irish TV and to read Irish writing), just because we read the same feminist theorists and listen to k.d. lang (I also get to hear Dolores Keane and Mary Coughlan and Zrazy . . .), just because there is so much that we share in terms of Western economic and cultural and political structures, it does *not* mean that our experiences are in every respect and context the same, nor yet altogether other. There are common elements in our histories but we give shape and sense to them in different ways and from different power positions.

> If I say I want (sometimes) to be more like you, I also want you to *want* to be more like me.

I get angry and fiercely defensive when I come to Britain and find Ireland and the Irish being ignored, denigrated, discriminated against and cast as mindlessly violent apes, hopelessly primitive peasants and raving religious maniacs. You don't believe that? Read The *Sun*, like millions of British people do every day. Remember, if you're old enough, the 'No Blacks No Irish' signs on boarding house windows. Read the latest report of the London Irish Women's Centre (1993):

> We've been shocked at the level of suffering [Irish] women have been prepared to put up with over extraordinarily long periods of time . . . More than 44 per cent of Irish women are concentrated in the lowest manual grades, compared to 28 per cent of British-born white women. (Conversation with Angie Birtill, in *The Irish Times*, 10 June 1993).

It is not easy to be Irish in Britain. It is downright difficult if you are poor. And Irish women have to live with the devalorization inflicted on them by older generations in their own ethnic community, who emigrated complete with all their traditional values, if nothing else. 'They're dinosaurs', as one young Irish women emigrant put it recently.

> The Irish community in Britain retains its heritage, yet within that community women continue to be misrepresented to the point of absurdity. In the dominant journals of the Irish in Britain, for instance, women are consistently used as smiling decorations, happy to remain on the sidelines of events and always to support the traditional values of Catholicism and motherhood. (Cross, 1989, p. 6)

But neither is it easy to be British in Ireland. That also needs to be said and not respectfully garnered into some storehouse of ancient colonial guilts. To let Irish xenophobia off the hook is to reinforce a historically-constructed relationship in which the victim, having less power than the victimizer, is absolved of reasonable ethical and political responsibilities. For you to expect less of me than I do of you is to perpetuate an inequality that we need to erase. I am angry, and so ought you to be, when British feminists in Ireland tell me they feel they cannot or may not speak publicly about the state of women in the country because they might be seen as doing an 'imperialist gig'. I'm angry with myself and other Irish women for being so exclusionary: nationality is not ownership. I am outraged when, in media reports of a recent and particularly brutal case of sexual abuse (the 'Kilkenny' case), I come across constant references to the fact that the family was English, as if that in any way accounted for the most horrendous and prolonged acts of sexual violence (see Shanahan, 1992).

It is entirely ironic that while the New English in fifteenth- and sixteen-century Ireland feared they would be tainted with degeneracy through contact with the 'barbarous rudeness' of the Native Irish (Cairns and Richards, 1989), Irish nationalist ideology casts the English as pollutants of the purity and respectability of the Irish nation[19] — whether through prohibitions against the playing of 'foreign games',[20] censorship of films and publications, or Constitutional prohibitions against abortions being performed on Irish soil.

I am neither complaining nor blaming when I say these things. The ambivalances each (differently) experiences about the other need to be acknowledged if they are to be resisted and overcome. 'Polite' silence —

the antithesis of Irish 'rudeness' — on these matters actually hardens the cement of centuries of inequality and separateness. Ann Rossiter (1992) argues that one of the major casualties of the war in Northern Ireland has been the disappearance of solidarity between the British and Irish women's movements. And, I would add, between the movements North and South. The function of Partition is indeed to keep us apart. But we should be resisting this politics of 'divide and rule' and actively seeking out those interests we have in common.

The Irish Question is not reducible to questions of Irishness. It is every bit as much about Britishness. It is therefore not actually the Irish Question at all, but the British *and* Irish Question. And it is, or ought to be, part of the political business of feminism to address that question.

> But how are feminists, here and there, to answer, in general and in particular? If it is not the wrong question and if, as feminists, we're equipped to answer it at all?[21]

3 Neither Question Nor Answer: The Particular Disrespects of Irish Women

I think I don't know any more what British feminists think about the question, so I'll stay where I'm coming from and talk about what I think feminism in the Republic is thinking, and doing. Therefore, reflecting on the troublesome connection between feminism and nationalism from a state of 'peace', not war. Because however much we (I mean, the Irish) trade on our history, living in 'the tombstone of the past' (Keane, 1992), notwithstanding the totalizingly bellicose aspirations of Articles 2 and 3 of the Constitution, the Republic of Ireland is not at war.

> *But on whose terms is peace made and 'kept'?*

Not to complicate matters, but following on from the business of British constructions of Irish 'homogeneity', let me emphasize again the non-homogeneity of the women's movement in the Republic. There are divisions around the issues of class and poverty, sexuality and — increasingly — ethnicity (see Crickley, 1992). In the past, the most damaging, or in any case prolonged, splits occurred over the issue of the

National Question. Some feminists argued that its resolution must be a priority for feminism, while others considered it to be less central or even altogether irrelevant (see Barry, 1988; Loughran, 1986; Smyth, 1993; Ward, 1987). While it remains a 'live' issue — how can it not while so many are still dying? — and despite all the passion and acrimony that the National Question has evoked among feminists over the years, it is no longer the case that feminist politics *in the Republic* is about having to make a choice between a politics of 'the womb vs. the border' (McCafferty, 1987).[22]

Almost imperceptibly, the National Question has ceased to be a major dividing issue within the women's movement in the Republic. This is due in part to the urgency of the economic situation, with official unemployment figures at 20 per cent, and in part to the immediate need to resist the onslaughts of the extreme right (O'Reilly, 1991; Smyth, 1992a). But it is also true that the National Question has become less of a defining issue in Irish social and political life as younger generations come to the fore whose sense of themselves and their 'national identity' has been shaped far more by the process of modernization (including Europeanization) which has occurred since the 1950s, (a process significantly retarded by the British colonization of Ireland), than by the struggle for Independence and the civil war which followed: a trajectory which has brought us from 'Die Irish' to 'Buy Irish' in less than a century, (see Connolly, 1993).

What I think is not generally recognized — except by feminists — is the extent to which feminism itself has been a crucial factor in shifting the centre of political debate in the Republic from an obsessive concern with nationhood and nationalism on to a much broader social and political basis. Feminism has not been the only movement for social change, but it has launched the most enduring, widespread and resonant challenge to the ideology and politics of our nation-state. I don't mean that feminist challenges to the institutions and practices of the state are necessarily explicitly articulated as challenge to nationalism, but their effect is to undermine the ideological bases of the 'nation-ness' on which the state was founded. Myths of the 'common good' and notions of national unity are exposed through and by feminist protest and resistance, as the oppressive, elitist, and homogenizing fabrications they are.[23]

Many Irish women are clearly no longer impressed by a rhetoric of martyrdom in the name of a manifestly male 'common good'; they are refusing to be the keepers of a national culture which reduces them to silent symbols; they are declining to be the reproducers of the nation on any terms but their own and no longer bend obediently to the intimately entwined dictates of state and church (Rossiter, 1992); they are vociferously and effectively demanding social and economic measures responsive to their diverse, self-defined needs. Irish women want jobs and training for jobs, as well as respect and equal treatment for home-based work; they want sex education in schools, reproductive health care, contraception and abortion when necessary. They want — and are having — fewer children, a decent and equitable social welfare system, and to leave a marriage when it is destructive or, quite simply, over. They want more women making decisions and policy and are electing them to do so. They are refusing to keep silent about the horrific damage wreaked on them by violent men; they are calling violence by its precise names — rape, sexual abuse, battering; physical, psychic and social coercion (Casey, 1987; O'Connor, 1992; Shanahan, 1992).

By 'going public', women are dislodging the cornerstone of control of the patriarchal state: women's privatized place in the sacrosanct family, foundation of the nation. Irish women, contesting traditional gender roles and sexual relations, and whether they acknowledge what they are doing as feminist or not or as 'anti-nationalist' or not, are refusing to pay their respects to the state they are in and are thus redefining the politics and meanings of 'Irishness'.

> I am Ireland / and I'm silenced
> I cannot tell my abortions / my divorces / my years of slavery /
> my fights for freedom
> it's got to the stage I can hardly remember what I had to tell /
> and when I do / I speak in whispers
>
> (Maighread Medbh: 'Easter 1991', 1993, p. 59)

But when silence finally speaks, it is never in a whisper. Once said, things can never be returned to their original state. They are there, public, voiced, acts of resistance and liberation.

The sense of dynamic feminist activism in the Republic is palpable: there is no question of the movement being 'dead', although it has certainly become more diffuse over the past two decades and radical feminists are still constantly 'under fire' (Smyth, forthcoming). Perhaps because women in Ireland have had such a blatantly traditional and repressive strain of nationalist patriarchalism to protest against, the movement has maintained a high level of visible activism. The desire and need for a new kind of politics, expressed through the election of Mary Robinson as President (O'Reilly, 1991; Smyth, 1992a) and, in 1992, by the election of twenty women (12 per cent) to Dail Eireann (Claffey,

Women, Violence, Culture and the State

1993) is significantly attributable to the strength of feminism as a social and political movement.

In Ireland, feminism has had a revitalizing effect on politics and a crucial role to play in the redefining of the terms of national identity. The historical tables have been turned, and it is nationalism which is now under pressure from feminism to demonstrate its value and relevance, rather than the other way around.

British women might well be forgiven for disbelieving what I say, for media representations of Ireland in Britain are scant and restricted to the endless regurgitation of the two Irish 'angles':

(a) conflict in Northern Ireland, the bloodier the better, because masculinity requires regular 'hits' of danger, risk and violence to remain in a state of inflated readiness: *We want the walking wounded*;

(b) the 'backwardness' of the Republic of Ireland, because it makes everyone else feel more forward: *We want the womb with a view*.

Such reductive representations are a powerful mechanism for maintaining the lie that Ireland is an (in)subordinate and inferior state — which does not mean that the lie is not contested and exposed by everyday realities and concrete practices. On the contrary:[24]

- There has been a dramatic decrease in the birth rate in the past few years (from 21.4 in 1980 to 15.3 in 1992).

- There has been a no less dramatic and clearly related increase in the number of married women in the workforce, from around 5 per cent in the 1960s to almost 30 per cent in the 1990s.

- The number of marital separations has spiralled over the same period.

- Whether the incidence of rape, sexual abuse and battering has actually increased, we do not know. But the number of reported rapes (i.e., women's public refusal to allow men to rape them quietly) has shot up from 76 in 1979, when the first rape crisis centre opened, to 1,479 in 1990, and in the 12-month period between November 1989 and October 1990, Dublin police had to respond to a total of 3,500 cases of 'domestic' violence. (Shanahan, 1992)

Change always and only ever comes at a price, and women are paying it, with incredibly high personal interest, literally carrying the burden of change personally. Just this time last year, a young woman, Lavinia Kerwick, took all her courage in her hands and made a public statement condemning the judge who had decided, in his wisdom, to adjourn sentence for a year on the young man who had raped her, by his own admission. The judge based his decision on the fact that, *inter alia*, the man had a clean record with good references from his employer. The young woman's pain, the violation of her person and of her right to bodily integrity, were apparently of no consequence to him. Lavinia Kerwick appealed publicly to the Minister for Justice. She identified herself (the first time a raped woman had done so) as victim of a violent crime perpetrated against her because she was a woman, because women are 'open territory'. She identified herself as the victim of a 'justice' system which denies women value and status as human beings, entitled to have their rights upheld and respected by the state and its agents.

Lavinia Kerwick's action revealed the dishonesty, double-dealing and injustice of a system based on profoundly unequal power relations between men and women. In such a system, women are set up to be the losers, unless and until they refuse to respect the rules of the power game and expose it for what it is. Lavinia Kerwick did this, but it is a terrible indictment of a society that can or will only change when extreme pressure is applied to its conscience and its public face, in the form of the publicly exposed pain of real flesh-and-blood women. Principles do not produce the same results as bodies: *Show us the blood*.

Despite the pain, and the price, women are not now prepared to keep their heads down and out of sight. The damage done is being named and condemned (although not by judges). That is a huge change.

The Irish and Catholic nation-state is being hauled, against the will of some of its citizens, out of the 'cold black shute of history' (Dooley, 1993), where heroes and priests ruled unchallenged. It is a fitful, complicated process, and often painful for those who refuse to be brutalized or excised in the name of the nation and the 'common good' (Smyth, 1992b).

I would be lying if I said that I know where we're going: I don't, although we seem very sure that we don't want to go back to where we've come from. At the very least, the foundations of the state are being unearthed and exposed, in the light of a differently organized day, as tattered and tired and altogether inadequate.

> God and nature never intended women to take advanced position in fighting for the emancipation of any nation. (*Connaught Telegraph*, 12 February 1881)

Whatever God, nature and the *Connaught Telegraph* intended in their omniscient fastnesses above, below and to the West, there is nothing more certain but that the state of the Irish Republic is being radically redefined by those who were allowed only the most circumscribed role in its foundation (see Hearne, 1992; Murphy, 1989; Owens, 1984; Ward, 1983).

Conclusion Without Evident Connections

I know that there are connections between the construction/destruction of women in war, in colonialism and in nationalism, although I do not know, yet, how to make them fit exactly. Perhaps they never do: for there are many contradictions and tensions, not always logical or rationally explicable. I do know there are cogent reasons, in particular contexts, for opposing nationalism as an ideology or a politics. But what you know in your head is not always echoed in your soul or followed by your feet.

As I understand them, through the prism of the history and contemporary reality of the state I inhabit, feminism and nationalism are antagonistic practices. For all that, it does not automatically follow that we should abandon the possibility of a national consciousness and national structures which can ensure social, political and economic rights for every member of the community. Living in an ex-colonial, peripheral and economically underdeveloped state does not make you want to jump into the jaws of an all-enveloping 'open' multi-national economy. I am acutely aware of the vulnerability of stateless communities in the contemporary geopolitical order, with its predatory superpowers, supra-national cartels and corporations and I do not for a moment under-estimate the significance of national independence for those who have been deprived of it. It is a good deal easier to envisage renouncing what you have than to give it up before you've even had it. But nation-ness is not an absolute value or a universal and fixed principle of social and political organization. If, in some of its contemporary manifestations (as in Ireland), it is found to be wanting as a path to freedom for all, then it must either be abandoned or radically transformed.

Ailbhe Smyth

In Benedict Anderson's (1983) over-worked phrase, nations are 'imagined communities'. Yes, but the question remains: who gets to do the imagining, and is imagining enough? Irish women have been protesting their exclusion from the elite task of 'imagining the nation' and simultaneously demonstrating that historical acts of imagination, translated into oppressive and violent social systems, have material consequences which must be resisted and transformed through acts of political will into very different systems which may, or may not, need nations to support them.

I believe — and it may be as much a matter of faith as of reason — that feminism does have the capacity to transform oppressive systems and the bloody states that women are in, which is why I will not surrender it, for any cause.

Notes

1 I categorically do not want to suggest that women never have an involvement or investment in the 'production and reproduction' of war. What I do want to stress, both generally and in relation to Ireland, is that the reverberations of war are different in *vital* respects for women and men, because of the inequality of gender-differentiated power structures. For further discussion of the implications of specific wars for women, see, for example, Aron *et al.* (1991); Drakulic (1993); Grech (1993); Sharoni (1992, 1993); Visser (1993).
2 At the World Conference on Human Rights, held in Vienna (May 1993), women organized a Global Tribunal on Violations of Women's Human Rights, and lobbied for the introduction of a UN Convention on the Elimination of All Forms of Sexual Exploitation of Women and for the adoption and implementation of the Draft Declaration on the Elimination of Violence Against Women.
3 Jyoti Punwani (1993), in an analysis of feminism, nationalism and the politics of violence in India, reports that 'In the city of Surat in early December 1992, mobs of Hindu men assaulted and gang-raped more than 13 Muslim women, and then killed at least seven of them by burning them alive'. She reports socialist leader Mrinal Gore as describing the 'targeting of women as the newest strategy for driving women out of their homes permanently — a strategy similar to the "ethnic cleansing" campaign in the territory that was called Yugoslavia' (p. 16).
4 Martyrdom and sacrifice are the 'life-blood' of the Irish Republican cause. Failure is redeemed by self-immolation which becomes the measure of victory. If the cause were to be successful on the battlefield, it would have no further *raison d'être*: 'It is not we who take innocent blood but we offer it, sustained by the example of our immortal dead and the divine example which inspires us all — for the redemption of our country' (Terence MacSwiney (1920), in Moran, 1991, p. 21).
5 About 500 women die of breast cancer alone in the Republic of Ireland every year. See *European Women's Almanac*, (Snyder, 1992, p. 193).
6 Report of a comment made by Sir Patrick Mayhew, at the opera in Belfast, after an explosion in which nearly thirty people were injured (*The Irish Times*, 3 July 1993).
7 While redrafting, I read about the death by an IRA bomb in Belfast of four adult

Women, Violence, Culture and the State

women, a 13-year-old girl and four men. The UFF (Ulster Freedom Fighters) immediately issued a statement declaring there would be 'indiscriminate retaliation against Catholics' (*Sunday Tribune*, 24 October 1993). And so it continues.

8 The *Observer* marked the twenty-fifth anniversary of the Northern Ireland Civil Rights Association with a colour supplement issue: 'Irish Special'. Only one of the six Northern Irish people interviewed for the 'Special' was a woman, and she was specifically represented as a 'Mother': 'The Mother's Tale'. In the interview, Sally McCartan remarks: 'If the Troubles ended tomorrow, it would make no difference financially to [our family], but an awful lot would lose easy money. The intimidation has increased recently. Why? Because before people always gave them what they wanted; now they're standing up to them. More and more people in the community see not Republicans or Loyalists but gangsters taking anything and everything. That's got to stop' (*Observer Magazine*, 11 July, 1993, p. 17).

9 'War' is the term used largely, and almost exclusively, by republicans.

10 Is it not remarkable that a recent collection of essays on Irish terrorism (Alexander and O'Day, 1991) contains no mention in its index of either 'war' or 'death'? That there is no reference to 'feminism' and only one to 'women' is less surprising.

11 The war zone is no more a fixed space than the front line: Cynthia Enloe (1988) writes that women '*as women* must be denied access to "the front", to "combat", so that men can claim a uniqueness and superiority that will justify their dominant position in the social order. And yet because women are in practice often exposed to frontline combat . . . the military has to constantly redefine "the front" and "combat" as wherever "women" are not' (p. 15). See also Enloe (1993)

12 See, for example, the report of Hugh Annesley's proposal to set up a 'National Anti-Terrorist Unit', and Edward Heath's speech to the British House of Commons on the 'security' response to the IRA (*The Irish Times*, 10 June 1993).

13 The 1980 amendment to the Northern Ireland domestic violence legislation excluded cohabitees. This was amended subsequently to bring the legislation into line with provisions in Great Britain (McWilliams, 1991, p. 82).

14 In an analysis of the Social Attitudes Survey results in relation to 'AIDS and the Moral Climate', not even a glancing reference is made to the existence of prostitution or pornography in Northern Ireland (Sneddon and Kremer, 1991). Research on both issues is also virtually non-existent in the Republic — presumably because such impure activities could not be pursued in such pure states.

15 While there is little recorded difference in the declared attitudes of women and men towards the withdrawal of British troops from Northern Ireland, women express far more ambivalence than men about UK membership of NATO, about the stationing of US nuclear weapons in Britain, and about superpower relations (Morgan, 1993).

16 Two large-scale peace initiatives have been developed and led mainly by women: the 'Peace People' in 1976 and 'Peace '93' following the Warrington bombing. While such initiatives are laudable in their efforts to unlock literally dead-locked doors, in both cases the leaders have 'mobilized' by appealing to women in terms of their nurturing/caring/protecting roles. Women are exhorted to cross sectarian lines in search of peace because of their common bond as mothers and wives. (see Edgerton, 1986; Mary Cummins, *The Irish Times*, 30 March 1993).

17 This is also true of the Republic of Ireland where the silence is only now beginning to be broken, although see Crone (1988) and Dublin Lesbian and Gay Collective (1986).

18 Nations, old and new, expend a great deal of their energy, and other resources, proving to themselves and everyone else that they are indeed 'different' and 'distinctive'. Long-established nations see themselves as *naturally* the 'way they are', and thus do not acknowledge their nationalism as such: they possess a kind of 'naturalized nationality'. But see the increasingly disruptive critique of 'Britishness' by black people and Asians in Britain, and growing awareness of (British) nationality as 'construct' on the part of whites (Grewal *et al.*, 1988; Colley, 1992).

19 Tifft quotes Hugh Kenner's observation that 'Irish womanhood [is] in its pure state a revolutionists' utility like gunpowder' (Tifft, 1992, p. 316). Nationalist ideology has thus no interest in unstating the 'purity' of women.
20 Until relatively recently, the GAA (Gaelic Athletic Association) forbade its members (all male) to play cricket, rugby, soccer and other 'foreign games'.
21 For a discussion of feminism and its strategies (or lack of them) *vis-à-vis* the state, see Delphy (1984).
22 See Theweleit (1993) for a discussion of the relationship between 'war and womb'.
23 I have some difficulty here in using the immensely more fashionable word 'fictions', which seems to me to be altogether too ethereal to convey the *materiality* of the consequences, in everyday life terms, of national myth-construction exercises.
24 Pauline Conroy Jackson points to the limits of such changes, however, arguing that although there is a crisis of 'some values, philosophical, religious and moral [in the Irish State], the profit and political systems are more or less intact, apart from some scandals' (quoted in Shanahan, 1992, p. 41).

References

ALEXANDER, YONAH and O'DAY, ALAN (Eds) (1991) *The Irish Terrorist Experience*, Aldershot, Dartmouth Publishing Company.
ANDERSON, BENEDICT (1983) *Imagined Communities*, New York, Verso.
ANDERSON, LINDA (1988) 'Gang-Bang Ulster Style', in KELLY, A.A. *The Pillars of the House*, Dublin, Wolfhound Press.
ANTHIAS, FLOYA and YUVAL-DAVIS, NIRA (Eds) (1989) *Woman-Nation-State*, London, Macmillan.
ARNOLD, MATTHEW (1962) *Lectures and Essays in Criticism*, Ann Arbor, University of Michigan Press.
ARON, ADRIANNE, CORNE, SHAUN, FURSLAND, ANTHEA and ZELWER, BARBARA (1991) 'The Gender-Specific Terror of El Salvador and Guatemala: Post-Traumatic Stress Disorder in Central American Refugee Women', *Women's Studies International Forum*, vol. 14, nos. 1/2, pp. 37-48.
BARRY, URSULA (1988) 'Women in Ireland', *Women's Studies International Forum*, vol. 11, no. 4, pp. 317-22.
BOLAND, EAVAN (1990) *Outside History*, Manchester, Carcanet.
BRADLEY, GERALDINE (1992) *Everything under the Sun: Feminism, Feminists and Local Women's Groups (Belfast)*, MA Dissertation, WERRC, University College Dublin.
BYRON, CATHERINE (1985) *Settlements*, Durham, Taxus Press.
CAIRNS, DAVID and RICHARDS, SHAUN (1988) *Writing Ireland: Colonialism, Nationalism and Culture*, Manchester, Manchester University Press.
CASEY, MAEVE (1987) *Domestic Violence: The Women's Perspective*, Dublin, Women's Aid.
CLAFFEY, UNA (1993) *Women on Top*, Dublin, Attic Press.
COLLEY, LINDA (1992) *Britons: Forging the Nation 1707-1837*, New Haven and London, Yale University Press.
CONNOLLY, CLARA (1993) 'Culture or Citizenship? Notes from the "Gender and Colonialism" Conference, Galway, Ireland, May 1992', *Feminist Review*, no. 44, pp. 104-11.
CRICKLEY, STASIA (1992) 'The Double Burden', *Irish Reporter*, vol. 8, no. 4, pp. 9-11.

CRONE, JONI (1988) 'Lesbian Feminism in Ireland', *Women's Studies International Forum*, vol. 11, no. 4, pp. 343–8.
CROSS, JEAN (1989) 'Irishwomen, Arts and Media', *FAN*, vol. 3, no. 3, pp. 6–7.
DAVIES, CELIA and McLAUGHLIN, EITHNE (Eds) (1991) *Women, Employment and Social Policy in Northern Ireland: A Problem Postponed?* Belfast, Policy Research Institute.
DELPHY, CHRISTINE (1984) 'Les Femmes et l'état', *Nouvelles Questions Féministes*, 6/7, pp. 5–20.
DOOLEY, MAURA (1993) *Explaining Magnetism*, Newcastle-upon-Tyne, Bloodaxe.
DRAKULIC, SLAVENKA, (1993) 'The Enemy Within', *Women's Review of Books*, X (8), May.
DUBLIN LESBIAN AND GAY MEN'S COLLECTIVE (1986) *Out for Ourselves: The Lives of Irish Lesbians and Gay Men*, Dublin, DLGMC/Women's Community Press.
EDGERTON, LYNDA (1986) 'Public Protest, Domestic Acquiescence: Women in Northern Ireland', in RIDD, ROSEMARY and CALLAWAY, HELEN (Eds) *Caught Up in Conflict*, London, Macmillan.
ENLOE, CYNTHIA (1988) *Does Khaki Become You? The Militarization of Women's Lives*, London, Pandora (First edition 1983).
ENLOE, CYNTHIA (1989) *Bananas, Beaches and Bases: Making Feminist Sense of International Politics*, Berkeley, University of California Press.
ENLOE, CYNTHIA (1993) 'The Right to Fight: A Feminist Catch-22', *Ms*, vol. IV, no. 1, pp. 84–7.
EVASON, EILEEN (1982) *Hidden Violence*, Belfast, Farset Co-op Press.
EVASON, EILEEN (1991) *Against the Grain: The Contemporary Women's Movement in Northern Ireland*, Dublin, Attic Press.
FAIRWEATHER, EILEEN, McDONOUGH, ROISIN and McFADYEAN, MELANIE (1984) *Only the Rivers Run Free: Northern Ireland: The Women's War*, London, Pluto.
FRENCH, MARILYN (1992) *The War Against Women*, London, Hamish Hamilton.
GILHOOLY, BRIEGE (1993) 'Lesbians in Belfast in the 1970s — An Oral History', MA paper, WERRC, University College Dublin.
GOLDRING, MAURICE (1993) 'Violence légitime', *Politis: La Revue*, 2, pp. 49–54.
GRECH, JOYOTI (1993) 'Resisting War Rape in Bangladesh', *Trouble and Strife*, no. 26, pp. 17–21.
GREWAL, SHABNAM, KAY, JACKIE, LANDOR, LILIANE, LEWIS, GAIL and PARMAR, PRATIBHA (Eds) (1988) *Charting the Journey: Writings by Black and Third World Women*, London, Sheba.
HEARNE, DANA (1992) '*The Irish Citizen* 1914–1916: Nationalism, Feminism and Militarism, *Canadian Journal of Irish Studies*, vo. 18, no. 1, pp. 1–14.
HÉLIE-LUCAS, MARIE-AIMÉE (1991) 'Les Strategies des femmes a l'égard des fondamentalismes dans le monde musulman', *Nouvelles Questions Féministes*, 16/17/18, pp. 29–62.
HIGGINS, RITA ANN (1992) *Philomena's Revenge*, Galway; Salmon Press.
JAYAWARDENA, KUMARI (1986) *Feminism and Nationalism in the Third World*, London, Third World Books.
KANDIYOTI, DENIZ (Ed.) (1991) *Women, Islam and the State*, London, Macmillan.
KEANE, DOLORES (1992) *On Solid Ground* (Compact Disc), Dublin.
LEONARD, MADELEINE (1992) 'The Politics of Everyday Living in Belfast, *Canadian Journal of Irish Studies*, vol. 18, no. 1, pp. 83–94.
LEONARD, MADELEINE (1993) 'Rape: Myths and Reality', in SMYTH, AILBHE (Ed.) *The Irish Women's Studies Reader*, Dublin, Attic Press.
LONDON IRISH WOMEN'S CENTRE (1993) *Roots and Realities: A Profile of Irish Women in London*, London, LIWC.
LOUGHRAN, CHRISTINA (1986) 'Armagh and Feminist Strategy', *Feminist Review*, no. 23, pp. 59–70.

LOVENDUSKI, JONI and RANDALL, VICKY (1993) *Contemporary Feminist Politics: Women and Power in Britain,* Oxford, Oxford University Press.
MCCAFFERTY, NELL (1987) *Goodnight Sisters,* Dublin, Attic Press.
MCLAUGHLIN, EITHNE (forthcoming) 'Women and the Family in Northern Ireland: A Review', *Women's Studies International Forum.*
MCWILLIAMS, MONICA (1991) 'Women in Northern Ireland: An Overview', in HUGHES, EAMONN (Ed.) Culture and Politics in Northern Ireland, 1960–1990, Buckingham, Open University Press; revised as: 'The Church, The State and the Women's Movement in Northern Ireland', in SMYTH, AILBHE, (Ed.) (1993) *The Irish Women's Studies Reader,* Dublin, Attic Press.
MEDBH, MAIGHREAD (1993) 'Easter 1991', *Feminist Review,* no. 44, pp. 58–60.
MEEHAN, PAULA (1991) *The Man Who Was Marked by Winter,* Oldcastle, Co. Meath, Gallery Press.
MOHANTY, CHANDRA (1991) 'Cartographies of Struggle: Third-World Women and the Politics of Feminism ', in MOHANTY, CHANDRA *et al.* (Eds) *Third-World Women and the Politics of Feminism,* Bloomington, Indiana University Press.
MORAN, SEÁN FARRELL (1991) 'Patrick Pearse and Patriotic Soteriology: The Irish Republican Tradition and the Sanctification of Political Self-Immolation', in ALEXANDER, YONAH and O'DAY, ALAN (Eds) *The Irish Terrorist Experience,* Aldershot, Dartmouth Publishing Company.
MORGAN, VALERIE (1993) 'Bridging the Divide: Women and Political and Community Issues', in STRINGER, PETER and ROBINSON, GILLIAN (Eds) *Social Attitudes in Northern Ireland: The Second Report. 1991–1992,* Belfast, Blackstaff Press.
MURPHY, CLIONA (1989) *The Women's Suffrage Movement and Irish Society in the Early Twentieth Century,* Brighton, Harvester.
NI GHLINN, AINE (1993) 'Racial Pride', in FITZMAURICE, GABRIEL (Ed.) *Irish Poetry Now: Other Voices,* Dublin, Wolfhound Press.
O'CONNOR, JOYCE (1992) *Breaking the Silence: Violence in the Home,* Limerick, Adapt Refuge and Mid-Western Health Board.
O'REILLY, EMILY (1991) *Candidate: The Truth Behind the Presidential Election,* Dublin, Attic Press.
O'REILLY, EMILY (1992) *Masterminds of the Right,* Dublin, Attic Press.
OWENS, ROSEMARY CULLEN (1984) *Smashing Times: A History of the Irish Women's Suffrage Movement 1889–1922,* Dublin, Attic Press.
PUNWANI, JYOTI (1993) 'India: Searching for Answers in the Wake of Religious Violence, *Ms,* vol. IV, no. 1, pp. 16–18.
RIDD, ROSEMARY (1986) 'Powers of the Powerless' in RIDD, ROSEMARY and CALLAWAY, HELEN (Eds) *Caught up in Conflict,* London, Macmillan.
ROSSITER, ANN (1992) ' "Between the Devil and the Deep Blue Sea": Irish Women, Catholicism and Colonialism', in SAHGAL, GITA and YUVAL-DAVIS, NIRA (Eds) *Refusing Holy Orders: Women and Fundamentalism in Britain,* London, Virago.
ROULSTON, CARMEL (1989) 'Women on the Margin: The Women's Movement in Northern Ireland', *Science and Society,* vol. 53, no. 2, pp. 219–36.
SHANAHAN, KATE (1992) *Crimes Worse than Death,* Dublin, Attic Press.
SHANNON, CATHERINE B. (1992) 'Recovering the Voices of the Women of the North', *The Irish Review,* 12, pp. 27–33.
SHARONI, SIMONA (1992) 'Homefront as Battlefield: Gender, Military Occupation and Violence Against Women', in MAYER, TAMAR (Ed.) *Women of the Occupation: The Impact of Israeli Military Occupation on Jewish and Palestinian Women,* London and New York, Routledge.
SHARONI, SIMONA (1993) 'Israel: Is Feminism a Threat to National Security?', *Ms,* vol. III, no. 4, pp. 18–22.
SMYTH, AILBHE (Ed.) (1989) *Wildish Things: An Anthology of New Irish Women's Writing,* Dublin, Attic Press.

SMYTH, AILBHE (1992a) ' "A Great Day for the Women of Ireland": The Meaning of Mary Robinson's Presidency for Irish Women', *Canadian Journal of Irish Studies*, vol. 18, no. 1, pp. 61–75.
SMYTH, AILBHE (Ed.) (1992b) *The Abortion Papers: Ireland*, Dublin, Attic Press.
SMYTH, AILBHE (1993) 'The Women's Movement in the Republic of Ireland 1970–1990', in SMYTH, AILBHE (Ed.) *The Irish Women's Studies Reader*, Dublin, Attic Press.
SMYTH, AILBHE (forthcoming) 'Haystacks in My Mind: Or How To Stay Sane, Feminist and Angry in the 1990s'.
SMYTH, CHERRY (1991) 'Cherry Smyth: Interview', in WALL, RITA (Ed.) *Leading Lives: Irish Women in Britain,* Dublin, Attic Press.
SNEDDON, IAN and KREMER, JOHN (1991) 'AIDS and the Moral Climate', in STRINGER, PETER and ROBINSON, GILLIAN (Eds) *Social Attitudes in Northern Ireland*, Belfast, Blackstaff Press.
SNYDER, PAULA (1992) *The European Women's Almanac,* London, Scarlet Press.
STEIN, GERTRUDE (1989) 'The Making of Americans', in GRAHN, JUDY *Really Reading Gertrude Stein,* Freedom, California, The Crossing Press.
THEWELEIT, KLAUS (1993) 'The Bomb's Womb and the Genders of War (War Goes On Preventing Women from Becoming the Mothers of Invention)' in COOKE, MIRIAM and WOOLLACOTT, ANGELA (Eds) *Gendering War Talk,* Princeton, Princeton University Press.
TIFFT, STEPHEN (1992) 'The Parricidal Phantasm: Irish Nationalism and the *Playboy* Riots', in PARKER, ANDREW, RUSSO, MARY, SOMMER, DORIS and YAEGER, PATRICIA (Eds) *Nationalisms and Sexualities,* New York and London, Routledge.
VISSER, WILLEMIEN (1993) 'Viols contre les femmes dans l'ex-Yougoslavie', *Nouvelles Questions Féministes,* 14 (1), pp. 43–76.
WARD, MARGARET (1983) *Unmanageable Revolutionaries: Women and Irish Nationalism,* London, Pluto/Brandon, Dingle.
WARD, MARGARET (Ed.) (1987) *A Difficult, Dangerous Honesty: 10 Years of Feminism in N. Ireland,* Belfast, Women's News.
WARD, MARGARET (1988) 'From Civil Rights to Women's Rights', in FARRELL, MICHAEL (Ed.) *Twenty Years On,* Dingle, Brandon.
WARD, MARGARET and MCMINN, JOANNA (1985) 'Belfast Women Against All Odds', in STEINER-SCOTT, LIZ (Ed.) *Personally Speaking: Women's Thoughts on Women's Issues,* Dublin, Attic Press.

Chapter 2

History of Women's Liberation Movements in Britain: A Reflective Personal History

Jill Radford

Attempting to over-view the history of the women's liberation movements in Britain is in one sense an attempt at the impossible. Women's Liberation was and is a huge, amorphous and diverse movement involving many thousands of women, and there can be no one definitive history.

Whilst my own life has been transformed through the Women's Liberation Movement, my personal contribution is minuscule. Through the years, I was present at some of the big national conferences, some of the Southern England regional ones, some of the marches and protests; but I missed many more.

But I have 'been around for a while'. This places me amongst the 'memory-bearing women' as Mary Daly (1993) recently put it. She attributed particular responsibilities to 'memory-bearing' women: to reflect on our memories, to enable the next generation of feminists to build on our strengths and learn from our mistakes in the voyage to the next wave of feminism.

Like Mary Daly, I think that now is the time to build the boat and start that voyage, to build a new, transformed, including, explicitly anti-oppressive, anti-racist and anti-homophobic, loud, active, liberatory women's movement. It is an urgent priority, given the state of the world.

Internationally, we see women and children killed by man-made war and famine in Somalia; desert storm, death and environmental destruction in the Gulf; organized and individual acts of femicide, organized and individual acts of rape and sexual torture, on an appalling scale, in former Yugoslavia, as warring patriarchal armies turn their weapons against women and children; fascism growing across Europe and in the UK, reflected in increasing numbers of racist attacks/attacks on

History of Women's Liberation Movements in Britain

foreigners, particularly in Germany, and the new immigration laws passed by French, German and UK governments (see *Rights of Women Bulletins,* 1993). The by-election win by the British National Party in London in September 1993, as this text was being edited, brings it into sharper focus. To be able to be heard saying 'not in our name', to be able to join international feminist protests and work to end these patriarchal abuses and look for different ways of preserving and sharing the world's scarce resources, we need a strong movement of women with a global vision.

Nationally, government policy has been orchestrated around moral panics scapegoating women, lesbians and lesbian mothers, black women, mothers who have never done it with men, single mothers, poor women, immigrant women, women who claim benefits — an illustrative but not excluding list.

The fear/threat and reality of sexual violence and racist violence against women and children is rising in our homes and neighbourhoods as individual men increasingly resort to sexual violence to control 'their' (*sic*-k) women and children. Femicide has become a legitimate penalty for 'nagging' and life imprisonment the penalty for resistance, for acts of self-preservation.

I think the time is right — right to make a transforming leap to the next wave.

So in reflecting on the past, I stand in the present, and look to the future. In the context of present visions for the future, I want to look back at threads from our past, in order to re-view, re-vise, re-new, re-connect and where necessary reject them, to ensure that in plotting the voyage forward, we are at least informed by our history.

As one of the memory-bearing women, I am accepting Mary Daly's 'dare' and presenting a personal and reflective history. Working in Women's Studies, I gained an insight into the complexities involved in constructing representations of women's lives in auto/biographical work. How much more so is the task of re-presenting something as huge and diverse as Women's Liberation.

I have valued enormously the ten years I have worked in community and academic women's studies. When I was first involved in community women's studies in the late 1970s in Winchester (of which more later), we saw it as an integral part of feminist process. Now, when we have to discuss whether we can even write the word 'feminist' in our validation proposals, I am concerned.

I am also concerned about the accessibility of Women's Studies. Much of our work is becoming inaccessible; inaccessible in the difficult language, fashionable within the academe; inaccessible in terms of who can get hold of it, given costs and the limited numbers of women allowed to use our library collections or to enrol on our courses. The questions we seem to be in danger of forgetting are those about 'why' and 'who': why we are writing, and who we are addressing when we write; why and who we are researching; what, why and who we are teaching; who is included and excluded in the setting of agendas and on our classroom registers? In explaining 'Why Women's Studies?' to students, as well as to college boards and funding bodies, are we forgetting to ask the question of ourselves?

I am concerned about some recent developments which are occurring in academic Women's Studies. For example, I am worried about the separations we have allowed to develop between Women's Studies and Feminism, and, probably as a consequence, the way Women's Liberation and feminism are being re-presented in Women's Studies — specifically, the way certain re-presentations are acquiring definitive status as they are handed on to a new generation. These re-presentations have acquired a heightened salience, now we can no longer assume the presence of memory-bearing women in our classrooms, women who can mediate these received her-stories/heracies.

In many of the accounts I read, connections fundamental to feminism, which gave it its meaning and dynamics, strength and energy, are hard to find. I am detecting an alarming process of de-construction afoot in academic re-presentations of feminism which write out the central notion of praxis. This has been accomplished through separations and exclusions. The academic is being separated from activism, and activism excluded; feminist politics are separated from feminist process, the process is lost and the politics rendered meaningless. Separations occur between policy and research, and without feminist politics, methodology is reduced to methods; theory is separated from practice, notions of practice flounder in institutional compromise and theory without a context is simply academic (binaries to be read as connected in all possible combinations).

In some re-presentations, within Women's Studies texts, feminisms have been defined, separated, and categorized into typologies to the extent that basic tenets are hard to decipher. In academizing feminism, there is a danger that, in abstracting theory from process and activism, the dynamism, the vitality, energy and chaos are written out, and as a result the strength and meaning of the movement are in danger of being lost.

Liz Kelly, Sheila Burton and Linda Regan of the Child Abuse Studies Unit recently made a similar point, in the context of debates around feminist methodologies:

History of Women's Liberation Movements in Britain

> Many . . . commentaries published in the 1980s interpret the first decade of 'second wave' feminism as an idealistic universalizing of women's experiences. While much of the more academic work published in the 1970s (and into the 1980s) can be read this way, activist literature and history tells a somewhat different story; a story in which differences between women were sometimes recognized and where conflicts and struggles about race, class and sexuality were commonplace within feminist groups, campaigns and organizations. (Kelly, *et al.*, 1994)

In this reflective and personal narrative I am seeking to remember some of those connections, and through them look again at some fundamental concepts of women's liberation as I understand them.

Personal Introduction

Given that this is a personalized account, I will introduce myself further, to indicate where I am coming from. I am a white woman, feminist and lesbian with a marginal position around class. I am an activist, campaigner, researcher, writer, involved in policy and support work, and tutoring Women's Studies at the Open University and the University of Westminster.

My engagement with feminism dates back to the end of the 1960s in a patchy sort of way. I was one of the women for whom feminist ideas, immediately I heard them, made some sense of my life — reached the parts male theory couldn't reach.

The memories I am reflecting on are drawn from two later periods: the first runs from 1975 to 1981/2, when with my daughter, then 5, and my son, then 4, I went to live in Winchester, Hampshire, a small, conservative town, then very much a part of Tory heartland; the second dates from 1986, when I became a paid worker, job-sharing, at Rights of Women. For me, both these experiences were transformative.

Winchester Women's Liberation Group

One reason for choosing to speak of this group is that many recorded histories have focused on national events and London-based groups, to

Jill Radford

the extent that local, autonomous women's liberation groups, great in number and diversity, have almost been written out of Women's Liberation histories.

The Wincheter Women's Liberation Group was six weeks old when I found it. It was a small group, rarely more than ten of us, with women moving in and out from time to time, though on occasions we drew audiences of fifty or more at campaigning meetings. Winchester was a white, middle-class town and this was reflected in the group, though the middle-class women were women with oppositional politics. There were also working-class women. Two of the founding women were black and there was a strong lesbian presence. So the group was predominantly white, middle-class and heterosexual, but to write out the contribution of black women, working-class women and lesbians would be a misrepresentation of the history of this group.

Issues of race, class and sexuality were frequently addressed in our c-r (consciousness-raising) meetings. Our diversity was often a source of strength, but at times tensions arose as we did not always find ways of fully recognizing or dealing effectively with differences in terms of our power and privilege within the group. These questions were discussed in the group, sometimes quite heatedly, but we behaved and spoke as if somehow these oppressive structures which contextualized our lives and our thinking could be overcome by good intentions and left with our coats at the door of the meetings. It is easier retrospectively to recognize some of the serious mistakes made over racism and heterosexism and access to wealth and resources than it was then.

Given this was Winchester, as a group we were fairly diverse in our backgrounds. In age we ranged from women who had reached their seventies to women in their early twenties; some of us had jobs or bits of jobs, some were unemployed and some were students, some of us had children and some not; some of us were married, others cohabiting with a male lover, some were single women and some lesbian. In fact by 1981/2, more of us had become lesbians and others had reached a decision not to have relationships with men.

None of our lives were unaffected by belonging to that women's group.

There were other differences. The group had been formed by women interested by the ideas of women's liberation. Some, not all, were also active within malestream political organizations: the Labour Party, the Liberals, the Greens, and left-wing groups such as the SWP (Socialist Workers' Party) and the IMG (International Marxist Group). So we spanned a range of competing political perspectives.

While we were very aware of political differences within the group, which at times became tense, we never split over issues — unlike groups in some larger towns. We could not, really, in such a small town. We might stay away from the group for a while when we were angry, but there was only the one group until 1981/2.

My memory of those days was of being part of a fairly small group of women of fairly diverse backgrounds, who came together as feminists, forming strong friendships, generating a lot of energy, excitement and anger, growing in strength, supporting each other in our hard times and at others having an incredible amount of fun.

The re-presentation of the Women's Liberation Movement as exclusively white, heterosexist and middle-class, maliciously racist and concerned only with our own opportunist self-interest, the sort of re-presentation I am finding in some student essays nowadays, to me feels over-drawn.

Feminism: Politics and Process

We came together as feminists. We understood feminism in a fairly straightforward way, along the lines of 'a recognition that women are oppressed, a concern to explore that oppression and a commitment to act to end it' (a definition constructed later by Liz Kelly, Jill Radford and Joan Scanlon see Kelly *et al.,* 1992). We did not assume that all women were oppressed in the same ways. We recognized differences in our relations to other power structures, of race, class, relationship to heterosexuality, and differences in terms of age, states of health and disability. We did not specify any precise ways of how oppression worked, the ways women were differently oppressed, or how women can behave in oppressive ways towards other women. We did not deal with these latter questions well or adequately, but they were not unaddressed, though all too often they were handled in patronizing and conflictual ways.

Racism and anti-lesbianism were talked about in consciousness-raising meetings as we shared lived experience. We never explored our personal complicity in it or the ways we played through those power dynamics within our own meetings. What we did attempt was to reject all power hierarchies by having no office holders, 'stars' or named leaders (though the mythical 'Ann Gree' gave a fair number of press statements), no bank accounts, sitting in circles, giving all women enough time to speak, while not excluding others. We aimed to find ways of working

Jill Radford

with each other that challenged, countered or minimized power oppressions with the group. Looking back, it is easier to see that we cannot locate ourselves outside the power structures that contextualize our lives.

Consciousness-Raising

Though sharing experience was important in our c-r meetings, it was never an aim in itself, as it seems to have become in some recent forms of identity politics and poststructuralist writings. The c-r process, as we understood it, included the sharing of lived experience, but as a part of a broader feminist political process. Importantly, our processes included reflection, discussion and working out how our experience was contextualized or fitted into the larger picture of things. We looked for connections and patterning in power structures and oppressive relationships. This formed the basis of our theorizing. Before the days of women's centres, building of theory took place in garage lofts, back rooms of pubs, women's kitchens, and loo queues, in making banners, songs and slogans rather than in formal academic settings. It was integrally linked to both c-r and activism and central to the struggle for change.

The Personal is Policital

We understood this as a statement of process as well as politics. In c-r, while we started from personal experiences, experience itself was not substituted for, or deemed equivalent to politics, in the essentialist way in which it has come to be used in some forms of identity politics and versions of poststructuralism. We did not hold that experiences of oppression *per se* made for critical awareness, which was to be achieved through reflective political processes, through the making of connections with and contextualizing our experiences within 'the big picture'.

Our political activism and the beginnings of feminist support work grew out of our c-r. For example, through sharing and reflecting on our experiences of sexual violence, we became aware of its prevalence, and in supporting each other when incidents happened, we recognized the limitations of law, legal processes and social services to provide adequate protection or redress for women. We experienced the ways in which woman-blaming ideologies trivialized women's experiences of violence and told us it was all our own faults anyway.

Of necessity we began to develop other understandings, more reflective of our experiences, and new ways of responding to them, i.e., developing feminist theories and practice. This process broadened out and led into networking with other groups, locating our experiences and awareness in a wider picture regionally and nationally.

We participated in regional conferences and networking meetings that were held in the south of England, from which Women's Aid, Rape Crisis and Incest Survivors groups were formed in Southampton, Portsmouth, Reading, Oxford, and Salisbury, though never in Winchester. We were able to make some contribution by providing political and personal support for women involved in cases which reached Winchester Crown Court. On one later occasion (see Radford, 1982), after being ejected from the court room for interrupting proceedings, we picketed the law courts, and made headlines in the national press.

Other issues I remember working around include a successful campaign for the appointment of a woman GP in the city, actions against the closure of the staff nursery at the Royal Hampshire County Hospital, for a woman's right to choose on fertility control and abortion, and against redundancies of woman workers in the local chocolate factory. With women from one of the Southampton women's liberation groups and the Ecology Party, we transformed an SWP bookshop into a community bookshop to enable us to begin to acquire the emerging feminist books. October Books — its name was never changed — is still trading as far as I know and remains the one alternative bookshop in the area.

Later, we set up a community education Women's Studies course, which recruited about 150 women for its first evening, following an advertising campaign which included leaflets in doctors' surgeries and the library, postcard adverts in every city post office and newsagents, and local radio and TV interviews. We were hoping to recruit the minimum of twelve students required by the WEA (Workers' Education Association). We were all surprised and totally panicked by our unexpected success. Our courses 'Time for Women' and 'More Time for Women' ran, I think, for three and two years respectively until about 1982/3. Subsequently, one of the fliers was produced in court in the course of a child custody dispute involving one of the women in the group, to demonstrate her alleged unsuitability as a mother!

We addressed painful issues sometimes, but our activism was often fun. We enjoyed having lengthy correspondences with each other in the letters page of the prestigious and respectable weekly newspaper, the

Jill Radford

Hampshire Chronicle, known to us as 'the Chronic'. We 'performed' in crazy street theatre events, and made home-made floats for all the many carnival events the city staged. We had picnics for women and children on St Catherine's Hill ecofeminist style, claiming a feminine spirituality for the hill and its ancient maze, and protecting it as part of the anti-M3 motorway protest (a struggle recently lost at Twyford Down). We flyposted to publicize our public meetings and organized lively marches and processions which included children, dancing, singing, bright colours and pageantry and lots of noise, not then so usual on political marches.

Networking, Alliances and Single-Issue Campaigns

We were always a small group, and knew that by ourselves in a small Tory town we could not always effect political change. But we did not exist in a social or political vacuum, and as a very small group in a Tory city we recognized a need to work politically on broad-based issues with other political and oppositional groups.

For illustration, in 1977, when the National Front and British National Party focused attention on Winchester, where racist Robert Relf was imprisoned in the city prison, the Women's Liberation Group played a strategic role in the networking with other oppositional political groups. This resulted in the formation of the Winchester Anti-Nazi League, which effectively resisted and protested fascist marches within the city, catching national headlines.

Another example was our work against Cruise and militarism. Newbury was only twenty miles up the road, and we often went to Greenham for weekend picnics and to express solidarity with women at the peace camp. In the city, the women's group again networked strategically across political party lines and played a founding role in establishing a Winchester Anti Cruise Group and later Cruise Watch.

Sisterhood is Powerful

In holding to a belief that sisterhood is powerful, we were under no naive illusion that we were all the same, with a total commonality of interest. But we learned through c-r about areas of common oppressions in the power relations of female subordination, for example in relation to domesticity, the experience of divorce and relationship breakdown and child custody decisions as well as violence against women which led us to ask wider questions about the oppressive nature of heterosexuality for women.

But it was not just talking about these things in c-r, it was moving beyond this, through providing support for each other when we were in trouble, that helped create the feelings of sisterhood. Staying over nights in each other's houses, when police refused to attend domestic violence calls and were reluctant to enforce injunctions, picking each other up from casualty departments, minding each other's children, brought us closer together, and enabled us to develop degrees of trust, across our differences.

Through c-r, through activism, through socializing together, laughing together, crying together, sharing pain, being there for each other, we became close and developed what could be called 'sisterly' feelings towards each other. Sisterhood wasn't such a bad word. It had both precedent as a political word and personal resonance. It didn't mean we always got along: we had heavy rows, sometimes behaved badly to each other — but sisters do. Sisterhood as we understood it did not presume equality of power. It is a concept drawn from a familial model of patriarchal power. As well as pointing to commonalities and closeness, it had the potential to explore power struggles between women, as well as paternal/fraternal power of men over women and power hierarchies amongst men. Its many-levelled meanings seem to be lost nowadays in some theoretical re-presentations of feminism. 'Sisterhood is powerful' was not for us true by definition, more something we could and to an extent did achieve through feminist processes and practices. It was also an expression of future ideals, not simply an expression of present materiality.

Ending and Moving On

Ultimately our group was not strong enough. In 1981 we were stunned, grieved, and angered by an act of femicide and its treatment by the law.[i] This was followed almost immediately by a difficult lesbian custody dispute, involving anti-lesbianism, violence and difficult issues around race. The group broke up amid sadness, anger, recrimination, and doubts. Many of us left the city. I went to London. Other, stronger women took on the task of rebuilding a new women's group in the city.

Jill Radford

After several years of involvement in women's liberation groups and working in community and higher education, I joined Rights of Women as a paid worker in 1986. This is the context of the second part of this personal and reflective narrative.

Rights of Women Today

For those unfamiliar with the work of Rights of Women (ROW), I quote from our information leaflet:

> Founded in 1975, Rights of Women is a feminist organisation which informs women of their rights and promotes the interests of women in relation to the law. Our recommendations have been presented to governments, lawyers, other voluntary sector groups, the media and women's groups. We also provide free, sympathetic, quality legal advice to women on a range of issues including relationship breakdown, sexual and domestic violence and employment rights.
>
> Rights of Women has been a part of several successful policy initiatives including defending child benefits, existing rights on abortion, promoting progressive amendments to the Sex Discrimination Act and the criminalisation of rape in marriage. We have worked consistently to oppose discrimination against lesbians within the law, particularly as parents.
>
> Both our management committee and our collective consists of black and white, lesbian and heterosexual women of different class backgrounds and ages. We are committed, where possible, to make our services available to all women.[2]

For the early history I am reliant on primary sources, fragments of ROW's archives that have survived our almost-twenty-year history and networking with 'memory-bearing women'.

History of Rights of Women

The idea for ROW came out of the Women's Liberation demand for financial and legal independence for women. Similar projects emerged in the 1970s around other Women's Liberation demands. An undated and non-attributed paper 'A short history of ROW — the first five years' explains that in 1974

> a group of women legal workers met together to discuss their own experiences of working in the white, bourgeois, male, heartland — the law. It was felt that women were getting a raw deal from legislation and the organisation of the legal profession and that for ourselves and for other women, we could and must do something about it.

This statement says quite a lot. It defined ROW as a feminist project. It recognized, without being drawn into complex debates about their nature, shifting articulations between patriarchy, racism, capitalism and the state. It did not presume that all women were oppressed in the same way. In fact ROW explicitly recognized difference by committing itself to work on lesbian oppression, specifically that of lesbian mothers. As our Lesbian Custody Project illustrates, this has remained a high-profile issue throughout ROW's history. Similarly, ROW's commitment to be non-excluding in relation to blackwomen dates from the appointment of the first workers, although these were temporary posts in 1975. This is not to say that ROW always got it right. At times in our history, we have been rightly criticized around issues of race, class and disability. We, like other women's liberation groups, have made serious and painful mistakes.

That early statement speaks of a commitment to women and a commitment to challenge the status quo in law, legislation and the profession. Its starting point is women's experiences of working in the law. ROW became something of a c-r or support group for women struggling in a white, male profession. Feminists working in law were often shocked at the ways the law systematically excluded, marginalized, stigmatized and degraded women, and failed to provide protections against discrimination, harassment or violence. But ROW was more than a c-r or discussion group. Women legal workers were well aware of the way the law oppressed other women, their clients, so women's own experiences of sexism and discrimination were contextualized in relation to wider power relations which recognized differences in the ways women are oppressed. The statement also included a commitment to make change.

ROW was formally launched in 1975, when a small, short-term grant was acquired from the EOC and a leaky office space in Islington obtained. From its beginnings ROW could never be contained within those schematic re-presentations of Women's Liberation which began the fragmentation processes by depicting feminism as composed of feuding factions, namely liberal feminism, socialist feminism and radical feminism. These labels can serve as a loose shorthand way of grouping some of the political strands within feminism, but is misleading as it fixes their meanings and does not identify their shifting interrelationship. ROW's history demonstrates that these differences existed and were negotiated within an organization without fragmenting it. From its beginning ROW was a broad-based umbrella group, containing and moving across and between these different positions.

The name Rights of Women most closely fits a liberal feminist paradigm, as it speaks to formal legal rights in the 'public' sphere. However, ROW never naively believed that acquiring formal rights in a racist and sexist society would be sufficient to bring changes in the lives of all women. Fighting for rights is nonetheless a strategically useful way of campaigning and forcing issues onto public agendas.

If working around workplace issues defined ROW as socialist feminist, then it was. For, as well as campaigning for equal pay for work of equal value, ROW worked with trades unions for better employment protection and against exploitation of women's labour, for better job opportunities and over childcare needs. Workplace issues included sexual harassment. This linked to ROW's work around other forms of sexual violence — rape, domestic violence, child sex abuse — an agenda which might define ROW as radical feminist. Forcing ROW into academic analytic categories can only be done by denying important elements of its early and present work, by failing to understand the connectedness of these issues in women's lives and by failing to understand feminist process or ways of working, of how feminist energy and attention may pick up on issues and transform them.

ROW began its advice line in 1976, providing free, quality, legal advice to women by telephone, one evening a week, later expanded to three evenings a week; now it is also open for two hours on four weekdays. Advice, policy and political work were closely interrelated. Our advice calls informed us of the areas of law which were causing the most urgent problems to women.

ROW was also concerned with accountability and outreach work which was progressed through newsletters, the Bulletin, organizing conferences, workshops, legal trainings, briefing papers, rights guides. We have been concerned to network with women in the communities, reaching community groups — black groups, minority ethnic groups and lesbian groups. This remains a central commitment in our present work, though funding, as ever, limits the amount of work we can do.

We remained activist and concerned with working for change, in a range of ways, including lobbying MPs and writing submissions for Parliamentary Select Committees and Royal Commissions; and the ROW banner was frequently seen on major WLM demonstrations.

Moving Into the Early 1980s

The 1980s saw great changes in ROW as the social and political context shifted with the arrival of Thatcherism and local government interventions into feminism.

ROW was one of the feminist groups which accepted considerable local government funding. The opportunity of receiving serious funding from local government, particularly in London with a progressive GLC (Greater London Council), was hotly debated within women's liberation groups. Some groups I was involved in, such as the *London Women's Liberation Newsletter* collective, decided to stand by the politics of an autonomous Women's Liberation Movement and never applied for funding. Others, like ROW, weighed up the possibilities and limitations and decided to go for funding.

Funding changed the organization, and relations within it, enormously. New structures and new approaches were needed as ROW reconstituted itself from a voluntary collective to an organization that employed and managed workers. Issues arose around the relationship between paid workers and the unpaid management/policy group formed from the membership. The members were drawn to ROW from a political commitment to the project; few had the skills or desire to be managers.

Nevertheless, this was a strong time for ROW. Our profile was raised enormously. Our publicity increased and we published several full-length books, upgraded our Bulletin and produced guides for taking action around a range of issues and legal briefing papers. ROW's submissions to Royal Commissions were given due attention and were not without influence. Funding injected a lot of energy into ROW and enabled more outreach work with schools and colleges; more networking with other women's and community groups. We held national conferences and workshops and facilitated training around a range of issues to do with women and the law.

Funding did present new problems. Accountability to funders created the need for a lot of bureaucracy. Working out relationships with local authority grants officers, between workers, policy and management group, voluntary advisors and individuals and groups which made up the membership, is an ongoing process which requires time. These structures were all new and constantly changing, and opened many new possibilities, but sometimes did and still do create problems and difficulties.

A condition of funding was that we are 'non-political' in our work. This was a stumbling block in many organizations — some found themselves with grants officers demanding access to minutes of meetings and access to confidential advice notes. ROW has been fortunate in this respect. While the organization has no party alliances, in a feminist sense all our work was and is political. The legal advice we offer is women-centred and our aim is to offer women possibilities and routes to making changes in their lives. We do not see ourselves as merely 'sticky plaster' to an ailing welfare state or as concerned simply with healing the wounds and putting women back on the front line. In our education and training work we promote feminist analyses of the law. In research and policy work, our aim is to monitor the impact of law on women's lives, including those groups often overlooked or discriminated against, black and minority ethnic women, lesbians, pensioners, women with disabilities, lone parents and homeworkers, not excluding categories. In looking to secure changes in law and judicial practice, our aim is to secure changes which will benefit all women. Changes which benefit only some women, often middle-class and white heterosexual women, and secured at the expense of black women, lesbians and poorer women are divisive. As well as working to secure changes in law and judicial policy, ROW is engaged in challenging negative discourses like those of woman-blame, racism and homophobia and those which define women as men's property.

Through the 1980s funding provided ROW with opportunities for development. Patriarchal conceptions of politics focused on the public sphere and located women and women's issues in the private sphere. The far-right-inspired moral panic which targeted lesbians and gay men, and defined lesbian mothers as 'pretended families' in Clause 28 (now section A of the Local Government Act 1988) marked a worrying shift.

In the mid 1980s we attempted to respond creatively to the emergence of identity politics. By sharpening our understanding of oppression and power relations between women, we strengthened our understanding of racism and anti-lesbianism and our work in these areas was revitalized.

The other face of identity politics, which defined identity in terms only of differences abstracted from any understanding of power relations, was more problematic. This formulation of identity promotes a fragmentation of interests, rather than attempting to study connections between oppressive forces needed to develop strategies for change. It seemed to generate an atmosphere of divisiveness and appeared to preclude possibilities of working politically across difference. The tensions which arose were reflected in some difficult and painful debates, which it was hard, but necessary, to learn from.

Working across difference required care and sensitivity and acquired a sense of urgency, given the rising forces of backlash in which government set the agendas and time-scales. ROW, like most groups, made mistakes as in trying to learn the tactics as opposed to the politics of working through alliances. The campaign against the CLAWS (Clause 28), while in many ways exciting, was full of contradictions for feminists working in mixed campaigns around lesbian issues.

Similar difficulties and contradictions arose later in CADI (Campaign for Access to Donor Insemination) — a feminist campaign to defend access to donor insemination for lesbians and single women, threatened by the Human Fertilisation and Embryology Bill. This attempted to define which women should be allowed access to and which women should be excluded from donor insemination and other assisted pregnancy services, i.e., which women are allowed to mother and which are not. The criteria for exclusion were informed by racism and negative assumptions around women with disabilities, women involved in prostitution or who had acquired criminal records as well as explicit anti-lesbianism. While defending the right of all women to choose in relation to fertility, many of us were also critical of high-tech pregnancy technology which does not, as FINNRAGE has demonstrated, serve women's interests. Holding together differences between lesbians and heterosexual women, black and white women with different class backgrounds was difficult. The legalistic damage limitation approach secured sufficient loopholes, but CADI was not the most successful of campaigning groups.

More recently the brilliantly successful campaign to free Kiranjit Ahluwahlia, inspired by Southall Black Sisters, demonstrates the positive potential of alliance and coalition politics. Personally, it has provided me with many wonderful and moving moments. The anger and energy of the pickets outside the Home Office, partial victories won and celebrated, brings back memories of the possibilities of sisterhood from earlier times, the strength, power and excitement of fighting together. Being invited to and warmly welcomed at Kiranjit's Freedom Party hosted by the Asian Community in Southall was an especially magical moment. It demonstrated that, in little but important ways, feminist visions can be realized and can help to generate the energy to take the struggle to force the law to be more inclusive of, and responsive to, women's experiences of oppression.

Working, with care, through the politics of alliances and coalitions is one way, though others will be needed, of working across differences, to combat patriarchal, racist and material economic oppression locally, nationally and internationally. In these difficult times we see in former Yugoslavia and Somalia the sexual atrocities and death camps of 'postmodern genocide' (MacKinnon, 1993). Here at home amid recession, cuts and attacks on women, single parents and pensioners, and rising homophobia and racism, in a culture celebrating and eroticizing subordination and fragmentation, make survival a real issue and one we may have to struggle for. Yet as Liz Kelly has put it, 'Survival was never not enough' (Kelly, 1992).

From my perspective at the interface of activism and academia I seek support from the Women's Studies academy in challenging political and institutional separations, re-working the connections to help with the building of an including women's anti-racist anti-homophobic liberatory and resistance movement. Women's Studies has an important potential in this project. Realizing this potential requires remembering the 'why' and 'who' questions. Why Women's Studies? Why does our teaching and research matter? I am suggesting that we need to think strategically about our work and about how we deal with the contradictions of working in the academy. We need to think about how we balance our commitments to the academy and the women outside our ivory towers; about how in our teaching and research we will be able to make a difference.

Liz Kelly, Sheila Burton and Linda Regan of the Child Sexual Abuse Research Unit at the University of North London made a similar point:

> Our desire to do, and goal in doing, research is to create useful knowledge, knowledge which can be used by ourselves and others to 'make a difference' . . . if we cannot speak of 'women' how can there be such a thing as 'women's oppression' or a political analysis of it? This is not answered by a sleight of hand — 'feminisms' since multiples are logically dependant on there being a singular.
>
> What troubles us most about the current 'romance with epistimology' is that it seems more concerned with attempting to convince the predominantly male academy that a privileged status should be accorded to 'women's ways of knowing' than with enabling us to better discover and understand what is

happening in women's lives, and how we might change it. (Kelly et al., 1994)

Combining academic with activist work, I often need to access Women's Studies writings and research, to assist understanding of the material realities of women's oppression and to explore possibilities for change. But when the texts contain chapter after chapter of difficult theory aimed at exploring the question of whether women exist, I am disappointed. If, as a consequence of taking Women's Studies into the academy, the voices of women are no longer heard, and our very existence has become a subject of academic debate, can I be forgiven for thinking something is going wrong?

At ROW we know women exist and, that, under present conditions, existence is becoming increasingly tenuous and difficult for many women nationally and internationally. Every day, women ring and tell their stories. Knowledge is rooted in lived experiences, grounded in feminist understandings and set in context. Knowledge is power. As academics, I think we need to recognize our power and ask ourselves questions about how we use it and let it be used.

Notes

I emphasize that this narrative is a personalized account, written in a specific context. It does not claim to be a definitive history. I take responsibility for this reading of events but I want to acknowledge the debt I owe to women from the Women's Liberation Group; to Rights of Women, particularly present and former co-workers including Anne Clark, Bernadette Baker, Jean Smith, Razia Aziz, Rita Rupal and Sibusiso Mavolwane; my friends in Women's Studies at the Open University, with particular thanks to the kitchen table options, and friends at the University of Westminster.

1 See Radford (1982)
2 Rights of Women welcomes new members and donations. We may be contacted at 52-54 Featherstone St, London EC1Y 8RT. Rights of Women is funded by the London Boroughs Grants Scheme for part of our work in London; for the rest we are reliant on donations, membership, and fundraising.

References

BOYE-ANAWOMA, MARGO (1993) 'The Asylum and Immigration Appeals Bill', *Rights of Women Bulletin,* Spring, available from Rights of Women, 52–54 Featherstone St, London EC1Y 8RT, 071 251 6576 (text of paper given at ROW AGM, 1992).

Jill Radford

DALY, MARY (1993) *Outercourse: The Be-Dazzling Voyage,* London, The Women's Press.
KELLY, LIZ (1992) 'Survival was never enough', *Bad Attitude,* January, Radical Women's Newspaper (bi-monthly) Issue 1, p. 25.
KELLY, LIZ, SCANLON, JOAN and RADFORD, JILL (1992) 'Feminism, Feminisms: Fighting Back for Women's Liberation', unpublished paper written for the Open University Women's Studies Summer School, 1992.
KELLY, LIZ, BURTON, SHEILA and REGAN, LINDA (1994) 'Researching Women's Lives or Studying Women's Oppression? Reflections on What Constitutes Feminist Research', in MAYNARD, MARY and PURVIS, JUNE (Eds) *Researching Women's Lives from a Feminist Perspective,* London, Taylor & Francis.
MACKINNON, CATHARINE A. (1993) 'Turning Rape into Pornography: Postmodern Genocide', *Ms,* vol. IV, no. 1, July/August.
RADFORD, JILL (1982) 'Retrospect on a Trial', *New Society,* 9 September; reprinted in RADFORD, JILL and RUSSELL, DIANA E.H. (Eds) (1992) *Femicide: The Politics of Woman Killing,* Buckingham, Open University Press.
RADFORD, JILL (1984) 'Womanslaughter: A License to Kill? The Killing of Jane Asher', in SCRATON, PHIL and GORDON, PAUL (Eds) *Causes for Concern,* Harmondsworth, Penguin, reprinted in RADFORD, JILL and RUSSELL, DIANE E.H. (Eds) (1992) *Femicide: The Politics of Woman Killing,* Buckingham, Open University Press.
RADFORD, JILL (1991) 'Immaculate Conceptions', *Trouble and Strife,* 21 (Summer).
RIGHTS OF WOMEN BULLETIN, available from Rights of Women, 52–54 Featherstone St, London EC1Y 8RT (071 251 6576).
SOUTHALL BLACK SISTERS (1991) *Against the Grain,* available from SBS, 52 Norwood Rd, Southall, Middx.
WOMEN'S AID TO FORMER YUGOSLAVIA (1993): leaflet (circulating at the conference and the international section), in WSN Newsletter, No. 15, July 1993.

Chapter 3

Nondecision-Making . . . A Management Guide to Keeping Women's Interest Issues Off the Political Agenda

Jennifer Marchbank

For the past century women in Britain and across the world have pursued policies to advance their position. This is, inherently, a threat to the position of men and to the maintenance of patriarchal society. In order to protect the status quo it is necessary to marginalize Women's Interest Issues (WIIs) (for definition and classification see Appendix, pp. 68-9) and to keep them off political agendas. One way that this can be achieved is to learn how to identify them and to employ tried and tested tactics. By providing examples of actual usage of these techniques this short guide will arm you with the basic tools (note the phallic language) to marginalize all WIIs and to remove feminists, femocrats and, if you wish, women from your field of work. The general name given to this practice is outright sexism but the tool I describe is much more than mere sexism — it is a system for the marginalization and defeat of any challenger. It is called *nondecision-making*.

The passage of women-specific legislation, the aim of the 'Equal Rights' feminists of the late nineteenth and early twentieth centuries, improved the social, economic and political position of women, though challenging gender relations was not the prime aim of this movement, or rather — conveniently for patriarchy — not the image of this movement that has been conventionally taught. On the other hand, the Women's Liberation Movement (WLM) of the latter half of the twentieth century set out to change society and how it is governed. 'The ultimate point of a feminist women's movement must be change in the way politics and the role of the state is conceptualised' (Lovenduski, 1986). Given this aim it is vital for the survival of patriarchy that WIIs are defeated.

Jennifer Marchbank

Nondecision-making

There is a general consensus among students of decision-making that decisions automatically involve power. Inequality in access to the decision-making process is related to the power that an individual or interest holds and affects the extent to which issues get onto agendas. In other words, power is inextricably linked to decision-making.

There is a longstanding debate on the theories of power. Concisely, Pluralists like Dahl (1961) concentrate on the observable, direct exercise of power — the *First Face*. But others, such as Bachrach and Baratz (1970) and Schattschneider (1960) focus on bias within a system and how that is maintained, which is the *Second Face*. Other theorists say that society may be structured in such a way as to prevent all opposition: Lukes (1974) and Gaventa (1980) support the view that bias can be supported by creating an atmosphere of quiescence — the *Third Face*. Lukes and Gaventa also discuss false consciousness, that is the mistaken belief that a certain policy benefits oneself. These Second and Third Faces are what are referred to as nondecision-making.

So what is nondecision-making? According to Bachrach and Baratz, who coined the term, a

> nondecision . . . is a decision that results in the suppression or thwarting of a latent or manifest challenge to the values or interests of the decision-maker. . . . nondecision-making is a means by which demands for change . . . can be suffocated before they are even voiced; or kept covert; or killed before they gain access to the relevant decision-making arena; or, failing all these things, maimed or destroyed in the decision-implementing state of the policy process. (1970, p. 44).

In simple English nondecision-making is the employment of power to maintain the status quo. However, rather than employing power in an outright and open conflict — which might get us into trouble with the law or the electorate — nondecision-making uses less direct methods, such as:

- threats to prevent an issue being raised;

- intimidation of the challenger;

- co-option of the challenger;

Nondecision-Making

Policy Making is a Series of Hurdles
A Policy may Flounder at Each and Every One

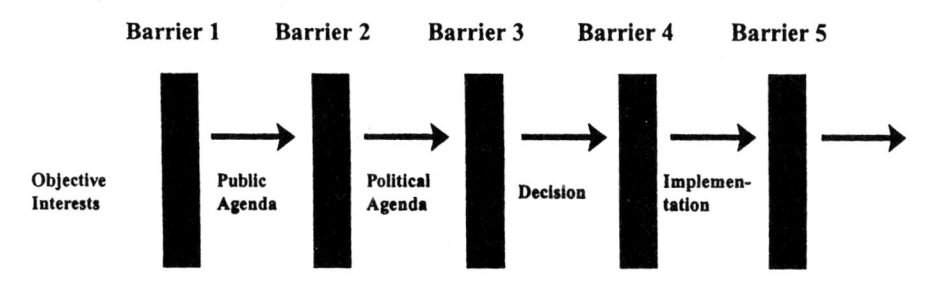

Figure 3.1: Policy-Making as a Series of Hurdles

- branding with negative symbols (e.g. 'loony left') to delegitimize;

- burying of demands in committee, or other delaying tactics.

Nondecision-making can occur at any stage of the policy life cycle. Given that the decision-making process is a series of hurdles which an issue must overcome before becoming a policy (see figure 3.1) there is an opportunity for nondecision-making (as well as outright opposition) at each and every one of these hurdles — and I urge you to use these opportunities.

The next section aims to provide appropriate examples of the successful application of nondecision-making techniques in the battle against the all-invasive WII.

Case Study of Successful Nondecision-Making

This case involves the creation of a childcare policy by a Scottish Local Authority and the subsequent pursuance of a women-orientated approach by a senior femocrat. In the late 1970s the Education Department of this Local Authority (LA) decided to develop policies on pre-school children. Various reports were written, systems investigated, corporate policy-making encouraged and boundaries between departments broken down. The end result of this was that a special unit was devised to deal with pre-school children. The Head of this newly formed

Unit became the only female member of an education Directorate of approximately twenty.

Various techniques of nondecision-making have been found to have been utilized, both in the formation of this policy and against the woman appointed to implement the policy. These will now be listed as illustrations of good practice in nondecision-making.

1 Issue Suppression

A major function of nondecision-making is to marginalize issues which challenge the status quo via the processes of suppression. Issue suppression may be utilized at every stage of the decision-making process and is effective in silencing debate.

Fortunately for this case childcare as an issue can have several definitions, which allows scope for nondecision-making in the form of issue suppression — for it can be defined as an education issue, a welfare issue, a deprivation issue or an issue of equality. Outshoorn's (1986) study of Dutch abortion policy highlighted how important it is to the final shape of a policy for women to have it defined in feminist terms. Therefore, conversely it is useful to patriarchy to be able to redefine issues as other than WIIs. In other words, defining childcare as an issue of social deprivation will have a very different result from defining it as an issue of equality.

This policy on children under 5 began in 1978 with the publication of a report by the Social Work Department (Strathclyde Regional Council, 1978). Among other proposals, this Social Work report recommended establishing an integrated, community-based daycare service offering flexibility and choice. Services for working mothers were included in the recommendations. From this background a Working Group on Under-Fives was established in 1981. After four years this Working Group produced their *Final Report* (Strathclyde Regional Council, 1985) focusing mainly on issues of social deprivation and child development.

The *Final Report* included two chapters of particular note here. In the first there is extensive detail on future policy directions for policy on under-5s. At no point in this chapter is any reference made to the needs of working parents yet it includes the statement: 'services for under-fives are also services for parents — the two are inextricably linked'. This appears to relate only to the educational and welfare needs of the child and parent for an examination of the provision recommended reveals that a facility for the children of working parents is excluded.

Nondecision-Making

Secondly, a later chapter of the *Final Report* deals exclusively with childminders and daycarers, noting that the service was less well developed in this Region than in other areas of Britain. *All* the recommendations in this section relate to the registration, recruitment and training of childminders. It should be noted that the Working Group avoided proposing any alternatives which might have been more woman-orientated. This is even more commendable given that the Group were aware that childminding was not universally available and that parents often stated a preference for other forms of daycare — they did not succumb to this pressure.

Issue Suppression can be endangered during the consultation stage of a policy. Consultation can revitalize the debate and force the reintroduction of suppressed issues. However, an examination of the different organizations invited to comment upon this policy and to proffer advice during the formulation period — detailed in an appendix of the *Final Report* — displays how this was avoided in this case. The 'interested parties' invited to respond included five institutions of higher education, three health organizations, several voluntary organizations and the British Association of Social Workers. Even if there had been calls from feminists for women's organizations to be consulted these were answerable: the Working Group did consult a women's organization — the Women's Royal Voluntary Service (WRVS) — though this appears to have been the only one — which focused on the need of expectant mothers for transport to ante-natal clinics.

Working mothers were not consulted at this stage, though the Group could argue that their needs had been recognized by inviting a response from the National Childminding Association — an interesting tactic, since, naturally, the NCA was more concerned with its members' interests than in advising the LA to provide a rival service to themselves and made little contribution towards the case of working mothers. In fact, the only organizations which put forward suggestions on the problems faced by working women were Gingerbread and the Scottish Council for Single Parents — both concerned with the economic position of single parents, the majority of whom are women — but their comments were not taken up. This itself is not an example of nondecision-making in that childminding was considered and suggestions made for the improvement of the service, the fact being that working mothers were simply not high enough up the priority list to justify funding.

Where nondecision-making did occur was in the Group's continual reference to the needs of working parents. From 1981 when the issue was first raised in the Group reference was constantly made but it became more and more peripheral until, by the time of the *Final Report* in 1985, it was of the lowest priority. It is difficult not to conclude that the habitual mentions of working mothers operated as palliatives for, when asked about on under-5s, all interviewees stated that working women were a policy priority, yet nothing was done about it. This suggests that nondecision-making did occur in that the failure to openly state that childcare for working mothers was *not* part of the policy can be seen as a successful attempt to avoid challenges to the policy. This is an example of nondecision-making through issue suppression.

2 Delay

My next example of nondecision-making involved a survey of community needs in 1987 undertaken by the principal femocrat to justify her actions in pursuing childcare from a feminist perspective. This very detailed survey covered all areas of under-5 care and parental requirements. One issue which the survey clearly raised was that one-third of mothers worked and that two-thirds of those who did not claimed that they would if they could only find suitable childcare — an uncomfortable finding for patriarchy. This resulted in the Under-Five Committee agreeing that all new developments would have to take the needs of working parents into consideration — a challenge to the status quo as well as being a femocrat and WII victory. However, not all was lost — when workplace nurseries were raised later in the same meeting regarding another project, the decision on action was remitted back, not to be dealt with for over two years. This then is an example of suppressing an issue through the tactics of delay and as the committee were on record as officially supporting the cause they were safe from immediate feminist criticism.

The femocrats were further placated by several successes between 1987 and 1989 when they managed to get the Under-Five Committee to revise its policy principles to include employment needs and to reflect equal opportunities regarding sex and race. Nonetheless, the categorization of the policy as primarily welfarist and educational is still accurate as equality was only included as a consideration within the *implementation* of the *existing* policy and did not mean that the actual nature of the under-5 policy was revised to include working mothers.

In conclusion, it can be argued that this under-5 policy is most certainly radical in a number of ways — most notably in tackling social deprivation. However, this radical policy is also paternalistic and welfarist and there is no way, given the inaction over providing better facilities for working mothers, that it can be called women-orientated. Therefore, it is an example of a defeat of a WII. It seems that politicians were keen to challenge class, but not sex, division and employed various nondecision-making techniques to guarantee the success of their position.

3 Bureaucratic Culture

Although not strictly a use of nondecision-making, creating a bureaucratic culture which is hostile to WIIs can be incredibly useful in creating and maintaining a bias against WIIs.

Swiebel (1988) shows how various factors within the bureaucratic culture can disadvantage attempts to devise and implement policy for women. Insufficient political support and an absence of career incentives within a bureaucracy can marginalize policy for women. Few bureaucrats will be willing to expend energy promoting policies which are not perceived as enjoying political endorsement or which would not be considered appropriate actions in promotion stakes.

In the LA described above there existed a political culture which did little to encourage Officers to anticipate that feminist demands would receive a sympathetic hearing. In fact, a clash existed between two political cultures, one welfarist and one radical, but both socialist — and the radical agenda lost out. In this LA, the fact that both agendas were socialist masked the lack of radicalism long enough for that agenda to be defeated. In the words of the Head of the Unit, 'we only gradually came to understand the differences and implicit as well as explicit assumptions about the purpose and directions of services' (Penn, 1992, p. 24). Although the values held by the staff of the Unit were a challenge to the status quo, the existence of such a bureaucratic culture, closed to radical suggestions regarding women's role, ensured that the prevailing bias towards the welfarist and paternalistic view prevailed.

4 Lack of Sympathy

Lack of sympathy is related to bureaucratic culture in that it operates to isolate, marginalize and exclude holders of positions which challenge the status quo. In our LA a lack of sympathy for, or understanding of, feminist issues ensured that anyone holding such views felt marginalized and excluded. As our 'defeated' challenger stated:

> For most of the time ... I felt uncomfortable as part of an all-male management team, not only with masculine assumptions about the relative importance of different aspects of the service, but with assumptions about hierarchy, status and worth. In retrospect, this is a familiar experience for women in management but at the time it was an isolating experience. (Penn, 1992, p. 107)

5 Branding and Delegitimization

In their list of nondecision-making tactics Bachrach and Baratz include the practice of branding. This means to label someone or something in negative terms so as to delegitimize what is being presented. Branding is a very common occurrence — the frequent cries of 'loony left' directed at certain actions of Labour-controlled councils by their opponents are too profuse to document but their effect is obvious — once labelled it is difficult for the target to regain status in the eyes of the public or of decision-makers. Although it is very crude this method is also very effective.

The subject of this branding — our femocrat — was a fairly easy target in that her personal politics regarding childcare were well-known since she had authored several articles advocating a more radical and equality approach to childcare.[2] This placed her outside of the Education Department and the Council. Further, her background as a politician was also public knowledge[3] as was her feminist viewpoint.[4] On top of these factors was a perceived difference between the needs of Scotland and London. The local tabloid media attacked her on the basis of her being an 'outsider' from another part of Britain (*Sun* (Scotland), 16 August 1988; 5 October 1988). Some councillors went as far as to confide in the press that '[her] appointment was certainly not a popular one' (Councillor Peter Edmonds, *Sun,* 5 October 1988).

This hostility was not limited to within the Council but also managed to filter into the community and thus delegitimize the Officer there too. An extract from an article in the *Sun* illustrates the employment of several brandings:

> Scots teachers are terrified of a new loony left regime — because a nursery boss has been employed from a notorious London council. . . . She is accused of neglecting nursery schools in favour of free creches for working mums. . . . One teacher said 'We're not having it — look at London. This is Scotland and we do not want politics in education. She is a feminist and I think she bases her ideals on her own background' (*Sun*, 5 October 1988)

This one quotation contains all of the negative labels used against this femocrat and relates them to her feminism and past political career to create an impression that any policy sought by this woman must be illegitimate. This illustrates that it is possible to marginalize a challenger, even one with high levels of political skill and experience. Although it is unclear whether or not this branding was deliberate, this is not important to the outcome for it justified the view that this Officer was not to be granted the respect commensurate with her position. This resulted in the blocking of reports and proposals at the stage of the Directorate (sometimes necessitating the bypassing of established procedures to get proposals discussed[5]) and in creating a generally unpleasant working atmosphere. This is a very clear instance of marginalizing a potential challenger through branding, conscious or unconscious, and as such is a beautiful example of the ways in which WIIs and their promoters can be isolated and totally discredited, and should be utilized wherever possible.

Conclusion

There is only one conclusion to be drawn from this paper — and that is that nondecision-making is a useful tool for patriarchy as it has a proven track record of success in marginalizing WIIs. In just this one case study it has been shown that WIIs, femocrats and women can be kept out of decision-making arenas and marginalized even if they do acquire certain levels of power. It is my recommendation that anyone wishing to defend patriarchy and gender power inequalities should look to nondecision-making as a weapon in this vital battle.

Jennifer Marchbank

Notes

1 It is only fair to point out that this was not strictly a fight between men and women, for this Officer did have the support of a senior male politician. However, he was not to remain influential in his field for long, thus heightening her marginalization and assisting in the maintenance of the patriarchal status quo.
2 See 'No Hope at the Nursery End' *Guardian*, 24 July 1984, p. 11, and 'State of Siege', *New Society*, 12 April 1984.
3 The *Glasgow Herald*, (21 May 1986, p. 11) reported that the Pre-Fives Officer had been a councillor for a London borough.
4 The *Glasgow Herald* (21 May 1986, p. 11), for example, reported that Penn was keen to change the perception that childcare was women's work and to encourage more men into the field.
5 Occasionally another Officer would 'sponsor' a paper to ensure that it achieved discussion at the Directorate level (private communication).

References

BACHRACH, P. and BARATZ, M.S. (1970) *Power and Poverty: Theory and Practice*, Oxford, Oxford University Press.
DAHL, R.A. (1960) 'The Analysis of Influence in Local Communities', in ADRIAN, C. (Ed.) *Social Science and Community Action*, Michigan, USA.
DAHL, R.A. (1961) *Who Governs? Democracy and Power in an American City*, New Haven, Yale University Press.
GAVENTA, J. (1980) *Power and Powerlessness: Quiescence and Rebellion in an Appalachian Valley*, Oxford, Oxford University Press.
LOVENDUSKI, J. (1986) *Women and European Politics*, Brighton, Wheatsheaf.
LUKES, S. (1974) *Power: A Radical View*, London, Macmillan.
OUTSHOORN, J. (1986) 'The Feminist Movement and Abortion Policy in the Netherlands', in DAHLERUP, D. (Ed.) *The New Women's Movement: Feminism and Political Power in Europe and the USA*, London, Sage.
PENN, H. (1992) *Under Fives: The View from Strathclyde*, Edinburgh, Scottish Academic Press.
SCHATTSCHNEIDER, S. (1960) *The Semi-Sovereign People: A Realist's View of Democracy in America*, New York, Holt, Rinehart and Winston.
STRATHCLYDE REGIONAL COUNCIL (1978) *Room to Grow*, Glasgow, Strathclyde Regional Council.
STRATHCLYDE REGIONAL COUNCIL (1985) *Under Fives — Final Report of the Member/Officer Group*, Glasgow, Strathclyde Regional Council.
SWIEBEL, J. (1988) 'The Gender of Bureaucracy: Reflections on Policy-Making for Women', *Politics*, vol. 8, no. 1, pp. 14–19.

Appendix
What Qualifies as a Women's Interest Issue (WII)?

WIIs cover three areas:

1 WOMEN-SPECIFIC policies, i.e., policies explicitly directed at women; for example the 1927 Act removing the marriage bar, electoral laws and the Equal Pay Act of 1970;

2 'newer category' of FEMINIST ISSUES which seek to change society's structure and assumptions regarding gender roles;

3 GENDER-RELATED — due to the differing strata men and women occupy in society the same policy may affect each differently, e.g., placing more revenue-raising emphasis on VAT (Value Added Tax) rather than Income Tax hurts women more as they tend to earn less than men but have to buy the same goods.

Such a broad definition of WIIs includes ALL issues which affect women's role in society.

Section II

Disrupting Sexual and Gender Identities?

Introduction

Over the past twenty years feminists have severely disrupted dominant discourses about gender and sexuality. We have argued, in both our theories and political practice, that gender and sexuality are socially constructed categories, closely, if not fundamentally, entwined with each other. Radical feminists, lesbian feminists and, more recently, poststructuralist feminists have emphasized that sexual and gender identities and practices are not rooted in nature, and hence are open to challenge and change. The chapters in this section engage in various ways with the notion that sexual and gender identities and practices are important sites for feminist intervention and struggle.

Sue Wilkinson and Celia Kitzinger's chapter develops a radical critique of heterosexuality which posits heterosexuality as the major way in which masculinity and femininity are produced in a relationship of domination and subordination. They examine the challenge posed to this critique of heterosexuality by recent arguments for a 'virgin heterosexuality' and a postmodern 'queer heterosexuality'. Although the proposal for 'virgin heterosexuality' claims to offer women a mode of heterosexuality which does not involve subordination, and that for 'queer heterosexuality' claims actively to 'fuck with gender', Wilkinson and Kitzinger reject both on the grounds that they ultimately fail to disrupt the processes by which heterosexuality constructs gender. They conclude that heterosexuality remains central to women's oppression, and must be opposed as such.

In contrast to Wilkinson and Kitzinger's scepticism about postmodern contributions to debates about sexuality, Angelika Czekay's chapter suggests that recent American feminist performance has been the site of powerful destabilizations of gender and sexual identities. She discusses the use three performers — Annie Sprinkle, Janice Perry and Kate Bornstein — make of their bodies in order to explore shifting gender identities. Czekay emphasizes that the many and varied representations of the female body in their performances self-consciously and playfully fetishize the body and in so doing assert the agency of the subject to challenge binary categories of gender and sexuality. Czekay's article can be seen as an exemplar of the emerging body of 'queer theory' with which British feminists, including Wilkinson and Kitzinger, are beginning to engage.

Like Czekay's chapter, Becky Rosa's article highlights women's power to challenge established sexual practices and institutionalized heterosexuality. She extends existing critiques of the role of heterosexuality in maintaining women's oppression by examining how monogamy, both heterosexual and lesbian, serves to keep women divided. In a passionate argument for the revolutionary potential of female friendship she suggests that lesbians should challenge the heterosexual couple model on which most of us base our relationships and build instead a community rooted in a variety of sexual and nonsexual relationships.

Taken together these three chapters illustrate that debates about sexual and gender identities and practices remain central to contemporary feminism.

Chapter 4

Dire Straights? Contemporary Rehabilitations of Heterosexuality

Sue Wilkinson and Celia Kitzinger

The Radical Critique of Heterosexuality

From the beginning of first-wave feminism on, feminists have produced searing critiques of heterosexuality, pointing in particular to the *abuses* associated with heterosexual sex: child sexual abuse, rape in marriage, clitoridectomy, wife-beating, sexual slavery (e.g., Mainardi, 1970; Russell, 1990; Delphy and Leonard, 1992); and to the *compulsory* nature of heterosexuality in a society which systematically inculcates and rewards heterosexuality while punishing and rendering invisible lesbianism (e.g., Rich, 1980). Many women, however, experience heterosexuality as pleasurable, supportive, and otherwise beneficial (i.e., not as 'abusive'); and many women also experience heterosexuality as 'freely chosen' (i.e., not as 'compulsory'). Do such experiences suggest that certain kinds of heterosexuality or heterosexual practice are, or should be, exempt from feminist critique? Alternatively, do they suggest that women who experience heterosexuality as 'non-abusive' and/or 'non-compulsory' are suffering from 'false consciousness'? We think not — rather, we argue that heterosexuality *per se* must be subject to analysis for its key position in the social construction of gender; and also that it is possible to develop such an analysis without resorting to notions of heterosexual women as suffering from 'false consciousness'.

Consider this description of the effect of a heterosexual feminist's first experience of heterosexual intercourse — an experience voluntarily chosen and enjoyed. Having, in childhood, taken 'delight in being mistaken for a boy', and in adolescence nurtured an 'inner conviction'

75

that she was 'not a "proper" woman', the writer — Alison Thomas — tells how:

> it was, several years later, my first 'proper' sexual experience with a man (as opposed to hesitant fumblings with adolescent boys of my own age) which made me finally identify myself as a woman ... I was totally intoxicated with the awesome realization that this grown man actually desired me, and it was this ... which allowed me to believe in myself as a woman for the first time ... this quintessential heterosexual seduction confirm[ed] my sense of womanhood (Thomas, 1993, p. 84).

Our analysis of heterosexuality addresses just such experiences. Following theorists like Judith Butler (1990), Marilyn Frye (1990), Sheila Jeffreys (1990), Catherine MacKinnon (1987) and Monique Wittig (1992), we argue that heterosexuality is a key site for the social construction of gender, and that heterosexual sex is a primary instrument through which we are constructed *as women* and *as men*, and hence as oppressed and oppressor.

We call this analysis the 'radical' critique, since it goes to the root of heterosexuality *per se*, as constitutive of maleness and femaleness — and does not depend upon heterosexuality being experienced as either abusive or compulsory. When heterosexuality is seen as the major way in which people with penises make themselves 'real' men and people with vaginas are made 'real' women (Frye, 1993, p. 134), it becomes possible — indeed, necessary — to critique it *even when* it is experienced as 'freely chosen' or as 'pleasurable'. Heterosexuality becomes subject to critique for its *reinscription of sex difference*, and hence, inevitably, women's subordination and men's power.

Heterosexuality reinscribes male/female divisions by its very definition: 'hetero' means 'other', 'different'; heterosexuality means sexual involvement with one who is other, one who is different — man with woman, woman with man. The otherness of the 'other' sex, the 'differentness' of man from woman, is thereby immediately reinforced. There are, of course, many ways in which human beings differ from each other: 'heterosexuality' *could* mean sex between two people of different racial or ethnic backgrounds (regardless of their sex), or between two people of different religious or political persuasions, or between two people from different socioeconomic groups. Instead, 'heterosexuality' marks what is seen, in some sense, as the fundamental 'difference' — the male/female division.

Moreover, to be a man is to be dominant, to be a woman is to be subordinate: not because it *has* to be this way, but because, in the sociopolitical context of patriarchy, it *is*. (Think of the counter-normative examples of the 'sensitive new man' or the 'aggressive, unattractive feminist'). Similarly, under *hetero*patriarchy, as lesbians — who don't have sex with men — we are 'not women' (cf. Wittig, 1992); and, indeed — as we don't do sexual intercourse — we may be said not to have 'sex' at all (cf. Frye, 1993). The meanings of heterosexuality/homosexuality, male/female and man/woman are what they are *made to mean* under (hetero)patriarchy. The radical critique of heterosexuality not only recognizes such meanings, but requires us to interrogate their sociopolitical functions.

Ever since feminists first began to advance critiques of heterosexuality, there have been heterosexual women determined to rescue it from any form of political challenge, from first-wave 'spinster-baiting' campaigns (Jeffreys, 1985, p. 95) at the turn of the century to second-wave responses to calls for political lesbianism — see the letters in *Love Your Enemy?* (Onlywomen Press, 1981). In response to the various critiques ('abusive', 'compulsory' and 'radical') to which heterosexuality has been subjected, contemporary feminists have continued to explain, justify and defend heterosexuality — and to denounce its critics: see, for example, responses to our own attempts to provide a forum for the theorization of heterosexuality (Kitzinger *et al.,* 1992; Wilkinson and Kitzinger, 1993) from Hollway (1993) and Swindells (1993). Indeed, some of the very theorists who propose the 'radical' critique, which would seem to render heterosexuality a political anathema for feminists, nonetheless retain the possibility of some kind of heterosexuality exempt from this analysis. In the rest of this chapter, we discuss and evaluate two such attempts — ironically, both (in their contemporary manifestations) originating from lesbian feminists. These are 'virgin heterosexuality' (a heterosexuality which does *not* reinscribe, but rather *resists* 'maleness' and 'femaleness') and 'queer heterosexuality' (a heterosexuality which not only does not reinscribe, but which actively *subverts*, 'maleness' and 'femaleness').

Virgin Heterosexuality: Resisting 'Sex'

Lesbian feminist Marilyn Frye (1990, 1993) offers the possibility of rehabilitating heterosexuality by reviving the historical meaning attached to the word 'virgins', which originally meant *not* women without experience of heterosexual intercourse but rather 'females who are willing to engage in chosen connections with males, who are wild females, undomesticated females, thoroughly defiant of patriarchal female heterosexuality' (Frye, 1993, p. 134). Other feminists have also pointed to the earlier meaning of 'virgin' as 'never captured: UNSUBDUED' (Daly, 1984, p. 262, her emphasis); 'belonging to no man' (Hall, 1980, p. 11); free 'to take [male] lovers or reject them' (Warner, 1978, cited in Mills, 1991, p. 251).

Can a contemporary woman become a 'virgin' in this sense? As Marilyn Frye (1993, p. 133) puts it:

> *Will* and *can* any women, many women, creatively defy patriarchal definitions of the real and the meaningful to invent and embody modes of living positive Virginity which include women's maintaining erotic, economic, home-making, partnering connections with men?

Or, put more bluntly, 'can you fuck without losing your virginity?' (Frye, 1993, p. 136).

Many women heard Marilyn Frye's own answer to this question as 'no', and as claiming lesbianism as an essential component of feminism. What she actually says is this:

> I think everything is against it, but *it's not my call*. I can hopefully image, but the counter-possible creation of such a reality is up to those who want to live it, if anyone does (Frye, 1993, p. 136, her emphasis).

Marilyn Frye's 'imaging' poses an important challenge to heterosexual feminists, and her analysis has far-reaching implications for feminist theory.

The Politics of Penetration

First, in suggesting that sexual intercourse is *compatible* with virginity, Frye's analysis runs counter to the long-standing feminist political analysis of heterosexual intercourse as *inherently* oppressive, and overlooks an important site of feminist resistance. It is *precisely* penile-vaginal penetration, rather than any other acts of heterosexual 'sex', which has been critiqued by those who point to the particular set of cultural and political meanings attached to penile penetration of women (being 'had', 'possessed', 'taken', 'fucked'), meanings which are 'oppressive humiliating and destructive' (Duncker, 1993, p. 148). The Leeds Revolutionary Feminist Group (1981, p. 7) argued that:

> No act of penetration takes place in isolation. Each takes place in a system of relationships that is male supremacy. As no individual woman can be 'liberated' under male supremacy, so no act of penetration can escape its function and its symbolic power.

The linguistic sleight proposed by some feminists in renaming penetration 'enclosure' (Ramazanoglu, 1989, p. 164) or 'penile covering' (Hite, 1989) simply serves to obscure the problem of the *institutionalized meanings* of penile penetration under heteropatriarchy.

This analysis of penile penetration is independent of whether or not a particular woman happens to *enjoy it* — although these two arguments have often been confused, as though the experience of 'pleasure' in sexual intercourse somehow mitigates against its oppressive function. Although for some women, penetration 'can feel like one more invasion . . . [and is] less pleasurable than other forms of sexual contact' (Gill and Walker, 1993, p. 70), many others can, and do, take pleasure from the experience and want to distinguish between 'compulsory' or 'abusive' penetration and 'consensual' penetration (e.g., Rowland, 1993, p. 77; Hollway, 1993).

It is not uncommon for heterosexual women to suggest that certain forms of 'consensual' sexual activity, whether welcomed penetration, or the 'politically correct blow job' (Dennis, 1992, p. 163), are exempt from the radical analysis of heterosexuality as oppressive *because they are pleasurable*. Commenting on the 'Heterosexuality' Special Issue of the journal *Feminism & Psychology* (Kitzinger *et al.*, 1992), which preceded our edited book (Wilkinson and Kitzinger, 1993), Wendy Hollway (1993, p. 412) laments 'the failure of this special issue to address questions of heterosexual desire, pleasure, and satisfaction'. We would reiterate our point that (although we were certainly struck by how *little* pleasure our contributors expressed), it is not 'pleasure', or the lack thereof, which constitutes our analytic focus. As Sheila Jeffreys says:

> An issue on housing would not be expected to focus on interior decoration at the expense of looking at homelessness. An issue on women's work would probably not just focus on individual fulfilment but on the issue of exploitation . . . [I]t is only in the area of sexuality that individual pleasure has taken precedence over the ending of oppression (Jeffreys, 1990, p. 264).

Or, put differently, since when is a good fuck any compensation for getting fucked? (paraphrased from MacKinnon, 1987, p. 61).

The refusal of coitus, whether or not accompanied by a more general refusal to do any form of sex with men, has long been a deliberate strategy of resistance for feminists (cf. Jeffreys, 1985). In seeking to revive a definition of 'virgin' which does not preclude penile-vaginal penetration, Frye renders invisible decades of feminist struggles around this issue: struggles related not just to the pleasure which may (or may not) be associated with penile-vaginal penetration, but to the *meanings* it has acquired, including those of being 'possessed' and 'had' — meanings which stand in direct opposition to those Frye wants to reclaim for 'virgin'. Moreover, some women are *real* virgins (in the modern sense of the term): women whose vaginas *are* untouched by any penis. The political imperatives guiding that choice are obscured by Frye's reversion to an archaic definition of 'virgin'.

Accepting the analysis of penile-vaginal penetration as inherently oppressive (and/or simply disliking the sensations it produces), other women — and, indeed, some men (e.g., Stoltenberg, 1990) — choose heterosexual sex which does not include intercourse itself. This rebellion against the 'coital imperative' is very difficult for women to achieve in the context of heterosexual relationships (see Sebestyen, 1982, p. 235). Nor is celibacy an easy solution (cf. Brown, 1993; Cline, 1993): a married woman who practises celibacy may be characterized as 'a ball-breaking feminist' (Gavey, 1993, p. 115).

If, as in Frye's analysis, heterosexual sexual intercourse is not seen as *a key site* of oppression, then women's valiant attempts to resist it (see Dworkin, 1987; Jeffreys, 1985) are reduced to mere acts of personal preference. Of course, some women happen to dislike sexual intercourse (and prefer not to do it), while others happen to like it — but liking or disliking it is not the point here: personal preferences do not address the key question of the function of intercourse in maintaining women's oppression.

(W)here are the Virgins?

Second, it is not at all clear how 'virginity' (in Marilyn Frye's terms) can be accomplished, or whether a woman can remain 'free', 'sexually and hence socially her own person' (Frye, 1993, p. 133), when engaging in heterosexual sexual intercourse and otherwise connecting with men. As Frye (1993, p. 133) points out, 'in any universe of patriarchy, there are no

Virgins in this sense': female children, lesbians, celibate and heterosexual women are *all* (in different ways) possessed by, and defined in relation to, men. If the *refusal* of penile-vaginal penetration can at least be conceptualized as resistance to heteropatriarchal oppression, then women's 'voluntary' engagement in coitus can be characterized as compliance with, or capitulation to, the enemy — rather than as free choice (Leeds Revolutionary Feminist Group, 1981). Adrienne Rich's (1980) concept of 'compulsory heterosexuality' has, paradoxically, been used to promote the notion of a 'freely chosen', 'consensual' heterosexuality (see Brunet and Turcotte, 1988, p. 455).

The 'choice' of heterosexual feminist virginity could begin to 'make sense' (according to Frye) if it included the following: refusal to attire or decorate the body in ways which signal female compliance with male-defined femininity; defence of women-only spaces; refusal of male protection and of the institution of marriage (despite the economic pressures); and ardent passion for, and enduring friendships with, other Virgins — including lesbians. Some women do attempt such 'virginal' strategies: 'woman-identified radical feminist' Robyn Rowland (1993), for example, takes responsibility for her 'choice' to be heterosexual; is not married; lives apart from her male partner 75 per cent of the time; and identifies her 'crucially important' commitment to 'putting women first'. But for most heterosexual feminists, their heterosexual relationships constitute a context in which woman-identified behaviours run counter to the interests of their male partners and/or cannot successfully be negotiated with them.

Moreover, many women have marriage and/or other heterosexual partnerships denied them for reasons of racism, class oppression, or disabilism (see Appleby, 1993; Griffin, 1993). Others are forcibly separated from their male partners (and children) by war, famine, political intrigue, scarcity of work, or economic necessity. The woman who, forced by her own poverty or the exigencies of her country's national debt, leaves her family to work as a domestic servant or as a migrant coffee picker, may well be apart from her husband for 75 per cent (or more) of the time, but where is *her* opportunity to 'invent and embody modes of living positive Virginity'?

Heterosex as Power Difference

Third, Frye's analysis fails centrally to address the 'radical' critique of heterosexuality which she herself advances: the function of heterosexuality in constructing us as 'men' and as 'women', and hence as oppressor and oppressed. Sexuality, as Catherine MacKinnon (1987, p. 149) says, 'is a social construct, gendered to the ground'. Heterosexuality is a key mechanism through which male dominance is achieved. Male dominance is 'not an artificial overlay' (MacKinnon, 1987) upon heterosexuality, which can somehow be stripped away to leave an uncorrupted, pure, sexual interaction; rather it is intrinsic to heterosex itself.

Many feminist theorists have analyzed the extent to which sex is eroticized power differences and have critiqued the phenomenon that Sheila Jeffreys (1990) labels 'heterosexual desire' — by which she means not just desire between women and men, but the eroticizing of dominance and submission. The problem, for feminists, is not just *men's* eroticizing of power, but also *women's* eroticizing of *powerlessness*. Erotic excitement, according to this analysis, is modelled upon a heterosexual paradigm constructed around power difference. When (as in lesbian or gay male sex) the 'sex' (as in 'gender') hierarchy is missing, other social stratifications ('race', class) or specially constructed power diffentials — as in sadomasochism — can sometimes be eroticized (cf. Clausen, 1991; Nichols, 1987).

As we have noted, critiques of heterosexual sexual activity often proceed as though sexual pleasure — or lack of it — were the sole criterion on which a feminist assessment could be made. Yet, for many women, the problem is rather their serious political concern about how sexual pleasure is produced, and the form that such pleasure takes. Lynne Segal (1983) points out that 'it does not feel like personal liberation to be able to orgasm to intensely masochistic fantasies'; and Sandra Lee Bartky's decision 'not to pursue men whose sadism excited me' (1993, p. 42) was made at the cost of 'the powerful erotic charge' found in such relationships. Sheila Jeffreys (1990, p. 314) recommends that women seek to shut down those sexual responses which eroticize subordination. Frye's acceptance of heterosexual desire and activity as unproblematic parts of the virgin's repertoire means that she utterly fails to engage with this kind of radical critique.

Queer Heterosexuality: Subverting 'Sex'

An alternative contemporary rehabilitation of heterosexuality comes from queer theory (and certain varieties of postmodernism). In recent years, the word 'queer', long used as a term of insult and self-loathing, has been reclaimed by lesbians, gay men, bisexuals, transvestites and transsexuals as a proud declaration of nonconformist sexualities: 'we're here, we're queer; get used to it!' The word 'queer' is seen as confrontational and as underscoring the fact that we are 'queer' ('deviant' and 'abnormal') to a world in which normality is defined in rigid and suffocating terms. The notion of 'queer heterosexuality' has come to refer to those people who, while doing what is conventionally defined as 'heterosexuality', nonetheless do so in ways which are transgressive of 'normality'. Just as Marilyn Frye and others have expanded the notion of 'virgin' to include (a particular way of doing) heterosex, so the queer theorists have expanded the notion of 'queer' to include — amongst other things — (a particular way of doing) heterosex.

Like 'virgin' theorists, 'queer' theorists start from the position that 'straight sex' *reinscribes* its participants as 'man' and 'woman'. Queer theory differs from virgin theory in that, whereas the concept of 'virgin' heterosexuality denotes the doing of (hetero)sex while *resisting* being 'sexed', 'queer' heterosexuality denotes the doing of (what used to be called) heterosex while *actively subverting* its constructive function. Rather than simply *resisting* the equation between sex (as activity) and sex (as 'gender'), queer theory explicitly acknowledges this link, and by deliberately drawing attention to and playing with it, attempts to denaturalize and hence subvert the equation. 'Fucking with gender' (a common phrase in queer theory) implies the possibility of doing sex in such a way that it not merely resists, but actively disrupts normative definitions of 'sex' and 'gender'.

Influenced by, and in many ways an offshoot of postmodernism, queer theory aims to deconstruct and confound normative categories of gender and sexuality, exposing their fundamental unnaturalness. There are no 'true' gender identities or natural sexes, rather maleness and femaleness are:

> *performative* in the sense that the essence or identity that they otherwise purport to express are *fabrications* manufactured and sustained through corporeal signs and other discursive means . . . an illusion discursively maintained for the purposes of the regulation of sexuality within the obligatory frame of reproductive heterosexuality (Butler, 1990, p. 136, emphasis in original).

There is no 'real' underlying maleness or femaleness on which we base our performances. 'Being' man or woman is conceptualized not as core identity, but rather as 'a put-on, a sex toy' (Schwichtenberg, 1993, p. 135) or as a 'temporary positioning' (Gergen, 1993, p. 64).

In conceptualizing what have previously been seen as 'core' identities (man/woman; heterosexual/homosexual) as no more than fluctuating fashions or performances, queer theory, like postmodernism more generally, expresses the hope for the future abolition of such divisive patriarchal binarisms, ushering in the age of the post-lesbian and — of course — the post-heterosexual. In this imagined world, man does not exist, nor woman neither; hence the concepts of heterosexuality, homosexuality and bisexuality are literally unthinkable. The 'sex' of the person you have sex with is not only irrelevant in terms of social meaning and identity: it is also unspecifiable, because 'sex-as-gender' is no longer a meaningful concept. Such a vision of the future is not, of course, specific to postmodernist and queer theory: it has a long (though rarely acknowledged) history within the gay, lesbian, and feminist liberation movements (e.g., Radicalesbians, 1970; Piercy, 1976). What is distinctive about postmodern and queer (as opposed to lesbian feminist) theory is the strategy envisioned for getting 'there' from 'here'.

The notion of 'queer heterosexuality' is one component of the postmodern strategy for transition into the brave new world of the future. Such a world would have no use for the concept of 'queer heterosexuality' because there would be no such 'thing' as heterosexuality, no 'men' and 'women' to perform it, nor any heteronormativity against which to be positioned as 'queer'. But in the interim, queer theorists give 'queer heterosexuals' a walk-on role. 'There are times', says queer theorist Cherry Smyth (1992), 'when queers may choose to call themselves heterosexual, bisexual, lesbian or gay, or none of the above'. According to Cathy Schwichtenberg (1993, p. 141), one could 'come out' and participate in a range of identities 'such as a lesbian heterosexual, a heterosexual lesbian, a male lesbian, a female gay man, or even a feminist sex-radical'. The notion of 'queer heterosexuality' has gained (a limited) currency in queer theory not, apparently, because many people are convinced of either its possibility or its desirability, or because it names significant contemporary identities, but because it is a necessary component of 'gender-fucking'.

Fucking with Gender

If all is artifice, simulation and performance, there is no point in opposing this by looking for some underlying reality or truth about 'men' and 'women'; rather the strategy becomes actively to participate in the artifice precisely in order to underscore the fragility of 'sex' and 'gender' *as artifice*. This strategy is often described by queer theorists as 'gender play' (Schwichtenberg, 1993), 'gender bending' (Braidotti, 1991) or, most popularly in the Queer movement, as 'gender-fuck' or 'fucking with gender' (Reich, 1992). The gender-fuck is supposed to 'deprive the naturalizing narratives of compulsory heterosexuality of their central protagonists: "man" and "woman"' (Butler, 1990, p. 146) and to illustrate the social constructedness of 'sex', in all its multiple meanings.

This key queer strategy, the gender-fuck, is about parody, pastiche, and exaggeration. It replaces *resistance* to dominant cultural meanings of 'sex' with carnivalesque reversals and transgressions of traditional gender roles and sexualities, which revel in their own artificiality. Media figures like Boy George and Annie Lennox have been cited as gender benders (Braidotti, 1991, p. 122-3), but the most famous example of contemporary gender-fucking is undoubtedly Madonna:

> Madonna, too, puts forth a disguise but less as a concealment than as a brash revelation of artifice. It is the essence of camp — cracking the mirror, dressing up and acting out to *expose* the constructedness of what in other settings passes as 'natural' male, female, or heterosexual (Henderson, 1993, p. 122).

This celebration of denaturalization is typical of the gender-fuck and Madonna has been described as both a 'postmodern feminist heroine' (Kaplan, 1987, cited in Mandzuick, 1993, p. 169; Schwichtenberg, 1993, p. 132) and as a 'queer icon' (Henderson, 1993, pp. 108, 119, 122).

A varied cast of characters has claimed (or been ascribed) the 'queer' label and lauded for its gender-fucking prowess. For example, in the name of 'queer', some lesbians reclaim butch-femme roles (as 'changeable costuming', MacCowan, 1992, p. 300), and some gay men reclaim camp (as 'the pervert's revenge on authenticity', Dollimore, 1991). Transvestism, transsexualism and even hermaphrodism are all celebrated for their transgression of the 'rigid binarism' (Williams, 1992, p. 261) of sexual identity (cf. Bristow, 1992; Sprinkle, 1992).

Queer (Per)Versions

From a feminist perspective, there are many objections one can raise against queer theory as a whole, not least its continuing fascination with violence and degradation, including claiming as its own supporters of pornography and sadomasochism (Merck, 1993, pp. 236-66); and the dominance of gay male concerns, including advocacy of lesbian emulation of gay men (Smyth, 1992, p. 42). Here we focus only on the specific implications of queer theory for the rehabilitation of heterosexuality — for more general critiques see Allen (1993); Jeffreys (1994); Parnaby (1993).

A major problem with 'queer heterosexuality' is that it is not clear either what it is — or, indeed that it is actually possible. For a 'lesbian' (or one who also has sex with women), it seems that merely the doing of sex with men is to be regarded as 'transgressive', in and of itself. Heterosexual sex for straight women cannot — *per se* - fulfil this allegedly transgressive function: does it then become a 'queer-approved' activity only if it violates some other purported taboos — if it is sadomasochistic or fetishistic, perhaps? Extrapolating from queer theory more generally, 'queer heterosexuality' would — at least — have to be a form of heterosexuality which 'fucks with gender', i.e., actively transgresses, parodies and subverts the 'woman subordinate', 'male dominant' sexual equation. It is not clear that, as a political strategy, this is any more sophisticated than is reclaiming as 'feminist' the female dominatrix scenes of male pornography or celebrating women's fantasies of 'raping' men. Further, it seems likely that, in current sociopolitical reality, a thoroughgoing 'queer heterosexuality' (i.e., one which *truly* subverts 'sex' and 'gender') cannot be envisioned. Only in a society *not* founded upon the subordination of women might such subversion be possible — except that then there would be nothing to subvert.

A second problem with the notion of queer heterosexuality is that, by definition, it presents heterosexuality and homosexuality as sexually — and hence politically — equivalent and interchangeable, betraying an underlying liberalism. The false equivalence imposed by queer theory (and liberal humanism before it — see Kitzinger, 1987) negates both the political force of lesbianism, as a refusal of the heteropatriarchal order, and the feminist analysis of heterosexuality as the key site of women's oppression. As the meanings of heterosexuality and homosexuality become blurred within a fantasy world of ambiguity, indeterminacy and charade, the material realities of oppression and the feminist politics of resistance are forgotten:

> It is difficult . . . to acknowledge the divided self and engage the pleasure of masquerade while at the same time fighting a strikingly antagonistic legal and social system for your health, your safety, your job, your place to live, or the right to raise your children (Henderson, 1993, p. 123).

Third, in promoting a flexible polysexuality (mono—, bi—, tri—, multi— trans—sexuality; categories to be transgressed and transcended) queer and postmodern theory provide renewed justification for heterosexual women's refusal to notice that they *are* heterosexual — or for their tendency to dismiss such an observation as unimportant, based on transitory and provisional attributions. Asked to identify themselves as heterosexual, many feminists react with defensive anger: 'How dare you assume I'm heterosexual?', 'Don't you think you are making one hell of an assumption?' (Wilkinson and Kitzinger, 1993, p. 5). Using such theories, then, the lesbian feminist insistence that heterosexual feminists make their choice intelligible (cf. Frye, 1993, p. 55–6) is, at best, sidestepped as unnecessary, at worst, dismissed as meaningless.

Finally, queer theory is centrally antagonistic to feminism. This is partly because queer theorists see feminism as a totalizing 'grand narrative', whose meanings and values must be subverted and thrown into question, along with the other explanatory frameworks in politics, science and philosophy, mere fodder for deconstruction in the postmodern age. More than this, however, queer politics is often expressed in terms explicitly oppositional to feminism, especially radical feminism, characterized as 'moralistic feminist separatism' (Smyth, 1992, p. 36). 'Queer' functions as apologia or justification for much behaviour seen by radical feminism as damaging to women and lesbians: imitation of gay male sexuality, the defence of pornography, and sadomasochism (Smyth, 1992, p. 38). 'Transgression' may be a convenient label to attach, and 'queer' a handy theory to invoke for those who are rather more interested in the hedonistic anarchistic possibilities of enhancing sexual 'pleasure' than in the political imperative of subverting 'sex' and 'gender'. This is sometimes made explicit, as for example when Lyndall MacCowan (1992, p. 323) wants to 'reclaim the right to fuck around with gender', but also insists that 'we need to take back "lesbian" as a sexual definition disburdened of any political justification'. There is no attempt to problematize pleasure, much less to engage with radical feminist attempts so to do (cf. Jeffreys, 1990; Kitzinger and Kitzinger, 1993; Kitzinger, 1994), other than to characterize these as repressive, restrictive and totalitarian in effect or intent. We cannot, then, as *feminists*, turn to queer theory in any attempts to salvage heterosexuality from feminist critiques, because queer theory simply ignores or mocks such critiques.

Rehabilitating Heterosexuality?

As we have shown, neither 'virgin' nor 'queer' theory offers a coherent feminist agenda sufficient for the rehabilitation of heterosexuality. At this point we would like to raise the question as to *why* heterosexuality is so vigorously defended, even (or perhaps, especially) — it seems — by lesbians? Why are some feminists apparently so desperate to continue the doing of heterosexual sex that they are prepared to accept dire concepts like 'virgin' and 'queer' heterosexuality in order to justify themselves? The lengths to which feminists (including lesbians) are prepared to go in defending sex with men is surely a clue to its political importance.

To some extent, and despite the bravado of the language in which both are couched, we see 'virgin' and 'queer' theory as defeatist. Recognizing the failure of lesbian feminism to communicate radical political analyses of heterosexuality, acknowledging the strong hold that heterosexuality apparently exerts on so many women (even those who *could* 'choose', even those who once *did* choose, lesbianism — see Bart, 1993), it is perhaps easier to revert to attempts to reform heterosexuality, exploring what feminist goals might be achievable *within* that institution, rather than attacking the institution *per se*. The abandonment of the radical critique of heterosexuality as inherently oppressive can be read as a tacit admission of defeat.

What seems to be missing in these continuing attempts to rehabilitate heterosexuality is any sense that it is still necessary to critique and analyze it as an oppressive mechanism of social control. 'Virgin' and 'queer' theories simply ignore, in equal measure, the 'compulsory', 'abusive' and 'radical' critiques of heterosexuality. For many women, heterosexuality still has the status of a compulsory institution; for many, it is still in the context of heterosexuality that they are abused. Any serious attempt to rehabilitate heterosexuality must, at the very least, address these material realities, making heterosexuality both 'safe' and 'optional' for all women. Any rehabilitated heterosexuality worthy of feminist support must be more than the luxury of a few socially and economically privileged partners of 'new men'.

More than this, given the radical critique of heterosexuality as a primary site for the reinscription of gender-based patterns of dominance and submission, the models of heterosexuality advanced by 'virgin' and 'queer' theorists are seriously incomplete or flawed. It is unclear how 'virgins' can mysteriously evade the implications of the heterosexual act; and implausible that 'queers', through 'playing' with gendered symbols of power and powerlessness, can hope to 'subvert' them. In the vast majority of heterosexual relationships, which are neither 'virgin' nor 'queer', heterosexual sexual activity continues to reinscribe biological and social maleness and femaleness, constructing women as women and men as men, in order to ensure male dominance and female subordination. In this way, nothing changes: heterosexuality continues to mean

Contemporary Rehabilitations of Heterosexuality

what it has always meant under heteropatriarchy, and to serve the same sociopolitical function.

References

ALLEN, L. (1993) 'Racism and Queer Identity', paper presented at the Annual Women's Studies Network (UK) Conference, Nene College, Northampton, 16–18 July.
APPLEBY, Y. (1993) 'Disability and "Compulsory Heterosexuality"', in WILKINSON, S. and KITZINGER, C. (Eds) *Heterosexuality: A Feminism & Psychology Reader*, London, Sage.
BART, P.B. (1993) 'Protean Woman: The Liquidity of Female Sexuality and the Tenaciousness of Lesbian Identity', in WILKINSON, S. and KITZINGER, C. (Eds) *Heterosexuality: A Feminism & Psychology Reader*, London, Sage.
BARTKY, S.L. (1993) 'Hypatia Unbound: A Confession', in WILKINSON, S. and KITZINGER, C. (Eds) *Heterosexuality: A Feminism & Psychology Reader*, London, Sage.
BRAIDOTTI, R. (1991) *Patterns of Dissonance: A Study of Women in Contemporary Philosophy*, Cambridge, Polity Press.
BRISTOW, J. (1992) 'Cross-Dress, Transgress', *Observer*, 3 May.
BROWN, L. (1993) 'Heterosexual Celibacy', in WILKINSON, S. and KITZINGER, C. (Eds) *Heterosexuality: A Feminism & Psychology Reader*, London, Sage.
BRUNET, A. and TURCOTTE, L. (1988) 'Separatism and Radicalism', in HOAGLAND, S.L. and PENELOPE, J. (Eds) *For Lesbians Only: A Separatist Anthology*, London, Onlywomen Press.
BUTLER, J. (1990) *Gender Trouble: Feminism and the Subversion of Identity*, London, Routledge.
CLAUSEN, J. (1991) 'My Interesting Condition', *Out/Look: National Lesbian and Gay Quarterly*, 7, pp. 10–21.
CLINE, S. (1993) *A Passion for Celibacy*, London: Bloomsbury.
DALY, M. (1984) *Pure Lust: Elemental Feminist Philosophy*, London, The Women's Press.
DELPHY, C. and LEONARD, D. (1992) *Familiar Exploitation: A New Analysis of Marriage in Contemporary Western Societies*, Cambridge, Polity Press.
DENNIS, W. (1992) *Hot and Bothered: Men and Women, Sex and Love in the 1990s*, London, Grafton/Harper Collins.
DOLLIMORE, J. (1991) *Sexual Dissidence: Augustine to Wilde, Freud to Foucault*, Oxford, Clarendon Press.
DWORKIN, A. (1987) *Intercourse*, London: Arrow/Century-Hutchinson.
DUNCKER, P. (1993) 'Heterosexuality: Fictional Agendas', in WILKINSON, S. and KITZINGER, C. (Eds) *Heterosexuality: A Feminism & Psychology Reader*, London, Sage.
FRYE, M. (1990) 'Do You Have To Be a Lesbian To Be a Feminist?', *off our backs*, August/September.
FRYE, M. (1993) *Willful Virgin: Essays in Feminism, 1976–1992*, Freedom, CA, The Crossing Press.
GAVEY, N. (1993) 'Technologies and Effects of Heterosexual Coercion', in WILKINSON, S. and KITZINGER, C. (Eds) *Heterosexuality: A Feminism & Psychology Reader*, London, Sage.

GERGEN, M. (1993) 'Unbundling Our Binaries — Genders, Sexualities, Desires', in WILKINSON, S. and KITZINGER, C. (Eds) *Heterosexuality: A Feminism & Psychology Reader,* London, Sage.

GILL, R. and WALKER, R. (1993) 'Heterosexuality, Feminism, Contradiction: On Being Young, White, Heterosexual Feminists in the 1990s', in WILKINSON, S. and KITZINGER, C. (Eds) *Heterosexuality: A Feminism & Psychology Reader,* London, Sage.

GRIFFIN, C. (1993) 'Fear of a Black (and Working-Class) Planet', in WILKINSON, S. and KITZINGER, C. (Eds) *Heterosexuality: A Feminism & Psychology Reader,* London, Sage.

HALL, N. (1980) *The Moon and the Virgin,* London, The Women's Press.

HENDERSON, L. (1993) 'Justify Our Love: Madonna and the Politics of Queer Sex', in SCHWICHTENBERG, C. (Ed.) *The Madonna Connection: Representational Politics, Subcultural Identities, and Cultural Theory,* Boulder, CO, Westview Press.

HITE, S. (1989) 'Love on the Rocks', *Marxism Today,* 14–19 December.

HOLLWAY, W. (1993) 'Theorizing Heterosexuality: A Response', *Feminism & Psychology,* vol. 3, no. 3, pp. 412–17.

JEFFREYS, S. (1985) *The Spinster and Her Enemies: Feminism and Sexuality 1880–1930,* London, Pandora.

JEFFREYS, S. (1990) *Anticlimax: A Feminist Perspective on the Sexual Revolution,* London, The Women's Press.

JEFFREYS, S. (1994) *The Lesbian Heresy,* London, The Women's Press.

KITZINGER, C. (1987) *The Social Construction of Lesbianism,* London, Sage.

KITZINGER, C. (1994) 'Sex and Power: A Radical Feminist Perspective', in RADTKE, H.L. and STAM, H.J. (Eds) *Gender and Power,* London, Sage.

KITZINGER, C. and WILKINSON, S. (forthcoming, in preparation) 'The Queer Backlash'.

KITZINGER, C., WILKINSON, S. and PERKINS, R. (Eds) (1992) *'Heterosexuality': Special Issue of Feminism & Psychology,* vol. 2, no. 3.

KITZINGER, J. and KITZINGER, C. (1993) ' "Doing It": Lesbian Representations of Sex', in GRIFFIN, G. (Ed.) *Outwrite,* London, Pluto Press.

LEEDS REVOLUTIONARY FEMINIST GROUP (1981) 'Political Lesbianism: The Case Against Heterosexuality', in ONLYWOMEN PRESS (Ed.) *Love Your Enemy? The Debate between Heterosexual Feminism and Political Lesbianism,* London, Onlywomen Press.

MACCOWAN, L. (1992) 'Re-collecting History, Renaming Lives: Femme Stigma and the Feminist Seventies and Eighties', in NESTLE, J. (Ed.) *The Persistent Desire: A Femme-Butch Reader,* Boston, MA, Alyson Publications.

MACKINNON, C.A. (1987) *Feminism Unmodified: Discourses on Life and Law,* Cambridge, MA, Harvard University Press.

MAINARDI, P. (1970) 'The Politics of Housework', in MORGAN, R. (Ed.) *Sisterhood is Powerful,* New York, Vintage Books.

MANDZUICK, R. (1993) 'Feminist Politics and Postmodern Seductions: Madonna and the Struggle for Political Articulation', in SCHWICHTENBERG, C. (Ed.) *The Madonna Connection: Representational Politics, Subcultural Identities, and Cultural Theory,* Boulder, CO: Westview Press.

MERCK, M. (1993) *Perversions,* London, Virago.

MILLS, J. (1991) *Womanwords: A Vocabulary of Culture and Patriarchal Society,* London, Virago.

NICHOLS, M. (1987) 'Lesbian Sexuality: Issues and Developing Theory', in THE BOSTON LESBIAN PSYCHOLOGIES COLLECTIVE (Ed.) *Lesbian Psychology: Explorations and Challenges,* Urbana, IL, University of Illinois Press.

ONLYWOMEN PRESS (Ed.) (1981) *Love Your Enemy? The Debate between Heterosexual Feminism and Political Lesbianism,* London, Onlywomen Press.

PARNABY, J. (1993) 'Queer Straits', *Trouble and Strife,* no. 26, pp. 13–16.

PIERCY, M. (1976) *Woman on the Edge of Time,* New York, Knopf (reprinted 1979, London, The Women's Press).
RADICALESBIANS (1970) 'The Woman Identified Woman' (leaflet), reprinted in HOAGLAND, S.L. and PENELOPE, J. (Eds) *For Lesbians Only: A Separatist Anthology,* London, Onlywomen Press.
RAMAZANOGLU, C. (1989) *Feminism and the Contradictions of Oppression,* London, Routledge.
REICH, J.L. (1992) 'Genderfuck: The Law of the Dildo', *Discourse: Journal for Theoretical Studies in Media and Culture,* vol. 15, no. 1, pp. 112–27.
RICH, A. (1980) 'Compulsory Heterosexuality and Lesbian Existence', *Signs: Journal of Woman in Culture and Society,* vol. 5, no. 4, pp. 631–60, reprinted by Onlywomen Press (1981) as a pamphlet.
ROWLAND, R. (1993) 'Radical Feminist Heterosexuality: The Personal and the Political', in WILKINSON, S. and KITZINGER, C. (Eds) *Heterosexuality: A Feminism & Psychology Reader,* London, Sage.
RUSSELL, D. (1990) *Rape in Marriage,* Indianapolis, Indiana University Press.
SCHWICHTENBERG, C. (1993) 'Madonna's Postmodern Feminism: Bringing the Margins to the Center', in SCHWICHTENBERG, C. (Ed.) *The Madonna Connection: Representational Politics, Subcultural Identities, and Cultural Theory,* Boulder, CO, Westview Press.
SEBESTYEN, A. (1982) 'Sexual Assumptions in the Women's Movement', in FRIEDMAN, S. and SARAH, E. (Eds) *On the Problem of Men: Two Feminist Conferences,* London, The Women's Press.
SEGAL, L. (1983) 'Sensual Uncertainty, or Why the Clitoris is Not Enough', in CARTLEDGE, S. and RYAN, J. (Eds) *Sex and Love: New Thoughts on Old Contradictions,* London, The Women's Press.
SMYTH, C. (1992) *Lesbians Talk Queer Notions,* London, Scarlet Press.
SPRINKLE, A. (1992) 'My First Time with a F2M-transsexual-surgically-made Hermaphrodite', in COOPER, D. (Ed.) *Discontents: New Queer Writers,* New York, Amethyst Press.
STOLTENBERG, J. (1990) *Refusing to be a Man,* London, Fontana.
SWINDELLS, J. (1993) 'A Straight Outing', *Trouble and Strife,* no. 26, pp. 40–4.
THOMAS, A. (1993) 'The Heterosexual Feminist: A Paradoxical Identity?', in WILKINSON, S. and KITZINGER, C. (Eds) *Heterosexuality: A Feminism & Psychology Reader,* London, Sage.
WARNER, M. (1978) *Alone of All Her Sex: The Myth and Cult of the Virgin Mary,* London, Quartet.
WILKINSON, S. and KITZINGER, C. (Eds) (1993) *Heterosexuality: A Feminism & Psychology Reader,* London, Sage.
WILLIAMS, L. (1992) 'Pornographies On/scene, or Diff'rent Strokes for diff'rent folks', in SEGAL, L. and MCINTOSH, M. (Eds) *Sex Exposed: Sexuality and the Pornography Debate,* London, Virago.
WITTIG, M. (1992) *The Straight Mind,* Boston, MA, Beacon Press.

Chapter 5

Flaunting the Body: Gender and Identity in American Feminist Performance

Angelika Czekay

Deconstructing notions like 'real' or 'true' identity has been poststructuralist feminists' primary objective for the past decade. Poststructuralism's concept of social and cultural constructedness has challenged and gradually replaced essentialist and universal notions of 'innate femininity' and 'true womanhood'. The focus on representation, the inquiry into what can be seen and who does the seeing, has complicated the original cultural feminist claim of women's uniqueness.

According to poststructuralists, the material body is always already within gendered representation, framed by a cultural and ideologically loaded sign system which signifies its gender through the discovery of its bodily markers. More specifically, dominant patriarchal culture insists on the identification of binary gender poles, male and female, and commonly equates gender with sex.

As part of the current larger feminist (poststructuralist) agenda in the US, feminist performers, like poststructuralist feminist theorists, have attempted to destabilize traditional representations of gender and gender identity. Many recent American performances have pointed to the cultural constructedness of 'male' and 'female', of styles, behaviours, and attitudes that are culturally mapped across the body.[1] Techniques such as cross-dressing and gender impersonation have provided powerful tools to complicate binary gender notions, to unmask conventional gender categories as cultural products and to point to the un-fixity of gender identities.

In such performances, the cross-dressed body becomes intelligible through the distinction between the performer's anatomy and his/her performed gender. Ideally, gender impersonation exposes male and female behaviours as products of cultural ideology, not biological difference, and, therefore, denaturalizes the equation of sex with gender. The spectator reads/sees both levels, the performer's 'real' sex and the performed gender. In fact, recognition of the performer's body as separate from the performance of gender determines the spectatorial pleasure of such performances.

In terms of feminist interventions into patriarchal discourse which defines man as 'subject' and woman as 'object', however, gender impersonation and cross-dressing have limitations. Through the body's signification within a representational apparatus of dominant cultural codes, a reliance on the spectator's referential system of gender recognition potentially reinforces the binary categories of male and female which it tries to subvert and the power dynamics which culture has invested in them.[2]

Poststructuralist feminist theory argues that gender — whether on stage or not — is continuously performed or enacted and that the body is always 'in drag', i.e., that a football player scratching his genitals on the field performs gender and sexuality just like a transvestite crossing the street.[3] However, in dominant discourse, this proposition remains theoretical. Cross-dressing, at least in mainstream venues, insists on the obvious difference between appearance and reality, or 'show' and 'substance'. It implicitly underlines an ontological status, a 'real' and gendered identity tied to the body, a correspondence between the body's signifiers and its 'normal' gendered behaviour from which the cross-dressed body suggests only a fictional departure. In most contexts, the transvestite is still considered a deviation from the norm while the football player is not.

If the body always already reads as gendered, how can live performance, using the body as its primary medium, subvert traditional images and assumptions about gender, gender identity, and sexuality? Can performance account for different positionalities that correspond to or diverge from the signifying body? For instance, can a woman in drag foreground the cultural construction of the gendered body when she reads as a man? How do gender, sex, and sexual preference intersect with the signifying body? How do bodily markers inform the reading of gender and sexuality? For instance, does a male heterosexual performance stripper having breast implants to shock his audience differ from a male to female transsexual having a sex change because he feels like a woman? If both bodies read as male/female why does the performer's position, his/her identity, matter? To what extent can the performer influence the reading of bodily markers on stage?

An assessment of these questions requires further investigation into the performer/spectator dynamics, into the techniques performers use to

Angelika Czekay

guide spectatorial responses, and into specific performance contexts. In this chapter, I will concentrate on the representation of the body in three recent American performance pieces and on the different strategies the performers employ to guide spectatorial responses. Following Jeanie Forte's argument (1992, pp. 249, 250), my proposition is that, to foreground assumptions about gender and gender identity, feminist poststructuralist theory needs to intertextually examine (1) the body as it is consumed through representation, and (2) the material body, the signifier itself, with the markings, functions, and desires that produce this consumption. Forte attempts to ground poststructuralist feminist concepts of representation by reinscribing the materiality of the (female) body into discourse without relying on essentialist categories and without reinforcing the heterosexist codes that place women as sexual objects. This juxtaposition, the attempt to differentiate between the performed and the performing body, potentially replaces dominant binary categories with a spectrum of genders and sexualities which resist unified identification and invest the body with a variety of identity positions. I would further suggest that a performance that knowingly fetishizes the body — one that writes the body's own narrative and lends itself self-consciously to spectatorial consumption while the performer is asserting her subject position — offers a subversive and politically powerful tool for feminist interventions in the traditional gender-biased apparatus of representation.

Three recent performance pieces by Annie Sprinkle, Janice Perry and Kate Bornstein focus on the body and its relationship to gendered, sexual identities, and, I suggest here, present a variety of performative devices that foreground the body as a locus of representation in dominant culture. All three pieces fetishize the body with its gender, sexuality, and gendered identity, and explore the verbal and visual representation of sexual markers. In all three pieces, the body itself becomes the spectacle of the performance.[4]

Ex-porn-star Annie Sprinkle's one-woman performance piece *Post Porn Modernist — Still in Search of the Ultimate Sexual Experience* (1990), which toured Europe and the US from 1990 to 1992, focuses on sexuality in many different forms and varieties. In thirteen brief episodes, Sprinkle tells her life and sexual evolution. While the main part of the performance focuses on Sprinkle's experiences as a sex-worker, slides also show the shifts in her position and identity, from Ellen Steinberg, the shy middle-class daughter who was 'afraid of . . . sex'(Sprinkle, 1991, p. 85), to Annie Sprinkle, the glamorous porn-star who 'wants fame and fortune' (Sprinkle, 1991, p. 188), to Anya, the 'ancient goddess' who 'makes love to the sky, mud and trees' (Sprinkle, 1991, p. 119). The performance displays sexually explicit material: Sprinkle describes her favourite sex toys, performs a bosom ballet (Sprinkle, 1991, pp. 66-7), urinates and douches, and invites the spectators several times to walk up to the stage and take photographs while she poses for the camera. In addition to her body display, Sprinkle presents sets of slides like the 'pornstastics', showing, for instance, a diagram that reveals in percentages her weekly income as opposed to that of the 'average' women (Sprinkle, 1991, p. 41) or a chart that reveals 'the reasons why I did it' (*ibid.*). Other slides show her different ex-lovers from straight women to gay men to transsexuals to amputees (Sprinkle, 1991, pp. 72-7, 96-9). Sprinkle ends the show with a masturbation ritual which she performs as Anya, the 'ancient Goddess who wants peace, love and freedom' (Sprinkle, 1991, p. 119).

The piece concentrates on the female body and its relationship to sexuality and sexual identity. It relies on the spectator's recognition of sexualized images of women, familiar from the porn industry and usually displayed for the male spectator. Sprinkle flaunts her body as the object 'to-be-looked-at' but interrupts conventional pornographic signification in several ways.[5]

First, she places enticing and sexually blatent images of the seductive female body into the theatrical conventions of performance art, thereby transforming the frame in which these images can be comfortably consumed into one in which they are unexpected.

Second, and more importantly, Sprinkle enacts the process of creating the pornographic female body, designed for sexual display, in front of the spectators. Putting on lingerie, garters, and high heels, she actively constructs her body as a site of sexual fantasies while commenting on the effects of special make-up or costume, specifically created for the porn consumer's desire.[6] During a different moment, called 'The Transformation Salon', Sprinkle shows slides of 'ordinary' women, housewives with children, secretaries, teachers, or saleswomen before and after they have dressed up as porn stars (Sprinkle, 1991, pp. 86-91). Both moments expose the constructedness of the female sexualized body, counteract easy identification of female sex stars, demystify conventional assumptions about pornography, and gear the spectator's attention towards representation itself.

Third, Sprinkle constantly relocates the place of the body, enacting the known — though culturally forbidden — pornographic body as well as the unknown, foreign one, the taboo within the taboo, or a different taboo. Sexually enticing, overexposed corporal images are placed in opposition to unspeakable, unexposed ones.[7] Both are enacted next to each other, contrasted, compared, performed side by side, mediated through the presence of the same body. After the bosom ballet, Sprinkle urinates and douches on stage, explains a chart of the female reproductive system and then invites the spectators to come up to the stage and look at her cervix (Sprinkle, 1991, p. 109). She sits down in the middle of the stage, inserts a speculum, and passes out a flashlight to the queued spectators, asking them individually to comment on what they've seen. Sprinkle confronts images from two discursive fields, one being the medical, gynaecological, culturally accepted but repressed, unconscious one; the other the obscene, pornographic, unacceptable but secretly interesting one — both culturally threatening, hidden, and obscured in different ways. By asking the spectators to come closer, hence forcing them to actively participate, Sprinkle uncovers the voyeuristic desire for both taboos, the curious urge to look, to watch, to consume what is usually not seen. By performing this contrast and contradiction between the sexual female and the reproductive female body, both consumed in the same space by the same spectators, Sprinkle exposes the gaze, the spectatorial complicity in the production of objectified bodily images as well as culture's sexual politics and its double standards in the representation of women.

Fourth, and most significantly, Sprinkle assumes a subject position that the porn-star does not have. Framing the show through an autobiographical narration, Sprinkle creates a metanarrative, implying the difference between a 'real' and a 'fictional' world, one suggesting authenticity, the other masquerade. The fictional world shows what Elinor Fuchs (1989), after watching an earlier Sprinkle show, called 'the obscene body'. It displays sexually arousing images but recontextualizes them through the contrast to the 'real', Sprinkle's life outside the performance. This framing device points to the difference between the performed body that signifies and the performing body that speaks and disrupts this signification with different layers of text.

When Sprinkle exhibits herself but repeatedly asserts her own sexual desires, constantly reminding the spectator of her presence, agency, and subjectivity, she — unlike the porn-star in traditional display settings — enacts both, the seen and the seeing simultaneously, presenting herself as a subject and an object. During the 'Public Cervix Announcement', Sprinkle responds to individual spectators' helpless comments 'Oh, the cervix is beautiful': 'I am glad you like it. Thanks for coming'.[8] This act of speaking, often of commenting on the construction of her body as a representation (as pointed out earlier, for instance, when she poses for the spectators and asks them which look they like best) becomes an act of mocking the spectators' obsession to watch but, more significantly, of returning their looks, of looking back.

Particularly the last part of the piece functions to assert Sprinkle's own sexual agency and desires. In a long masturbation ritual for which she has created an environment of candles, incense, and spiritual music Sprinkle 'breathe[s], undulate[s] and masturbate[s] [her]self with a vibrator into an erotic trance, often to full-bodied and clitoral orgasms' (Sprinkle, 1991, p. 112) while the spectators shake rattles to support her. And while Sprinkle offers her trance and sexual energy as a shared ritual, she claims the performance space for herself, expressing and asserting her own sexual pleasure and agency. That the show ends with this autoerotic act, that Sprinkle perhaps even gets a sexual kick out of exhibiting her sexuality fuses the narratives between 'real' and 'fictional' and reverses the pleasure dynamics between her and the spectators.

Overall, the performance uncovers conventional representations of 'pornography' in which the displayed female body is valued because it has no identity. Sprinkle's body speaks. Far from being subjugated to silence or passivity or a victim status, Sprinkle promotes 'active female sexual desire and audacious sex positivity' (Straayer, 1993, p. 161). Through layers of presenting herself as representation, revealing the process of creating pornographic display, insisting on her own sexual desires, and shifting in and out of the porn-star position, Sprinkle foregrounds the sexualized female body's discursive constructedness and subverts traditional connotations of 'pornography' with women as submissive objects. Instead, she assumes and offers a position of female sexual agency.[9]

Moreover, the final stage image of the masturbation ritual undermines the complete co-option and essentialization of the female body in performance. Forte (1992, p. 256) argues that 'women artists, manipulating imagery in order to inscribe themselves in discourses as erotic agents . . ., may transgress the limits of representation and construct a different viewing space in which both the spectator and performer become differentiated subjects'. Whether Sprinkle really experiences sexual pleasure or just pretends to is not what matters here. The significance of this moment is that by asserting her subject position she presents a body with its own narrative, pleasure, history, and agency.[10] With her own position constantly shifting — from show entertainer to educator to sex-worker and porn-star to performer to autoerotic New Age feminist — Sprinkle offers a gendered identity that is constantly in flux, reembodied, and reperformed but always invested with agency.[11]

Structurally similar to Sprinkle's piece but different in content, Janice Perry's show explores different images and representations of the female body. In her one-woman performance *World Power Sex Control* (1991) which toured Europe, London, and the United States from 1991 to 1993, Perry presents a combination of cabaret, music, comedy, and satire, covering a variety of topics from current politics to literature and culture. Although Perry covers diverse issues like censorship in the US or German reunification, she infiltrates her performance with a deconstruction of gender and reveals sexual politics as perpetuating misogynist notions and gender biases.

In numerous short sketches, Perry uses her body, physical attitudes, and a minimum of props to establish images drawn from a variety of cultural, political, and social spheres. She assumes the cultural codes while constructing her body accordingly, then offers her own alternative readings of the images which often parody common-sense assumptions, and provoke political and social reflection. Much of the performance consists of Perry layering her body with different clothes before the spectators but — unlike Sprinkle — without ever undressing in front of the audience. In one her sketches, for instance, she performs the difference between butch and femme. She explains that her wearing a mini-skirt, make-up, and pumps gives her the appearance of a 'femme' woman, asking the audience to repeat several times 'My, what a femme woman!'[12] Then, she dons a suit over the skirt, explains that this is what a butch looks like, and again invites the audience to repeat after her: 'My, what a butch woman!' But since she is still wearing pumps, earrings, make-up, and stockings, she contemplates that she is, in fact, wearing signs of a butch and a femme, provoking the audience to repeat 'My, what a fascinating combination of butch and femme!' Perry's manipulation of the spectator mocks and exposes costumes as signifying and actually producing different gender and sexual identities.

Moreover, her constant enactment of changing clothes in front of the spectators, her insistence on putting a pair of trousers over a skirt or donning a T-shirt over a dress before removing the dress — sometimes a quite sophisticated endeavour — stages an exhibitionism similar to Sprinkle's. The paradox with which Perry works is that she exposes her body and hides it at the same time. She apparently creates moments of intimacy for and with the spectators which, depending on the contexts, she emphasizes or ignores, at times pointing to the clothes, at others telling a story and creating a second narrative that is independent of her act. This particular illusion of emphasizing intimacy between performer and audience and at the same time undercutting it strangely perverts the gaze, implicitly asserting the performer's control over the spectator's curiosity and compulsive desire to look.

Like Sprinkle, Perry establishes her own erotic agency, but she employs a parodistic, almost self-ironic style. In the beginning of the show, she constructs the entire audience as object of her desire: 'The moment I came in here I was in love with you. I can't stop thinking about you. I'd like to sing you a love song'. What follows is a love song that mocks American love ballads. Perry assumes the subject position — traditionally male-gendered — and inverts the usual power dynamic with the performer on display for the spectators.

Later, while still in her 'butch' outfit, she reads an erotic story, substituting neutral descriptive terms, including names of parts of speech: 'It was lying beside me, verbing quietly. I could hear its steady breathing and the soft sounds of its verbing. I began to get adjective, so I turned to it and put my body part around it'. Perry can safely rely on the spectators to fill in the gaps of the act but leaves her fictional lover's gender undefined. Although the story is written in the first person, Perry avoids clearly identifying the gender and sexual identity of both herself and her lover. The story's 'it' represents both possible genders, depending on different spectators' interpretations. With the butch costume, Perry invites a variety of readings but privileges none of them. The humour of this sketch does not only lie in the evocation of the sexual act but also in her deliberate refusal to satisfy the spectator's curiosity about her partner's gender identity.

Perry, again like Sprinkle, frames her show through a personal narration. She recalls seemingly arbitrarily chosen situations and impressions from her recent past and draws on references from popular culture, exposing the gender ideology behind them, along with the racism, capitalism, and sexism. In one of the first sketches, for instance, she wears a black dress emblazoned with red hands on her left breast, her right thigh, and her left hip, producing an image of a female body surrounded by touching hands. Then, she describes the display of a mannequin in the window of a German fashion store: 'When I was in Düsseldorf, the fashion center of Germany, I saw a woman doing this . . .'. She assumes a broad-legged, slightly bent position and puts her right hand on her crotch. 'Her other hand was on the head of a large gorilla, both wearing the same clothes. What are they trying to tell us? Wear our clothes and you will look as good as this gorilla? Wear our clothes and you will have sex with yourself, next to a gorilla?' Costume and speech provide a juxtaposition that foregrounds the gender bias in everyday images as well as the sexual objectification of women's bodies. The display's misogyny — the beauty and the beast — as well as the sexualization of women in advertising that here invites the female customer to identify with the mannequin in order to buy the dress, is foregrounded by the ironic graphic commentary of Perry's own costume.

By layering and relayering different clothes and/or sexual markers on the body and by giving attention to gender costuming, Perry subverts

Angelika Czekay

gender identification as stable, continuously pointing to the discursive production of gender roles and cues. Throughout the performance, her body is in flux. It becomes a medium that can be reconstructed, negotiated, transformed, recreated, and readorned, always signifying diverse, unfixed, changing sexualities and identities. Perry's focus on clothes as producing bodily images and gender representations confronts mass culture's construction of identity and sexual politics. Clothes — as opposed to nudity — become the actual markers through which the body is identified.

By enacting different, contrasting representations of the body both Sprinkle and Perry expose gender and gender identity as culturally learned and mapped across the body. But where Sprinkle works with taboos, Perry uses culturally safe images which she invests with a different reading, unravelling meanings that are taken for granted and remain unquestioned in common-sense knowledge. Both performers use exhibitionism as a strategy to remind the spectators of their own responsibility in the production of sexual meaning, Sprinkle by exposing nudity, Perry by avoiding it. The performers' material bodies, though not tied to one monolithic gender or sexual identity, maintain the signifiers of the female gender against which the different representations are evoked and read.

In contrast to these performance pieces, Kate Bornstein's performance *Hidden: A Gender* (1989) explodes the very notions of binary gender and gendered identity. The piece was first produced in association with Theatre Rhinoceros in San Francisco in 1989 and then toured the United States for about two years. Although more traditional than Sprinkle's and Perry's performance pieces in terms of presenting a linear narrative, *Hidden: A Gender* explores a variety of sex and gender positions and provides a compelling contrast to the other two performances.[13]

In a complex interplay of historical narrative, Brechtian alienation techniques, and references to current gender issues, Kate Bornstein, a male-to-female transsexual, Justin Bond, a gay man, and Sydney Erskine, a lesbian, produce their stories of a nineteenth-century hermaphrodite, Herculine Barbin, and a contemporary male-to-female transsexual, Herman Amberstone.[14] The basic structure consists of two fragmented but linear, parallel narratives about the girl Herculine who later becomes the young man Abel, played by the male actor (Bond), and the young man Herman Amberstone who later becomes Kate, a transsexual lesbian, played by the female actor (Erskine). While Herculine is forced by nineteenth-century medical discourse to accept her 'real gender' and become a man, Herman decides himself that he wants to

100

change his gender. Both Herculine and Herman are originally and after their transformations sexually attracted to women. But while Herculine, after becoming Abel, commits suicide, Herman, after becoming Kate, decides that he/she is 'fluidly gendered' and that gender and sexual preference are 'two separate issues': 'I used to have a cock and now I don't. Now I have a cunt. And I still fuck women and women still fuck me. And if the right man came along I just might fuck him'.[15]

The different scenes on Herculine and Amberstone are interrupted by the commentaries of Doc Grinder, heterosexual male narrator and talk master of the show. He comments on the scenes and directly addresses the audience with issues triggered by the plot: 'We don't think about gender. It's not until we see somebody walking on the street and we can't tell whether it's a man or a woman. Did you ever wonder why you can't stop staring until you decide whether it's one or the other?'

One of the ironies of the piece is that Grinder repeatedly tries to sell the spectators his product, the 'Gender Defender, the pink bottle for the girls, the blue bottle for the men' (Barnes, 1992, p. 314), suggesting they buy into the binary gender distinction to be safe in their gender identity. In contrast, Bornstein herself continuously takes on different gender identities by changing her body language but, particularly, by layering her body with different markers, make-up, earrings, glasses, or a tie while wearing her shoulder-length hair either loose or in a pony-tail.[16] These markers rarely correspond to one another, and combined with Bornstein's ambiguous body language mean that Bornstein can seldom be identified as entirely male or entirely female. Likewise, while Herculine and Herman slowly transform into Abel and Kate through changing voice, demeanour, physical action, and gender markers such as hairstyle, they are not limited to one stable gender, refusing to present a clear 'before/after effect'. While contained or open gestures, higher or deeper vocal pitch are defined as distinct gender attributes, they are not assigned to one single character or one single moment. Instead, all three characters are marked by gender cues that are discontinuous, shifting, blurred, bent. The effect is to disrupt the illusion of clearly definable gender categories or distinctly intelligible gender attributes. At one point, Kate and Abel engage in a dance — the only time they meet in the piece — both wearing trousers and shirts and with their shoulder-length hair loose. Because their movements are also similar in style and gesture, it is impossible to decide if either one performs the male or the female gender. The show's theme of 'gender blur' is further explored both verbally and visually, for instance, when Grinder asks Amberstone in the fictive talk show 'What's your Gender?' 'Herman, can't you just dress up as a woman?' and Amberstone, dressed and acting as a man, responds: 'I'm a woman, no matter what I'm wearing'.

Angelika Czekay

Destabilizing the boundaries of the sex/gender system and exploding clear gender distinction, mapped on the body by medical, philosophical, and psychological discourse, is the piece's central agenda. After a medical examination, Herculine says, 'I cannot bear children. This mysterious uterus is present nowhere in my body. According to the doctor, it's all the reading I did as a child. Too much knowledge is incompatible with the innocence which is to be a woman's nature'. This moment confronts the inscription of nineteenth-century medical discourse on the body but also explores how the insistence on a bipolar gender system influences the individual's identity.[17] When Herculine cannot decide whether she is 'really' a man or a woman, she concludes: 'I think I'm becoming a vampire'.

Hidden: A Gender explores the absence of transsexual identities from dominant representation, but also points to the gender bias in the representational apparatus of today's ideology that is maintained in the interest of keeping gender polarities and identities distinct.[18] Performing gendered bodies that cannot be read as either entirely female or entirely male, the performance confronts cultural identity politics and discursive authority. Gender impersonation is explored without relying on a point of origin, without relying on a fixed body as the locus against which the performance of gender is read.

Sprinkle, Perry, and Bornstein flaunt the body as a site which, although consumed by signification, can self-consciously signify. All three performances invest the body with different, shifting gender and sexual identities that do or do not correspond to the sex the body signifies. Despite these overall similarities, however, differences remain which have important political ramifications.

Sprinkle stages and constructs different images of female nudity while Perry layers the body with different clothes, one performer reinscribing female erotic agency on the body, the other pointing to and parodying different gender significations within the cultural apparatus. Both performers use their bodies to point to attitudes towards women's bodies, and to expose and deconstruct socially constructed gender roles. Both bodies come to resignify, invested with the performers' agency and authority. In contrast, Kate Bornstein's performance destabilizes the very notion of a clearly gendered body, confined by a unitary gender construction. In her performance, biological sex, gender identity, and sexual preference all become shifting, flexible categories, as does the body itself.

The reconstruction of gendered images in all three performances, the use of the body as a rewritten text, throws into question the very location of gender and gender identity. By self-consciously lending

Gender and Identity in American Feminist Performance

themselves to the gaze, all three performances present a body that is not completely graspable, a body that can be reconstructed and destabilized and layered with different shifting identities and subject positions. This body has its own history, and writes its own narrative; it is a body that is being reclaimed and resists total consumption.

Notes

1 I use 'performance' here in a wider sense that includes postmodern (as opposed to early) performance art as well as alternative performance pieces. In their opposition to mainstream theatre, institutionally and ideologically, they can be linked together through their critical assessment of dominant liberal politics and a departure from traditional theatrical forms (in the US mostly realism). These performances are predominantly produced in alternative venues or contexts that draw very specific audiences. Feminist performances generally imply a critical examination of gender and identity politics and a focus on the representation of the body. For a comprehensive discussion of feminist theorizations of performance, see Sue-Ellen Case (1990). For a discussion of the intersection between poststructuralist feminist theory and the representation of identity in performance, see Jill Dolan (1989). For a discussion of theory and practice with regard to different women performance artists, see Jeanie Forte (1990).
2 See, for instance, a recent revision of Dolan's (1992) article 'Gender Impersonation on Stage', in which she differentiates between the meanings of gender impersonation in different production contexts. Similarly, Kate Davy's (1992) essay 'Fe/Male Impersonation: The Discourse of Camp' provides a historical account of the ideological and political differences between male and female impersonation.
3 See, for instance, feminist postmodern theorist Judith Butler's widely quoted statement (1990b, p. 270) 'gender is in no way a stable identity or locus of agency from which various acts proceed; rather, it is an identity tenuously constituted in time — an identity through a *stylized repetition of acts*'. For a more detailed and comprehensive theoretical discussion of the subversion of gender identity, see Butler (1990a, pp. 128-49).
4 Although it is beyond the scope of this essay to look at specific performance contexts, I want to mention that all three performances were produced in non-mainstream venues which shaped their meaning significantly.
5 My use of 'pornography' refers to Eileen O'Neill's definition (1989, p. 69). O'Neill differentiates between ' "pornography" to refer to sexually explicit representations that have arousal as their aim' and 'the erotic' which ' "expresses" sexual arousal and desire rather than being what causes them'.
6 See also 'Anatomy of a Pin-up Photo' (reprinted in Straayer, 1993, p. 160) in which Sprinkle labels the different items of the lingerie she is wearing with explanations, as for instance, 'Corset makes my waist look four and a half inches smaller, but I can't breathe (*sic*)'. See also Chris Straayer (1993, p. 157) who describes these images as a 'form of body art to display the constructed "nature" of sexiness'.
7 The term 'overexposed' relates to Johannes Birringer's (1991) discussion of the postmodern body. Birringer analyzes cultural practices in visual and performance art (for example, Karen Finley's one-woman performance) and examines the body as a

Angelika Czekay

referent for diverse 'discursive, aesthetic, and technical productions' (p. 205) in postmodern American consumer culture. With regard to the body in postmodern performance, Birringer argues: 'The question of the body (Who is posing? What is being posed?), then, cannot be answered except . . . by observing how reconstructions of the body in postmodern performance have become subject to the enormous pressures of constantly multiplying screens and false mirrors . . . the performing body as a self-reflexive, aesthetic production . . . has lost its privileged position or separate autonomy . . . largely because the ideological encoding of the body slides across all the media of American pop art culture and makes it nearly impossible to locate or reclaim *ruptures* in terms of oppositions between "truth" ("authenticity") and "spectacle" ("surface")' (p. 215).

8 Unless noted otherwise, all quotes from Sprinkle are taken from an undistributed videotape (*Annie Sprinkle: Post Porn Modernist*, 1990).
9 As I have pointed out elsewhere (Czekay, 1993), Sprinkle's piece read differently when she performed in Berlin in 1991. Because of the different discursive and cultural manifestation of pornography in Germany, the performance did not effectively deconstruct traditional representations of the porn-star or prevent the objectification of Sprinkle's body. See also Jill Dolan's (1988) chapter 'The Dynamics of Desire' in which she examines desire as a key category for the representation of gender and sexual identities in different performance contexts.
10 See also Straayer (1993, p. 161): 'Through her assertion of desire, she [Sprinkle] consciously claims prostitution and pornography as her own sexual experiences. The tricks, the experiments, the knowledge, the exhibition, the pornographic discourse, the pleasure belong to her. Her aim to please the client is not in conflict with her other sexual aims'.
11 Linda Williams reads Sprinkle's performances through Butler's (1990a, pp. 142-9) comprehensive discussion of identity. Butler (1990a, p. 145) argues that 'the rules that govern intelligible identity . . . operate through *repetition*', and that ' "agency", then, is to be located within the possibility of a variation on that repetition'. According to Williams (1993, p. 180), Sprinkle's agency consists in the articulation of her own desire *within* the nomination of 'whore' which she accepts: 'Annie Sprinkle neither denies that she is a whore nor fights the system that so names her . . . but in that acceptance also sees room for what Butler calls "subversive repetition". This subversive repetition becomes an articulation of something that is not named in "whore": her own desire'. While I agree with Williams (and Straayer) that Sprinkle asserts her agency through expressing her desire, I would also caution against the potential danger of commodification in the representation of female sexual desire on stage (which, I think, can definitely be part of a traditional pornographic display like, for instance, a peep-show). Sprinkle's performance is subversive not only because she articulates her sexuality, but because — through constantly negotiating and shifting her position — she provokes a reading of her identity, one in which the subject is suggested and becomes visible in representation.
12 All quotes from Perry are taken from an undistributed videotape (*Janice Perry AKA Gal: World Power Sex Control*, 1990).
13 Bornstein has recently also performed a solo piece called *The Opposite Sex . . . Is Neither!*.
14 For a production history and critical analysis of *Hidden: A Gender*, see Noreen C. Barnes (1992).
15 Unless noted otherwise, all quotes from Bornstein are taken from an undistributed videotape (*Hidden: A Gender*, 1991).
16 See Barnes (1992, p. 314).
17 For a critical analysis of Foucault's publishing of nineteenth-century hermaphrodite Herculine Barbin's journals, especially Foucault's introduction to the journals, see Judith Butler (1990a, pp. 93-111).

18 For a comprehensive historical account of the different scientific discourses written on the transsexual body, see Sandy Stone (1991). Stone (1991, p. 289) mentions phenomena such as the necessity for transsexuals to pass 'directly from one pole of sexual experience to the other' without 'any intervening space in the continuum of sexuality'. See also Judith Shapiro (1991) who uses the discursive formations around transsexuality to investigate the relationship between sex and gender in Euro-American and other societies.

References

BARNES, N.C. (1992) 'Kate Bornstein's Gender and Genre Bending', in SENELICK, L. (Ed.) *Gender in Performance: The Presentation of Difference in the Performing Arts*, Hanover, NH, and London, University Press of New England, pp. 311–23.
BIRRINGER, J. (1991) 'The Postmodern Body in Performance', in BIRRINGER, J. *Theatre, Theory, Postmodernism*, Bloomington and Indianapolis, Indiana University Press, pp. 205–31.
BUTLER, J. (1990a) *Gender Trouble: Feminism and the Subversion of Identity*, New York and London, Routledge.
BUTLER, J. (1990b) 'Performative Acts and Gender Constitution: An Essay in Phenomenology and Feminist Theory', in CASE, S.-E. (Ed.) *Performing Feminisms: Feminist Critical Theory and Theatre*, Baltimore and London, Johns Hopkins University Press, pp. 270–82.
CASE, S.-E. (1990) 'Introduction', in CASE, S.-E. (Ed.) *Performing Feminisms: Feminist Critical Theory and Theatre,* Baltimore and London, Johns Hopkins University press, pp. 1–13.
CZEKAY, A. (1993) 'Distance and Empathy: Constructing the Spectator of Annie Sprinkle's "Post-POST PORN MODERNIST — Still in Search of the Ultimate Sexual Experience', *Journal of Dramatic Theory and Criticism*, 7.2, pp. 177–92.
DAVY, K. (1992) 'Fe/Male Impersonation: The Discourse of Camp', in REINELT, J. and ROACH, J. (Eds) *Critical Theory and Performance*, Ann Arbor, University of Michigan Press, pp. 231–47.
DOLAN, J. (1988) 'The Dynamics of Desire: Sexuality and Gender in Pornography and Performance', in DOLAN, J. *The Feminist Spectator as Critic*, Ann Arbor and London, UMI, pp. 59–81.
DOLAN, J. (1989) 'In Defense of the Discourse: Materialist Feminism, Postmodernism, Poststructuralism . . . and Theory', *TDR*, vol. 33, no. 3, pp. 58–71.
DOLAN, J. (1992) 'Gender Impersonation on Stage: Destroying or Maintaining the Mirror of Gender Roles?', in SENELICK, L. (Ed.) *Gender in Performance: The Presentation of Difference in the Performing Arts,* Hanover, NH, and London, University Press of New England, pp. 3–13.
FORTE, J. (1990) 'Women's Performance Art: Feminism and Postmodernism', in CASE, S.-E. (Ed.) *Performing Feminisms: Feminist Critical Theory and Theatre*, Baltimore and London, Johns Hopkins University Press, pp. 251–69.
FORTE, J. (1992) 'Focus on the Body: Pain, Praxis, and Pleasure in Feminist Performance', in REINELT, J. and ROACH, J. (Eds) *Critical Theory and Performance*, Ann Arbor, University of Michigan Press, pp. 248–62.
FUCHS, E. (1989) 'Staging the Obscene Body', *TDR*, vol. 33, no. 1, pp. 33–58.
O'NEILL, E. (1989) '(Re)Presentations of Eros: Exploring Female Sexual Agency', in JAGGAR, A. and BORDO, S.R. (Eds) *Gender/Body/Knowledge: Feminist Reconstructions of Being and Knowing*, New Brunswick and London, Rutgers University Press, pp. 68–91.

SHAPIRO, J. (1991) 'Transsexualism: Reflections on the Persistence of Gender and the Mutability of Sex', in EPSTEIN, J. and STRAUB, K. (Eds) *Body Guards: The Cultural Politics of Gender Ambiguity*, New York and London, Routledge, pp. 248–79.
SPRINKLE, A. (1991) *Post Porn Modernist*, Amsterdam, Torch Books.
STONE, S. (1991) 'The Empire Strikes Back: A Posttranssexual Manifesto', in EPSTEIN, J. and STRAUB, K. (Eds) *Body Guards: The Cultural Politics of Gender Ambiguity*, New York and London, Routledge, pp. 280–304.
STRAAYER, C. (1993) 'The Seduction of Boundaries: Feminist Fluidity in Annie Sprinkle's Art/Education/Sex', in CHURCH GIBSON, P. and GIBSON, R. (Eds) *Dirty Looks: Women, Pornography, Power,* London, BFI, pp. 156–75.
WILLIAMS, L. (1993) 'A Provoking Agent: The Pornography and Performance Art of Annie Sprinkle', in CHURCH GIBSON, P. and GIBSON, R. (Eds) *Dirty Looks: Women, Pornography, Power*, London, BFI, pp. 176–91.

Videos

Annie Sprinkle: Post Porn Modernist, Excerpts from a Live Performance at 'The Kitchen' (1990), unpublished videocassette, dir. Emilio Cubiero, New York City, The Kitchen.
Hidden: A Gender (1991), undistributed videocassette, San Francisco, Theatre Rhinoceros.
Janice Perry AKA Gal: World Power Sex Control (1990), undistributed videocassette, Burlington, VT, Burlington City Hall.

Chapter 6

Anti-Monogamy: A Radical Challenge to Compulsory Heterosexuality?

Becky Rosa

Whilst lesbians and feminists have explored the dynamics of societies which push women into sexual relationships with men (e.g., Rich, 1980), and have theorized the revolutionary challenge of lesbianism (e.g., Leeds Revolutionary Feminist Group, 1981; Hoagland and Penelope, 1988; Jeffreys, 1990),[1] the form our relationships take has not been as carefully analyzed. Compulsory heterosexuality is not the complete package. All women, both heterosexual and lesbian, are expected to buy into a whole way of life that goes far beyond being involved in sexual relations with men. One of the most important parts of the package is monogamy.

In this chapter I propose that anti-monogamy provides a positive and profound challenge to the institution of compulsory heterosexuality. Lesbians and feminists have long engaged in intense discussions about monogamy and nonmonogamy, but thus far little has been committed to paper on the subject.

We have no adequate or positive language to describe our relationships that do not fall into the monogamous partner category nor are 'just' friends. Instead of there being a continuum of behaviour considered appropriate to different relationships, it confuses people if we hold hands walking down the street with a friend, slow dance with them at a disco or regularly share a bed — this is behaviour that signifies a sexual relationship, or an impending sexual relationship. Conversely, if we choose to go on holiday separate from our partner, or both go to a party with different people and do not talk to our partner most of the night, it is assumed that we have problems and may be in the process of splitting up.

There is a problem in defining monogamy purely in sexual terms. I would like to describe monogamy as the ideology that as adults we should primarily bond with one person, meeting most of our needs from

107

them (sexual, emotional, physical etc.). This is enforced by cultural products (the media), economic restraints (tax incentives, the high cost of single living), social factors (the provision of support and companionship, or social status and privilege) and by the notion that this is 'how it is', this is natural.

Theory of the family has generally included theory around child-rearing and motherhood, and the functions of the nuclear family in this process. Family theory has therefore often ignored childless women and lesbians.[2] A cursory examination of any sociology of the family textbook, for example Elliot (1986), will confirm this. Many women do not choose to have children yet still live and get their support predominantly in couple relationships. It is outside the scope and the intent of this paper to consider how child-rearing would be carried out in a nonmonogamous society.[3]

Women's monogamy has repercussions for their friends, for nonmonogamous women, and for feminism. Women living outside what have been recognized as families (or 'the family') have traditionally been ignored, so each woman trying to relate to people in a different way feels as if she is the first. Women have been controlled through our sexuality, and have been separated from each other through monogamous heterosexuality. Men have almost constant access to women through various mechanisms, marriage, harassment, violence, the organization of work and so on, which women do not necessarily have to each other. Women's friendship is vital for feminism and for an end to women's oppression, and the means by which we are divided from each other need to be examined as a prerequisite for women's liberation.

Falling in Love

Love is set up to be a highly individualized emotion free from the social determination of other aspects of our lives, to love or not to love is seen as a free choice, and the notion of 'arranged marriages' where the participants are not perceived to be given this choice is often looked down on by white Westerners. However, we are not free to make choices based on our (socially constructed or otherwise) feelings for other people. If we are in a couple it is assumed that we 'love' our partner, particularly if the couple is heterosexual. However, many people do not 'love', or even like, their partners. In the opposite direction, the love for our same-sex friends and colleagues is minimized. Like the word 'family' many feminists seem to feel that the word 'love' is too highly loaded with meanings to be able to reclaim, and instead use terms such as Gyn/affection, passion, and female friendship (Daly, 1978, Raymond, 1986).

For monogamy to exist, there needs to be a division between sexual/romantic love and nonsexual love. Since our friendships are generally with people of the same sex as us (Nardi, 1992; Garrett, 1989), homophobia plays a part in keeping our friendships non-genitally-sexual. We believe that there is a distinction between the romantic/sexual love people feel for their partners, the love people feel for their friends and the love we feel for our biological families, yet this is not quantified nor qualified. The existence of such a large number of women survivors of childhood sexual assault shows that many men at least are unable to keep within the boundaries of family 'love'. It is not universally expected that family members will 'love' each other. Girls in modern Zambia are expected to confide in and seek advice from an older woman relative, not their mothers. Similarly, Cheyenne Indian girls of the last century had 'strained' relations with their mothers and instead received affection from their father's sisters (Collier *et al.*, 1982, p. 29).

Once this division has been established, different types of relationships with different roles and positions in our society are created as separate and distinct from one another. Romantic love is given precedence over platonic love. We are asked if we have a partner, but information about our friends (where we met them, how long they've been our friends) is not commonly solicited with such vigour. Even though society may not specifically dictate that we can only *love* one person, other social structures (such as emotional support, sex, levels of intimacy, passion, sharing of finances) are linked specifically with romantic love. Sex is seen as an intrinsic part of romantic love, and it is made inevitable that we will be in, or want to be in, a sexual relationship. Because norms exist about who we are allowed to have sex with, and because sex is linked with this superior form of love, the effect is that we are only really allowed to properly love one adult person (who is not part of our biological family).

It has not always been the case that passionate love and sex were congruous. Women's romantic friendships, Chinese marriage resisters and nuns are examples of this. British feminists around the turn of the century praised passionate non-genital love, perhaps an early recognition of the role of 'love' in women's oppression and an attempt to break out of the clearly defined notions of 'love' and redefine bonds of affection in a less oppressive way. Sex was viewed as something they avoided or were coerced into with men, or purely for reproduction, and the 'love' they felt for their friends often may not have been associated with genital sex (Jeffreys, 1985; Faderman, 1981; Raymond, 1986).

The powerful link between sex and love seems to have emerged with the writings of the sexologists during the first half of the twentieth century. With greater economic choices for upper-class and middle-class women, a new way had to be found of enticing women into marriage. The link between love and sex, and the stigmatized categories of the lesbian and the frigid woman were created (Jeffreys, 1985; Faderman, 1981). Women were now expected to enjoy sex with men, and find the companionship, previously gained from other women, from their husbands.

Women were not just forced into compulsory heterosexuality, but also into compulsory *sexuality*. Women are expected to be in, or to want to be in, a sexual relationship. This pressure exists inside and outside of the lesbian community. Sex has become an important organizing principle of our society and we feel it is necessary to ascertain whether someone's relationship with someone else is sexual or not. If a woman does not have a sexual relationship, we want to know why, and how she intends to go about finding one. Physical affection for friends is expected to exist within certain boundaries, to be 'nonsexual'. This compulsory sexuality is maintained by ensuring that certain needs can only be met within a certain kind of relationship, the couple. Physical contact is equated with genital-sexual contact, and the orgasm seen as the goal. Firestone writes: 'Isolation from others makes people starved for physical affection; and if the only kind they can get is genital sex, that's soon what they crave' (1970, p. 140). It is also very difficult for people not in couple relationships to get the love and caring they want if other people are absorbed in their pair-bond.

Romance and love legitimize women's sexual relationships with men and with women, exonerating women from being called 'slags' and similar names, serving to keep women in unsatisfactory and even violent relationships ('But I love him/her') and allowing women to maintain their 'good girl' reputation (and thus reinforce the division between 'good' and 'bad' women) whilst participating in sexual activity. For lesbians, love can act to justify sex which is named as unnatural: if two women really love each other then their sexual relationship is justifiable. Lesbians can conform to the dominant belief (that love is inevitable, natural, and universal) to explain 'deviant' behaviour, reinforcing the dominant morality relating to love, and fitting into the 'feminine' stereotype of being governed by our emotions.

Conversely, there is also an expectation that if you are in a close relationship with someone of the appropriate gender and sexual orientation, it does or should involve a sexual element. Faderman says:

'[i]t is no doubt unlikely that many women born into a sex-conscious era can conduct a lesbian relationship today without some sexual exchange' (1981, pp. 328-9). Joyce Trebilcot writes that 'we need not assume that erotic feelings should lead to love making or that love making ought to occur only where there are erotic feelings' (quoted in Douglas, 1990, p. 166). It is the former of these links that is least challenged.

Monogamy is seen by women as a means of security, both economic and emotional. One lesbian in Johnson's study of long-term lesbian relationships says that in a nonmonogamous relationship, 'the security isn't there' (Johnson, 1990, p. 181). However, in nonmonogamous relationships, the security 'isn't there' only in the context of a society that pressures women into loving only one person at a time. A question that arises out of this is *how* exactly a monogamous relationship gives more security: do obligations of various kinds mean that people stay in relationships they do not really want to be in? Is this what 'security' means to women — staying in a relationship no matter what the quality of it is, and hiding the fragility of it? Lesbians and survivors of family rape know how 'unconditional love' from our biological families can disappear on coming out or confronting the attacker.

In a lesbian-hating world it is vital that heterosexual definitions of relationships, invented for the benefit of men, do not divide us; our relationships are too precious to fall out over the issue of 'sex'. We need to question each stage of our relationships, including the usefulness and the results of 'falling in love'.

When we meet a women to whom we are 'attracted', why does this indicate to us the start of a sexual relationship, rather than friendship? What if we already have a sexual relationship (remember we are only allowed to have one)? Within a monogamous framework, if we 'fall in love' with a woman and we already have a girlfriend[4] our choices are to finish with our current girlfriend and start a new relationship, to have 'an affair' or to openly continue two relationships with little or no support, and few models of how other lesbians may have made them work. Our energy is taken up trying to sort these out rather than in engagement with the wider lesbian community, and this often ultimately causes the break-up of relationships. However, since we can have an unlimited number of friends, it would serve us better if we did not separate off feelings of lust/ attraction from feelings that we might like to get to know a woman better and be her friend.

Johnson says:

during the early months of an infatuation, we almost completely misrepresent ourselves to our new love. . . . It isn't until we calm

> down a few weeks, months or years later that our true, sober selves emerge. . . . Falling passionately in love is about bonding; it is not about accurate self disclosure (Johnson, 1990, pp. 143-4).

But with what are we bonding, if we assume that our new lover is also not projecting her true self? This suggests that we know what roles we should play in sexual/romantic relationships, at least at the beginning, which is different from the more honest representations of self that occur in emergent friendships.

There is also evidence that sex is used as a short cut to making friendships (Becker, 1988; Nardi, 1992; Ramey, 1974). Perhaps this is because of the different patterns in becoming friends and becoming lovers with someone. When we become friends, this tends to happen over a longer period of time, perhaps at work or in a political group, without the same intense contact that is usually characteristic of a new lover relationship. Nonsexual friendships are likely to take longer to establish purely because of the lesser time and energy put into them over any period.[5] Raymond suggests that it is in friendships that women are most able to be themselves (1986, p. 227). Ti-Grace Atkinson explains: '"[f]riendship" is a rational relationship which requires the participation of two parties to the mutual satisfaction of both parties. "Love" can be felt by one party; it is unilateral in nature, and . . . is thus rendered contradictory and irrational' (1974, p. 44). Friendship is more compatible with autonomy, independence and freedom, and perhaps has more of a voluntary nature than the obligations of lover relationships.

Sexual monogamy has a double standard built into it. It is more acceptable for men than women to engage in extra-marital relationships (Buunk and van Driel, 1989, p. 97). As well as having affairs, many men also see prostitutes. The link between sex and exclusivity then is often broken, more often by men but also by women. It is reported that during the so-called 'sexual revolution' of the 1960s 'free love' was available, but it might be more aptly described as 'free sex'.[6]

Being sexually non-exclusive is not good enough to change society. With heterosexuality, the presence of a minority of lesbians does not prevent most women being coerced into relationships with men; there needs to be a strong enough challenge to overthrow the whole system. Many lesbians have assimilated into heterosexual culture, talking about their girlfriends as a personal sexual choice. Similarly, plenty of people (including many infamous Tory politicians who espouse values of *the* family) claim to be monogamous but are in fact nonmonogamous. However, they do not challenge the system which says that we ought to be in couple relationships. It is anti-monogamy, perhaps analogous to political and radical lesbianism, which aims to break down this very system that dictates how we should conduct our relationships and that makes 'free choice' impossible.

Lesbian Monogamy

Lesbians are well placed to break down these false boundaries between love, sex and friendship. Nardi found that of lesbians who had lesbian best friends, 77 per cent were at least minimally attracted to them, 59 per cent had had sex with them at least once and 54 per cent had been 'in love' with their best friends (Nardi, 1992, pp. 110–11). Also, 45 per cent of lesbians said that their best friend was an ex-lover (Nardi, 1992, pp. 113–14). Weston in her interviews noted that 'both men and women featured early attractions to friends in their coming-out stories' (Weston, 1991, p. 121). The boundaries between sexual and nonsexual love are not as clear as we might believe when we examine our experiences as lesbians.

Although lesbians challenge the patriarchal rules that try to force us into heterosexuality, other aspects of the way in which we are supposed to conduct relationships, for example monogamy, remain largely unchallenged. Various studies bear this out. According to a 1978 study (reported in Johnson, 1990, p. 19), 60 per cent of the 'women-identified-women' who were part of this large research project said a permanent relationship is either 'very important' (25 per cent) or 'the most important thing in my life' (35 per cent). She also reports a study by Schwartz and Blumstein which documents a high break-up rate amongst lesbian couples: 48 per cent had broken up a year after the survey, compared with 14 per cent of the married couples, and 36 per cent of gay male couples. In a recent survey in *Lesbian London*, filled in by 250 lesbians, only eight women were attempting more than one relationship. Lesbians tend to fall into a pattern of (usually short-term) serial monogamy.

In Becker's book (1988) about lesbian ex-lovers, she writes that lesbians who were not in a new relationship at the time of the interview still expressed hope that they would be. Joani says she was 'developing friendships, maintaining my own interests and cultivating a sense of myself apart from being lovers with someone. Faith in some future lover relationship gave me the courage to do those things' (Becker, 1988, p. 180).

It is not as easy for lesbians as for heterosexuals to define what we mean by being in a couple. We cannot fall back on the well worn stereotypes and patterns of heterosexuality where engagement and marriage mark commitment, and there is more of a blurring for lesbians between lovers and friends. In her study of lesbian ex-lovers, Carol Becker shows that lesbians do not fall into exactly the same patterns of serial monogamy as heterosexuals, remaining in touch with ex-lovers and 'includ[ing] them in a family of friends that provides a reference point for personal continuity and growth' (Becker, 1988, pp. 18–19). Weston found that lesbian and gay families 'resembled networks . . . based on ties that radiated outward from individuals like spokes on a wheel' (1991, p. 109). Boundaries were fluid, and one 'family' could overlap with another — that of a lover or a friend. There were no easily identifiable units, which Weston (*ibid.*) comments 'might represent a nightmare to an anthropologist' but which make perfect sense to lesbians and gay men. She found that when lesbians and gay men were asked to list the members of their families, these mostly comprised other lesbians and gay men. With such loose, often unarticulated definitions of families there can be problems in who lesbians and gay men include in their families — and of reciprocity — 'do they include me?'

As lesbians individually and collectively we have to invent our own relationships — we are not shown how these should be as we grow up. However, heterosexism and homophobia serve to divide lesbians from each other, so it is very difficult for us to imagine and recreate different relationships. The heterosexual norms we learn are carried over into our community where it is made difficult for us to develop and communicate our own.

Lesbians face extra pressure to be monogamous because of anti-lesbianism. Many lesbians stay in monogamous relationships for the support they provide from an anti-lesbian world. Others stay with a lover simply because they do not know any other lesbians. Some lesbians feel the need to be in a relationship to maintain their lesbian identity in a world which wishes to invisiblize us. Many lesbians are disowned by their families or feel unable to be in contact with them because of their heterosexism. There is thus pressure on lesbians and gay men to create alternative 'family' structures, and monogamous relationships may be one of the easiest ways to gain this security that heterosexuals are more likely to be able to take for granted in their families of origin.

There is also a pressure on lesbians to be as 'normal' as possible. Many lesbians and (probably more) gay men take the line that we are just like heterosexuals except for the sex of our lovers. The aim of lesbian and gay politics then becomes the assimilation of lesbians and gay men into the mainstream, so we have campaigns for lesbians and gay men to be able to get married just like heterosexuals.

Johnson found that lesbians in long-term couples emphasize the importance of having friends also in long-term couples (1990, p. 280). This reinforces the primacy of a woman's partner, and sees friends as a function of that partnership. Barrett and McIntosh point out that '[w]hen a marriage breaks up . . . the partners often find themselves friendless and isolated. A second marriage, replicating the first, is the easiest solution, and so a pattern of serial monogamy is set up' (1982, pp. 54–5). Women tend not to prioritize their own friendships and as a result leave themselves with fewer choices upon the break-up with their partners.

Friendship and Autonomy

It is not easy for women to live alone. Factors such as cost, fear for safety, social stigma and lack of emotional support all act against us. Yet studies show that single women achieve higher educational qualifications and are more highly qualified on average than women in couples and that single women are happier than married women. The reverse is true for men: single men tend to be 'uneducated' blue-collar workers, they do not live as long as married men, and married men are happier than single men (Houseknecht *et al.*, 1987: Buunk and van Driel, 1989; *Shocking Pink*, no date). It is in men's interests and to women's detriment that women are in monogamous heterosexual relationships, yet popular knowledge would have it the other way round, that men are 'nagged', 'tied down' etc. whilst women are lucky, do no work and spend all their partners' money. Houseknecht found that 'even highly dedicated professional women indicate that they limit their career strivings in deference to their husbands' careers' (1987, p. 335).

Single women, similarly to lesbians, dispel the myth that women should be dependent on a man, and are thus penalized for it. However, unlike single or coupled lesbians, heterosexual single women are not necessarily creating structures for women to bond with other women to provide real alternatives to heterosexual monogamy. Feminist writers have not generally challenged the stigma attached to the single woman, being concerned more with women's rights to be lesbians. For example, when Valverde talks about heterosexual feminists talking about their relationships with men, she writes: [c]learly, *tact is needed so as not to make single women feel left out*' (1985, p. 63, emphasis added). She makes an assumption that single women *will* feel left out, thus reinforcing the idea that single women *are* missing out. She also does not ask heterosexual women to challenge a relationship form that leaves other women feeling 'left out' to the benefit of men. Turning this statement around to tell single women that tact is needed when talking about their singleness so as not to make women in heterosexual couples feel left out seems slightly ridiculous, because of course the stereotype contends that women in couples *choose* to live like that, whereas single women are out of control of their lack of a partner.

Female friendship has been given a bad press — when it is mentioned at all. Women and girls have always formed bonds of affection and necessity, but there is little sociological study on friendship. Stephanie Garrett (1989) suggests that the lack of non-Western research on friendship is because most research on relationships has focused on kinship ties, and the same may be true for the West. Feminist writing on radicalizing women's friendship, such as that by Mary Daly (1978) and Janice Raymond (1986) has also been largely marginalized, yet feminism is based in a fundamental way on women's friendships.

Our socialization as girls teaches us to accept the role of second best to our friends' boyfriends (Griffin, 1985; Lees, 1986). Does this conditioning carry over to lesbian communities where we accept that we are going to be second best to our friends' lovers? Friends are often used by people in relationships to support those relationships. For single people this most frequently means an unequal flow of energy. According to Becker '[f]riends were the greatest source of support for ex-lovers during their breakups' (1988, p. 69) as practical help, providing a place to stay, help with moving etc., and also a shoulder to cry on. Most women turned to their friends when they broke up with a lover as it 'left an empty hole in a formerly-full life'. So friends are turned to in a crisis, but who do single women turn to in their crises, when many of those same friends are with their partners? Pat says of her ex-lover Marcella: 'If I had a lover, I might have less energy for her. She has less energy for me, but that's fine because she has a husband and son' (Becker, 1988, p. 207). The energy that Pat is giving to Marcella is not being reciprocated, but being directed into her husband and son.

Conclusions

The individual needs that people meet in monogamous relationships are real needs, which may or may not be socially constructed. However, monogamous relationships then become not *a* way of meeting them, but *the* way. Because many of these needs (for affection, physical contact, someone to share things with) are considered 'natural', and a couple relationship is the main socially sanctioned way in which they are met, the couple itself is then considered to be a 'natural' method of structuring society.

The breaking down of the barriers between sexual and platonic love does not necessarily mean promiscuity or casual sex. In fact, with less pressure on individual relationships as a result of our needs being met by different people, relationships would be likely to be longer-term than at present. It would also mean a recognition that sex does not equal sexual intercourse, but a whole range of sensual experiences instead of the categories and rigid definitions currently forced upon us. At present, although we could describe women's sensual/sexual practice as being on a heterosexual-lesbian continuum, the lesbian exists as a social category *not* on a continuum but as a distinct identity with its own sub-culture, oppression and political significance. This means that women who identify as lesbians make choices and take risks which are different from those of a self-defined bisexual or heterosexual women. Misogyny and the oppression of lesbians makes identification as a lesbian important, a political act rather than purely classification of our sexual behaviour.

It has recently become difficult for lesbians/feminists to discuss lesbian sexuality. The debate has been simplistically polarized into 'pro-sex' and 'anti-sex', with lesbians who critique lesbian sexuality being subject to criticism similar in tone to the abuse lesbians suffer for refusing to service men, with non-SM sex often derogatorily referred to as 'vanilla' or 'bambi'.[7] In redefining women's sexuality it is important not to fall into the trap of starting from the premise that men have 'a sexuality', therefore women have to have one as well, separating this from other spheres of our lives. On the other hand, there is also a need not to theorize women's sexuality out of existence, reaffirming the stereotypes of the passive woman, victim to and defined by men's active sexuality.

If divisions were broken down between friends and lovers, it is improbable that compulsory heterosexuality could remain since women's friendships are at present predominantly with other women and there is no reason to expect that these close same-sex bonds are likely to disappear. It seems very difficult to envisage how an anti-monogamous society would still retain its hetero-relational imperative. However the necessary destruction of society's homophobia and woman-hatred to enact more fluid relationships between women is an enormous task. The practicalities of a nonmonogamous lifestyle would require massive changes in society, necessitating a radical rethinking in social policy.

Advocating nonmonogamy does not mean that a lesbian's relationships must all be the same and equal. It is possible that women will still feel closer to a particular person at any point in time than they feel to others. However, it is also likely that women will choose different people to meet various needs (some people are good at cheering us up, others at providing a sympathetic ear, some enjoy going to the cinema, others prefer eating out and so on). A nonmonogamous society would not presume that because a woman felt closer to someone one day she would necessarily feel closest to them the next day, week, month or year, and it would not assume to know how that relationship was constructed nor would it elevate that relationship over all others.

It is important that lesbians do not replicate current oppressive heterosexual models. As Weston (1991, p. 208) says, 'major institutions ... will find it easier to validate domestic partnerships, custody rights for lesbian and gay parents, and the right to jointly adopt children, than to recognise gay families that span several households or families that include friends'. Without the legal and social recognition of friends as 'family', the privileging of some family forms, including biological families, whilst others are subordinated, will reinforce the social order which oppresses lesbians.

Monogamy ultimately serves to keep women divided. Heterosexual women are divided from each other by being 'policed' by individual men. Lesbian energy is used in individual relationships instead of building our communities. Day-to-day anti-lesbianism is absorbed within the couple relationship instead of being transformed into movements to fight our oppression and reaching out to connect with other lesbians. Many lesbians struggle for their relationship to be accepted into heterosexist society, instead of creating a place where *all* lesbians are safe. This redirection of energy from a lesbian community to the individual ultimately benefits the patriarchy in its different forms.

It is not going to be easy to achieve, but the resolution for lesbians must be the creation of women's 'passionate friendship' (Raymond, 1986), where women act from a position of independence and autonomy, and 'sex', in a wider definition of what is 'sexual', becomes one way amongst many of demonstrating love.[8] 'For female-identified erotic love is not dichotomised from radical female friendship, but rather is one important expression/manifestation of friendship' (Daly, 1978, p. 382), and as Firestone stated over twenty years ago, 'we demand . . . not the elimination of sexual joy and excitement but its rediffusion over . . . the spectrum of our lives' (1970, p. 147).

Notes

1 See Douglas (1990, pp. 137–84) for a review of feminist/lesbian writing on the politics of lesbianism and heterosexuality.
2 Lesbians may or may not have children, from previous heterosexual relationships, as co-mothers, or from artificial insemination. Lesbians are often ignored in 'family' policies and studies because we are assumed to be childless. However, a large proportion of lesbians do not have children, for political reasons, because it does not 'just happen' as it apparently does for heterosexual couples, and because lesbians choose to put our time and energy into other things.
3 However, Marge Piercy (1976), in her novel *Women on the Edge of Time*, provides one futuristic vision of how nonmonogamy and a child's need for stability may work.
4 I use 'girlfriend' as it is the word I use in my community of working-class dykes. Whilst being aware of its drawbacks, there is no other term I prefer, as 'girlfriend' emphasizes our lesbianism whereas gender-neutral terms such as 'partner' do not. I suspect that 'partner' is used more in middle-class circles than among working-class people.
5 Little research has been done around lesbian friendships; however, women's friendships in general are not encouraged and it could be that lesbians find it hard to make friends with other lesbians as we have few models as to how to do this. How do lesbians make friends? When does someone become a friend as opposed to an acquaintance/colleague/neighbour?
6 See Smith and Smith (1974) for a collection of articles on sexual behaviour during the 'sexual revolution'.
7 See Jeffreys (1990), particularly chapters 5 and 6 for further discussion of this.
8 This may or may not co-exist with relations with men. It is vitally important that men also have close emotional relationships with each other, and are able to be in close emotional relationships with women without expecting sexual intercourse. This chapter however, is not primarily concerned with this.

Refrences

ATKINSON, TI-GRACE (1974) *Amazon Odyssey*, New York, Link Books.
BARRETT, MICHÈLE and MCINTOSH, MARY (1982) *The Anti-Social Family*, London, Verso.
BECKER, CAROL S. (1988) *Unbroken Ties: Lesbian Ex-Lovers*, Alyson Publications.
BUUNK, BRAM P. and VAN DRIEL, BARRY (1989) *Variant Lifestyles and Relationships*, London, Sage.
COLLIER, J., ROSALDO, M.Z. and YANAGISAKO, S. (1982) 'Is There A Family? New Anthropological Views', in THORNE, BARRIE and YALOM, MARILYN (Eds) *Rethinking The Family*, New York and London, Longman.

DALY, MARY (1978) *Gyn/Ecology*, London, The Women's Press.
DOUGLAS, CAROL ANN (1990) *Love and Politics: Radical Feminist and Lesbian Theories*, in press.
ELLIOT, FAITH ROBERTSON (1986) *The Family: Change or Continuity*, Basingstoke, Macmillan.
FADERMAN, LILLIAN (1981) *Surpassing the Love of Men*, New York, Marrow (reprinted 1985, London, The Women's Press).
FIRESTONE, SHULAMITH (1970) *The Dialectic of Sex: The Case for Feminist Revolution* (reprinted 1979, London, The Women's Press).
GARRETT, STEPHANIE (1989) 'Friendship and the Social Order', in PORTER, ROY and TOMASELLI, SYLVANA (Eds) *The Dialectics of Friendship*, London, Routledge.
GRIFFIN, CHRISTINE (1985) *Typical Girls? Young Women from School to the Job Market*, London, Routledge and Kegan Paul.
HOAGLAND, SARAH LUCIA and PENELOPE, JULIA, (Eds) (1988) *For Lesbians Only: A Separatist Anthology*, London, Onlywomen Press.
HOUSEKNECHT, S.K., VAUGHAN, S. and STATHAM A. (1987) 'The Impact of Singlehood on the Career Patterns of Professional Women', in *Journal of Marriage and the Family*, 49(2), p. 353-66.
JEFFREYS, SHEILA (1985) *The Spinster and her Enemies: Feminism and Sexuality 1880-1930*, London, Pandora.
JEFFREYS, SHEILA (1990) *Anticlimax: A Feminist Perspective on the Sexual Revolution*, London, The Women's Press.
JOHNSON, SUSAN E. (1990) *Staying Power: Long Term Lesbian Couples*, Naiad Press.
KITZINGER, CELIA (1987) *The Social Construction of Lesbianism*, London, Sage.
LEEDS REVOLUTIONARY FEMINIST GROUP (1981) 'Political Lesbianism: The Case Against Heterosexuality', in ONLYWOMEN PRESS (Ed.) *Love Your Enemy? The Debate between Heterosexual Feminism and Political Lesbianism*, London, Onlywomen press.
LEES, SUE (1986) *Losing Out*, London, Hutchinson.
LESBIAN LONDON (1992) Issue 9 (September) and Issue 10 (October).
NARDI, PETER M. (1992) 'That's What Friends Are For: Friends as Family in the Gay and Lesbian Community', in PLUMMER, KEN (Ed.) *Modern Homosexualities*, London, Routledge.
PIERCY, MARGE (1976) *Woman on the Edge of Time*, New York, Knopf (reprinted 1979, London, The Women's Press).
RAMEY, JAMES (1974) 'Emerging Patterns of Innovative Marriage Behaviour' in SMITH, JAMES R. and SMITH, LYNN G. (Eds) *Beyond Monogamy*, Baltimore and London, Johns Hopkins University Press.
RAYMOND, JANICE (1986) *A Passion for Friends*, London, The Women's Press.
RICH, ADRIENNE (1980) 'Compulsory Heterosexuality and Lesbian Existence', in RICH, ADRIENNE *Blood, Bread and Poetry*, London, Virago; also reprinted as a pamphlet by Onlywomen Press (London, 1981).
SHOCKING PINK (no date) *Don't Get Married!*, Issue 11.
SMITH, JAMES R. and SMITH, LYNN, G. (Eds) (1974) *Beyond Monogamy*, Baltimore and London, Johns Hopkins University Press.
VALVERDE, MARIANA (1985) *Sex, Power and Pleasure*, Canada, Women's Press.
WESTON, KATH (1991) *Families We Choose: Lesbians, Gays, Kinship*, Columbia University Press.

Section III

Imaging and Imagining

Introduction

The three chapters in this section demonstrate the diverse ways in which *imagining*, that is how women and men perceive and think, influences *imaging*, i.e. how they construct and consume cultural products. In this process a dialectic is at play between the subject, whether this be the producer or the consumer, and the object, the text or image, whereby continuities of vision are achieved through the fashioning of the object in the image corresponding to how we imagine the object to be. Imagination thus presides over materiality, offering an engaged perspective which simultaneously conceals and reveals its biases.

Thus Kim Clancy's chapter 'Angry Young Women? Sex and Class in Nell Dunn's *Up the Junction*' analyzes the ways in which working-class women's sexuality is both celebrated and reviled in *Up the Junction* by a female observer. This observer, fascinated and horrified by the spectacle of otherness presented by her working-class female protagonists, establishes the latters' identity through marking her self as different, less promiscuous, less working-class.

Difference is a key concept here, as indeed it is in Women's Studies as a whole. Difference of both sex and class is topicalized and historicized in Clancy's article, revealed in its relation to time and culture. In *Up the Junction* difference arises in the context of a post-war middle-class preoccupation with working-class habits on to which the middle classes could project the fears and desires they found within themselves. Thus Dunn's *Up the Junction* does not offer a documentary or realist account of working-class women's lives but one informed by a middle-class woman's desire to transgress. This desire encourages the female flâneur/ narrator of Dunn's text to move into working-class territory and engage

123

voyeuristically with women posited as different from her whom she adores and reviles precisely on account of that difference.

The question of how empowering for the objects (or rather, referents) of the female flâneur's gaze the latter's presentation of their lives is, is a question also raised in Sue Thornham, Elaine Brown and Angela Werndly's chapter, '"Not Happy but Hopeful": Readers of Catherine Cookson in the North-East of England'. Here the authors discuss the responses to Cookson's novels of predominantly working-class women readers from the region of England in which her novels are set. Strikingly, the readers reveal a desire for identification with Cookson's heroines whom they regard as resilient and ultimately truimphant in the face of suffering. Simultaneously, while differences between the readers' present and the past depicted in Cookson's novels are emphasized by the readers, their responses reveal the continuities in gender-related attitudes between that imagined past and their lived present; identification with Cookson's heroines is thus established on the basis of an understanding of continuing inequalities between the sexes on the one hand, and the celebration of bonding among women, on the other. Among the many female voices interviewed by Thornham, Brown and Werndly who record the escapist function Cookson's writings have in their lives, one lone voice of female protest stands out strongly, pronouncing her rejection of the Cookson image of a heroine because the structure of the narratives, centred as they are on the overcoming of adversity, condones female suffering as inevitable and ennobling. Cookson's texts thus do not appear to mobilize their readers to become agents of change; rather, they disempower these readers by projecting the notion that adversity can be overcome and that this overcoming will be its own reward.

Issues of agency also play a role in Margrit Shildrick and Janet Price's 'Splitting the Difference: Adventures in the Anatomy and Embodiment of Women'. Shildrick and Price argue that 'ways of seeing and ways of knowing are not predicated on a reality somehow beyond discourse, but are deeply implicated in the construction of bodies and selves'. They show how anatomical presentations at different historical moments offer an image of prevalent ideologies of femininity and masculinity whereby the female body, always re-constructed in relation to an image of the male body, is inevitably presented as secondary, incomplete, passive, void, receptive. Such imaging, Shildrick and Price argue, operates irrespective of the state of knowledge of the human anatomy, thus reinforcing its ideological basis. An understanding of this implicatedness allows the questioning of biology as a given, a position often suggested in contexts where biology is contrasted with socialization. But nature is always nurtured, constructed by the imagination of those who image it.

This continuity between the imagination of the producer/consumer and the image does not deny the possibility of an intervening other gaze which exposes that continuity and refuses it on the basis of a different and differently engaged perspective. The possibility of such an intervention, more partisanly: 'debunking', reinstates the agency of the female subject, reacting to images of women by women and men, in order to mobilize different images which challenge the ones under scrutiny. This generates debate and openings for change, allows for shifting territories and refuses the dominance of any one position.

Chapter 7

Angry Young Women? Sex and Class in Nell Dunn's *Up the Junction*[1]

Kim Clancy

Introduction

A central project of feminist cultural theory has been to locate and name a female 'gaze', a female 'voice', be it that of the writer or reader, producer or consumer, of cultural texts. What happens when a woman looks, when a woman speaks? Does the familiar landscape of the female body, as constructed from a male perspective, radically shift? Or does it depend on the nature of the woman who looks, her reasons for doing so, and the institutional structures, the historical, cultural and linguistic boundaries, within which her gaze/voice is permitted, mediated, shaped?

It is with such questions in mind that I approach a particularly fruitful historical and cultural moment, Britain in the early 1960s. It is here, amidst something of a feminist wasteland, devoid of all but a handful of self-consciously feminist voices, that the writing of a number of women began to demand attention. A concern to explore openly the experiences of women in relation to sexuality, femininity, reproduction and female friendship informs much of the work of Nell Dunn, Margaret Drabble, Maureen Duffy, Shelagh Delaney, Edna O'Brien and others. Their books swiftly became films, the titles of which — *A Taste of Honey, The L-Shaped Room, Up the Junction, Georgy Girl* and *The Knack* — still conjure up a mythical sixties landscape of permissiveness and adventure. However, for all its radical potential, this work, with the notable exception of Duffy's (Duffy, 1962, 1966), remains largely white, heterosexual and middle-class in its articulation of female desire — hardly surprising, given the cultural backgrounds of those women able to find a voice, and the historical moment of their speaking.

127

Kim Clancy

In this chapter I intend to do two things: firstly, explore the cultural landscape of early 1960s Britain, examining, in particular, social realist representations of working-class women; secondly, provide a reading of Nell Dunn's *Up the Junction* with a view to affirming its radical attempt to applaud the lives of working-class women. However, I also want to draw attention to the contradictions which are manifest in the body of this text. When a female writer, in 1963, attempts to speak the unspeakable, to name and celebrate an active female heterosexual desire existing outside the confines of marriage and monogamy, and accorded lesser importance than camaraderie between women, such contradictions are inevitable.

Hello Ingrid, Goodbye Vic

For the liberal/left imagination of the late 1950s and early 1960s, working-class culture offered a romanticized image of 'authenticity' and 'realism'. Films such as *Look Back In Anger* (1959), *Saturday Night and Sunday Morning* (1960) and *A Kind of Loving* (1962) were adaptations of the published work of so-called 'Angry Young Men' such as John Osborne, Alan Sillitoe and Stan Barstow. The 1957 publications of Richard Hoggart's *The Uses of Literacy*, the cultural and historical writings of Raymond Williams and E.P. Thompson, the 1960 launch of the Granada soap *Coronation Street* and the fashion spreads of some of the glossier magazines suggest that working-classness was in vogue, both literally and metaphorically.

This foregrounding of working-class culture occurred in the context of the postwar era of slum demolition and city reconstruction programmes, of 'grammar school boys' and supposed upward mobility, of the 'winds of change' of a liberal political consensus. It expressed concern at the perceived 'embourgeoisement' of the working class, the erosion of 'traditional' working-class values by Americanized popular culture and consumerism.

In fact, the majority of these texts focus specifically on working-class masculinity. With the exception of Shelagh Delaney, and to a lesser extent Doris Lessing and Ann Jellicoe, women were not allowed into the 'Angry Young Man' club. The role of the working-class woman as character was limited. She represented the girlfriend, unable to share the ideals of the male hero. Instead she 'craved' the very consumer durables — semi-detached house, washing machine, fridge, television — that the

Sex and Class in Nell Dunn's Up the Junction

'Angries' denounced as undermining traditional working-class communities! Frequently she become pregnant and 'forced' the hero into marriage, thereby putting an end to his finer aspirations. A shining example of such a narrative is Barstow's *A Kind of Loving*. Here, first-person narrator Vic passes judgment on his wife, Ingrid: 'As for Ingrid, I don't think she had a serious thought to call her own before she met me and I gave her something to think about, except what colour of coat she wanted for winter and whether she liked "Criss Cross Quiz" better than "Double Your Money".' (Barstow 1991, p. 243)

There was a space — small and stereotypical — in which to celebrate 'Our Mam'; but no such space for the voices of those I might call the 'Grammar School Girls' or the 'Angry Young Women'. In the words of Terry Lovell (1990), 'the adult daughter is silent'. It is within this somewhat depressing scenario that the female voices of *Up the Junction* offer liberating possibilities.

1963: The Year of 'Sex'

The year of its publication, 1963, was a highly contradictory cultural moment. The sixties were not yet 'swinging' with any confidence; sex was both out in the open, and still undercover. The Pill, first put on the market in 1956, was becoming widely available; yet the 1957 Wolfenden Report into male homosexuality and prostitution saw its recommendations on the latter, that prostitutes should be less publicly visible, become law (Weeks, 1983, p. 168). 'Suddenly you could talk about sex at dinner parties, because it was in the newspapers' (Maitland, 1988, p. 151); but, although 'spoken', sexuality was not being 'owned'. Instead it was massively projected elsewhere: onto the bodies of the establishment — adulterous cabinet minister John Profumo, and divorcing couple the Duke and Duchess of Argyll — the latter described by the judge as 'a completely promiscuous woman whose sexual appetite could only be satisfied by a number of men' (Wheen, 1982, p. 93); onto the bodies of high-class call-girls Christine Keeler and Mandy Rice-Davies; onto the bodies of juvenile delinquents and West Indian communities; and onto literary characters such as Lawrence's Lady Chatterley and Dunn's Rube and Sylvie.

From this perspective the exponents of social realism stand accused of excessive voyeurism. The 'kitchen sink' dramas, particularly in their cinematic forms, exhibit a fascinated interest in working-class sexuality.

For Hill 'Riding on the back of the "social commitment" to observe "ordinary people" . . . [there] . . . emerges a kind of sexual fascination with "otherness", the "exotic" sexualities of those it now has a licence to reveal' (1986, p. 136). Lovell (1990) suggests that Hoggart's *The Uses of Literacy* in its address to an assumed middle-class audience 'resembles an anthropological study written by an exiled native informant'. In similar vein, I will argue that the middle-class gaze of *Up the Junction* inadvertently constructs the inhabitants of Battersea as exotic working-class Other.

Useful to such an analysis is the work of Stallybrass and White (1986) on Victorian reforming texts. Here they argue that as the nineteenth-century bourgeoisie began to regulate their own bodies — both organic and social — they wrote eagerly of the body of the city slum and its inhabitants. This latter body became the site of middle-class fantasies and fears, a place of contagion and pollution, depraved desire and disease, a source of both horror and fascination; in other words, a place of projection for all that the bougeoisie sought to repress of their own physical functions and sexual desires. For Wilson, the body of the working-class woman served as a 'touchstone' for nineteenth-century debates on 'civilisation and progress' (1991, p. 28). The jostling crowds on the city streets held dangers of pollution and contamination, for a 'respectable' woman might be accidentally detained as a prostitute! The images of working-class woman, woman walking the streets and prostitute were thus collapsed into one category, indexing an ambiguity of reading much in evidence in the critical reception of *Up the Junction*.

This then is a colonial discourse, seeking to observe, explain and contain the threat of the Other. As in discourses of Empire, oppositions between the 'savage' and the 'civilized' are employed to articulate the working-class as beyond the pale. In the nineteenth century, reformers such as Josephine Butler and Octavia Hill ventured into the 'darkness' of the London slums, their object to do good. Dunn's journey into the backstreets of Battersea owes something to this ancestry. In the language of reviewers she, too, was represented as an intrepid explorer (Jones, 1963): 'Nell Dunn . . . [is] on safari through the south suburbs, accompanied by trustworthy native guides'. Certainly, Dunn's publishers sought to encourage such a reading: 'In 1959, Nell Dunn . . . crossed the bridge from fashionable Chelsea and bought a tiny house in Battersea. . . . The exuberant, uninhibited life she found in the tired old streets and under the railway arches enchanted her, and she recaptures it in these closely linked sketches which are funny, witty, bawdy and gorgeously human' (Dunn, 1966). In this sense *Up the Junction* can be placed alongside Doris Lessing's *In Pursuit of the English* (1960), Margaret Lassell's *Wellington*

Sex and Class in Nell Dunn's Up the Junction

Road (1962) or even the 1962 reprint of Jack London's *The People of the Abyss*. In each of these texts there is a meeting of the respectable and the rough, as middle-class writers submerge themselves in a working-class milieu, writing with fascination of their adventures.

Up the Junction

The publication of *Up the Junction* was itself a junction in terms of cultural constructions of female sexuality. In its various textual forms — article, book, TV drama, film — it spans the period 1960–67, and several sites of institutional production. Between 1961 and 1963 four of the stories appeared in the political journal *New Statesman*; in 1963 it was published as a collection of semi-autobiographical 'sketches' or short stories; in 1965, Ken Loach's drama-documentary was broadcast by the BBC and in 1967 Peter Collinson's film adaptation was released. It is safe to assume, therefore, that the published text powerfully articulated shifting discourses around gender, sexuality, class and race, providing something of a bridge between the 'austerity' of the fifties and the 'permissiveness' of the sixties. Not surprisingly, therefore, it is a site of massive contradictions, transgressing the boundaries of 'fact' and 'fiction', of 'author' and 'subject', of social class, and of high and low culture. Its range of potential readings also crosses boundaries. Is it a lurid exploitation of its working-class subjects or a celebratory account of working-class women? How far did discourses of working-classness already in circulation construct the very nature of Dunn's gaze, what it was capable of 'seeing', remembering, interpreting and judging worthy of recollection?

Up the Junction was Dunn's first book. It was followed in 1965 by *Talking to Women*, a series of interviews with, amongst others, artist Pauline Boty and writer Edna O'Brien, and in 1967 by *Poor Cow*, the story of working-class Joy and her young son, Jonny. As a member of the Young Communist Party, Dunn had a commitment to exposing and challenging social and economic deprivation. She was familiar with the writings of Simone de Beauvoir, and, having seen Osborne's *Look Back In Anger*, asked herself who was writing the story from the woman's point of view? Her commitment to speak to, and on behalf of, women is clearly evident (Dunn, 1993).

In this sense the text enjoys impeccable credentials. A female author writes of working-class women within whose community she chooses to live. She utilizes stylistic devices which enable her 'characters' —

marginalized from mainstream cultural production — to speak 'in their own words', unedited, unfettered, unsilenced. Constructed as a series of 'sketches', the women's stories are told through anecdotes, dialogue, reportage. The 'I' of the first-person narrator is present, but is anonymous, effaced, rendered of lesser importance than the 'named' working-class characters, in particular, sisters Rube and Sylvie. However, as I will show, the effacing of this authorial voice is counterposed by an extremely powerful authorial 'presence', a narrative structure and a use of language which critiques the very lives that it seeks to celebrate.

Celebrating Working-Class Female Sexuality

There is much to celebrate in the verions of female sexuality constructed in *Up the Junction*. A close-knit community of women is represented. Men are peripheral to their lives. The women earn their own money and thus possess economic and sexual independence. On numerous occasions men become objects of exchange between female characters, featuring within the sex stories and jokes that they swap: ' "Anyone lend me their husband for the weekend?" "Yeah, you can 'ave mine, he's a dirty sod on the quiet" ' (23). The women are depicted as having control over their own bodies. They have sexual relationships when they choose, on their own terms, for their own pleasure: Rube at a party: ' "I don't half fancy a snog tonight". . . ."After going steady for six months you get a bit fed up, snoggin' with the same bloke every night" '. (30). Monogomy, married life and husbands are not recommended: ' "No", says Sylvie, "straight — if I have it once I want it three or four times . . . Remember I got married when I was sixteen. Now I've got rid of him I like to be out and about" '. (38–9).

The camaraderie between the women is of crucial importance. In the factory, in the pub, shopping, at the laundry, they enjoy one another's company, listen to one another's stories. Such positive representations of female friendship remain rare, even in women's writing!

Discourses around femininity and consumerism, referred to above, are here given a different twist. In the 1962 film, *Live Now, Pay Later*, for example, a combination of advertising, HP inducements and sexy salesmen persuade naive 'housewives' to run up debts that they cannot afford to repay, on consumer items that they do not really need. In contrast, Rube and Sylvie are depicted as having the money to pay off their debts, but simply refusing to, unless caught out by the debt collector. Women take the goods, a new bedroom suite, for instance, but

Sex and Class in Nell Dunn's Up the Junction

refuse to pay the remaining instalments. Rube takes the narrator to a pay-as-you-wear shop: and outlines the complicated series of lies and evasions by which Sylvie avoided further payment on 'a fabulous two-piece' she purchased there: 'one pound down and she wasn't going to pay no more' (21).

An image of the celebrated Viv 'Spend, Spend, Spend' Nichols is evoked; the working-class woman, much beloved by the right-wing press, who won a million on the pools, spent the lot, and became, once again, penniless. Working-class women, such discourses imply, are not capable of handling money with any responsibility or ethics. The emphasis on Rube and Sylvie having the necessary money, but *choosing* not to pay up, obscures precisely the poverty which has historically forced working people to make their purchases on the slate. At the same time it is possible to read this 'battle' between Tally Man and women as a highly gendered resistance to patriarchal capitalism and male authority. The women refuse to be denied consumer items that they desire, and resist regulation by male agencies of consumer capitalism. Sylvie's response to a Tally Man waiting in the street for payment is: 'You can go and tell him to piss off' (16).

A Female Flâneur?

'My writing comes from the streets of the city; from the everyday street theatre of life, with me as its anonymous observer' (Neustatter, 1981).

The women are active. They walk the streets, day and night, between factory, pub, club, laundry, shops, home. In this sense they occupy a public space, loudly and raucously, are not quietly confined to a domestic arena. Watching them, writing them, it could be argued that the narrator occupies the position of the classic flâneur, a male figure of the late nineteenth century, conventionally depicted as lounging in the streets, observing the women, passing judgment, writing his gaze.

The possibilities for transgression here are evident: Nell Dunn/ narrator as female flâneur; the objects of her gaze, not passive passantes who coyly look away, but Rube and Sylvie, with 'sultry' stares and active sexual desires. There are possibilities for the naming and celebrating of a lesbian gaze. Not only does Dunn construct women who move freely on the streets and act openly on their sexual desires; she, too, in the very act of 'looking', is transgressing the gendered boundaries which maintain that the flâneur is male. The line between desiring to 'become' and desiring to 'possess' the women who are the objects of her gaze, is a fine one.

However, it is as if this very act of transgression renders the streets grotesque for the narrator. They overflow, both metaphorically and literally, with piss, stench and debris. A constant link is made between the working-class women's bodies, piss overflowing, and the streets which they walk. The streets, in effect, become a urinal: 'The alley don't belong to you. It's a public convenience 'ent it?' (80); 'Outside in the yard the toilet is aswim with piss. Rube blacks her eyebrows' (32); 'Sylvie squats behind a ten-ton truck for a piss and the truck moves off' (53). Here there is matter out of place, fluids oozing from the margins of the women's bodies and from the margins of the streets.

The women who inhabit these streets are rendered nightmarish, horrific. The gaze which attempts to pin them down, which attempts to speak of their bodies, is fascinated, appalled: 'Rube is running towards me, bulging out of her bra, a pink jelly' (12). The narrative constantly constructs women's flesh, especially older women's, as mottled, veined, purple, bursting out of its clothing: 'thick red fingers, swollen with the cold' (23); 'Fat Lil stamps her old feet, blue veins bulging out of broken shoes' (51).

The masquerade of femininity is exposed again and again as descriptions of the working-class women's bodies are juxtaposed with references to toilets, food being consumed or ashtrays overflowing: 'We were crushed in the toilets. All round girls smeared on pan-stick' (10); 'While she dresses I look out the window over the lavatory' (17); 'She is pretty in the dirty cafe; full ashtrays and dripping sauce bottles' (22). This rhetorical structuring device is found throughout the text, a shift of perspective from the description of a woman's body to some other object which is overflowing, messy, dripping. It may well be that this is an attempt to provide the characters with a certain poignancy, a fragility, by juxtaposing them with vivid images of an urban, socially deprived environment. Nevertheless, I would argue that these powerful visual images stand in for the negative critique that the narrator does not overtly speak, and the author did not *intend* to suggest. The text passes its own judgment!

Opposed to these fluids are the fluids that the women avoid — soap and water, symbolic of cleanliness and hygiene. The narrator draws attention to signs which the women deliberately ignore: 'WASH YOUR HANDS AFTER USING THE TOILETS. THIS IS A FOOD FACTORY' (26) and 'LADIES! WILL YOU PLEASE PULL THE CHAIN!' (62). The story 'Wash Night' juxtaposes imagery of the purification process of cleansing: 'The huge damp room, the smell of boiled sheets in the soapy, steamy air' (73) with the voices of Rube and Sylvie recounting sexual anecdotes: ' "He kept pressin' himself against me, then his hands began to wander. 'You ain't half hot-blooded', he says . . . 'I can't help being sexy', I says" ' (74). The purification process of the laundry is less powerful than the women's stories. The women refuse to be 'cleansed'.

This female gaze then, this female flâneur, walks the streets, observing the women, remaining herself unobserved. But, in order to observe, to speak, to write, the narrator must occupy what I will call — for want of a better term — a 'male' gaze. She must construct the working-class women's bodies as grotesque, in order to atone for her own active gaze, her transgressive position as flâneur. Like Virginia Woolf in her essay 'Street Haunting: A London Adventure' the narrator must construct another Other, one based on class and racial difference, in order to, herself, be freed from objectification.

Good Girl/Bad Girl

In keeping with her position as flâneur, and to utilize Woolf's image, it is difficult to locate the 'eye' of this text. The narrator seldom breaks cover. Voices flow together, comments are unattributed. However an analysis of the fleeting instances when the power dynamic is briefly reversed, and a character speaks of/to the narrator, suggests that she is constructed as the antithesis of the working-class women she observes.

Such moments are made available only to male characters. The narrator is positioned by a male voice, a male gaze, not a female one. The comments draw attention to her status, her sensitivity, her lack of sexual availability, her 'difference'. They do not provide physical description. Unlike the bodies of Rube and Sylvie, the body of the narrator is not presented to us in the flesh, so to speak. It remains effaced, hidden, unavailable. The only physical detail of the narrator we are given is the presence of a wedding ring on her finger. Early in the first story: 'Rube points to my wedding ring' (10). This moment has a direct inversion in a later story when Rube defiantly states: "I ain't got no rings on my fingers 'cept me own!" (32). Her sister Sylvie is divorced, and brawls violently in the street with her ex-husband. The narrator, therefore, is constructed as married (sexually unavailable?), in contrast to Rube and Sylvie.

In the first story, each woman pairs off with a man. The narrator's partner comments: ' "I don't know what to say to a decent girl. If you was an old slag, I'd just say 'Come 'ere. . .' " ' (13–14). She is defined by what she is not. If she is not an 'old slag', then who is? In the fourth story, they again pair off. Her male partner, Dave, comments: ' "When I saw yer sittin' there I began to sizzle . . . Then you began to talk and I realised you were a nice girl" ' (35) and a few lines later: ' "You smell as if you never sweated in yer life" ' (35–6). In a later story she is told: ' "I've bin with all sorts of girls but it's the decent girls like you that I prefer . . ." ' (111). These moments suggest that although the narrator seeks to 'pass' in the London slums in much the same way as Jack London did in *The People of the Abyss* her essential 'difference', her greater sensibility, her 'purity', her lack of bodily odour(!), is recognized — and named — by the authoritative male observer. A good-girl/bad-girl dichotomy is set up in the first story and subsequently reinforced. This dualism serves implicitly to position the activities of Rube and Sylvie as 'bad'.

The fact that it is male characters who offer this perspective of the narrator could possibly be read as irony: the attempt by men to categorize female sexuality into 'good' or 'bad'. Nevertheless, the narrative itself is complicit in this process. The possibility of possessing a gaze, of judging women's bodies, is constructed within a hierarchy of textual power relations. The narrator possesses a gaze which frequently reduces her working-class characters to their bodily parts. On the few occasions when the gaze is reversed and held by a male observer, the narrator's body is not held up for exposure. Compare the following: a male character comments on the narrator's ankles: ' "That's a posh pair of swanky ankles someone's got" ' (84). No physical description. No voyeuristic detail. Only an allusion to her class position and status. In contrast, here is the narrator's earlier description of Sylvie's ankles: 'The hard little balls of her ankles are black with dirt. Her feet are thin in the cheap shoes one size to big' (37). The description is one of fascinated voyeurism, the emphasis on the hardness, dirtiness and cheapness of Sylvie's body.

Whose Gaze?

In common with many social realist writers and filmmakers of the period, Dunn employs elements of poetic realism in her work, as evidenced in the following lines: 'Outside the dawn slides over the gasworks, slips over the rubble through the window' (36); and 'Great gusts of black smoke blow sideways out of the four chimneys of Fulham gasworks across a streaky sky' (122-3). Interestingly enough, it is here that the text constructs a landscape without people, as if moments of 'beauty' only become available when the Battersea landscape is emptied of the working-class people who inhabit it.

In contrast to the poetic moments to which the narrator draws the reader's attention, we can compare the subjects to which Rube and Sylvie draw her attention: ' "See him? Patsy Chubb had it with him twice in his car and his wife's carrying" ' (19); ' "See her: she done her house up all posh and filled it with Coloureds" ' (20). Their world is constructed as narrow and blinkered, filled with gossip and prejudice. The only metaphors that they utilize are euphemisms for the female genitals such as 'hold onto yer halfpenny' and 'hands off me crumpet'.

In this sense the working-class inhabitants of this textual Battersea once again do not possess a gaze. They cannot both *be seen* and *see*. They are an integral part of this ugly/beautiful landscape, so firmly embedded *in* the landscape as artefacts, exhibits, curiosities, that there remains no place from which they can speak of it. The 'difference', the huge gap separating narrator and narrated, is thus further emphasized. Unlike her subjects, the narrator is not restricted to a single, limited, linguistic code. She ranges widely across the colloquial, the factual, the poetic, just as she also moves more freely across moral and sexual codes of behaviour.

Other 'Others'

The central characters are constructed as white and unproblematically heterosexual. Their fascination, their Otherness, for the narrator/reader, lies in their working-classness and their excessive heterosexuality. Overtly racist or homophobic remarks are attributed to working-class characters; they include Sylvie's comment on 'queers': ' "They say a lot of them's mentally disturbed" ' (77); Rube's casual racism: ' "I reckon all our germs come from them foreigners. You don't know what they bring over with them" ' (76); and that of the Tally Man: ' "You see the blacks have only got half the brain cells to what we've got. They never had a civilization" ' (120). The manner in which the comments are inserted into the text tends to suggest disapproval emanating from the narrator. She is able to disassociate herself — and by implication, Dunn — from the views expressed, by implying that she is merely providing an unmediated snapshot of the prejudice she encounters. However, by unproblematically reproducing such comments, the text itself circulates racist and homophobic views.

Similarly, in the story 'Sunday Morning', Moira, a young black woman resident in a home for unmarried mothers, is the object of the Matron's racism. While the author undoubtedly sought to use this story to critique racism, the narrative actually exploits racist discourses which associate blackness with animality, physicality, and the exotic, by constructing a sensationalist tableau of Otherness, the spectacle of a black woman's body giving birth to a dead baby: Moira 'barefooted on the glazed tile floor, screaming while the baby's head emerged' (47); 'She stood stiff and screaming till the black baby slipped out with a soft thud onto the stone floor' (48). In white Western culture the bodies of black women are circulated in cultural texts as sources of fantasy, fear and desire; the emotions they arouse are subsequently contained, and rendered safe, as is the case in this story. By the narrative closure Moira has been marched away by the forces of authority — ambulancemen and police: 'Nobody ever saw black Moira again' (48).

Bang on the Common

The pivotal story of *Up the Junction*, the point at which my arguments find their most obvious expression, is 'Bang on the Common', the story which recounts Rube's botched backstreet abortion. It is this story which readers tend to recall most vividly, due in part, no doubt, to the harrowing detail of the TV and cinema adaptations.

'Bang on the Common' is accorded a central place in the text. It is the ninth of sixteen stories, and therefore falls midway in the sequence of individual narratives: a middle point, at the heart of the text, which, not surprisingly, focuses in the closest detail on the working-class woman's body. It is sandwiched, interestingly, in between 'The Clipjoint', in which the narrator comes closest to the life of the hostess/prostitute, and 'Wash Night', with its narrative of cleansing and purity.

Rube is pregnant. Abortion is not legally available. A friend suggests that she tries quinine: ' "This Barry, he gets it from the chemist. Tells him he's got a mate just back from Africa with a touch of the malaria, then he sells the tablets ten bob each to the girls" ' (67). A link is established between women's bodies, abortion, Africa and disease — the cure for all forms of Otherness being quinine.

The narrator accompanies Rube to see Winny, a backstreet abortionist. Winny 'wore a red dress above her knees showing her varicose-vein

Sex and Class in Nell Dunn's Up the Junction

legs. . . . She had delicate arms and huge bony hands with long red fingers' (68–9). One Sunday morning, after several trips to Winny, Rube begins to abort painfully. The imagery renders her animal: 'Rube was shrieking, a long, high, animal shriek' (71). Allusions to the earlier malaria are invoked: 'Her jet-black hair stuck to her face and tiny rivulets of blue rinse coursed down her white cheeks. She was semi-delirious' (70). A direct link is made between the Sunday roast that the Macarthy family are consuming, and the abortion: 'The smell of Sunday dinner cooking floated up the stairs. Rube bent up tight with pain . . . Sylvie came in. ' "I'll hold her now, Mum, if you want to go and have yer dinner" ' (70). The family itself is depicted as able to sit and watch a woman abort, in between grabbing mouthfuls of Sunday roast. The emphasis on the smell of meat further implies that Rube herself is animal, is meat. 'In the kitchen everyone was eating' (71), except for the narrator who is busy phoning for a doctor.

'The baby was born alive, five months old. It moved, it breathed, its heart beat' (71). The Macarthy women all refer to the baby as 'it'. The narrator however, in the closing sentence, alters 'it' to 'him': 'They took Rube away, but they left behind the baby, which had now grown cold. Later Sylvie took him, wrapped in the *Daily Mirror*, and threw him down the toilet' (71).

This final sentence stands as a summary for the points I have been trying to make: the reference to working-class popular culture: the *Daily Mirror*, being 'wrapped' in newspaper, suggesting fish and chips, to a baby disappearing down the drain, a life/death directly equated with excrement, urine. The implication is that the baby is left to die, and then disposed of. There is a suggestion of sacrifice, of some inverted religious ritual: the day is Sunday, the carving and eating of the Sunday roast, the flushing of the toilet. As with the story of Moira, 'They took Rube away' suggests authority, punishment, guilt. It is a harrowing narrative, constructing working-class women as animal, and positioning the reader forcibly with the narrator, outside Rube's experience, watching/reading with horrified fascination and condemnation.

Conclusion

How does one make sense of a text which, on the one hand, appears to crudely sensationalize working-class female sexuality, yet, on the other, overtly sets out to celebrate the very same? These two aspects are inextricably entwined. In attempting to see — and celebrate — working-class women's bodies, desires, sexualities in 1963, the text also finds a place to speak its fear, loathing, anger and repulsion. Its overt project is to affirm, so there can be no overt critique. Therefore the critique spills over into the way working-class vernacular is used, into the construction of imagery and the structuring of narrative, just as the fluids spill out of the women's bodies and the debris spills onto the streets. Groping for a voice, Dunn produces a text which slips between affirmation and repulsion, celebration and disgust. What I might call the 'conscious' voice of the text, Dunn's alter ego, the narrative first person, seeks to celebrate. But the 'unconscious' of the text is structured by discourses more powerful than the author's overt intentions. It is here, perhaps, that Dunn 'speaks' her own fears and anxieties around her own body, her own sexuality, her own desires.

Up the Junction transgresses many boundaries — but not necessarily those it set out to. It is not so much an individual author, such as Nell Dunn, who should be held to account, as the specific configurations of class, gender and racial identity which authorize certain women to speak, while limiting what they are able to say. Dunn had the opportunity — and courage — to extend her own boundaries, linguistically, socially and creatively. Not so her working-class subjects. Their boundaries were still being drawn, by somebody else's pen and somebody else's fantasies.

Note

1 References made to Dunn (1966) throughout this chapter are indicated by the page numbers in parenthesis.

References

BARSTOW, S. (1960) *A Kind of Loving*, London, Penguin.
DRAKE, N. (Ed.) *The Sixties: A Decade In Vogue*, New York, Prentice Hall.
DUFFY, M. (1962) *That's How It Was*, London, Panther.
DUFFY, M. (1966) *The Microcosm*, London, Hutchinson.
DUNN, N. (1966) *Up the Junction*, London, Pan.
DUNN, N. (1965) *Talking to Women*, London, Macgibbon and Kee.
DUNN, N. (1967) *Poor Cow*, London, Pan.
DUNN, N. (1993) interview with author.
HILL, J. (1986) *Sex, Class and Realism: British Cinema 1956-63*, London, BFI.

JONES, D.A.N. (1963) Review of *Up the Junction*, *New Statesman*, 22 November, pp. 750-1.
LANDAU, C. (Ed.) (1991) *Growing Up in the Sixties*, London, Macdonald Optima.
LASSELL, M. (1962) *Wellington Road*, London, Routledge.
LESSING, D. (1960) *In Pursuit of the English*, London, Granada.
LONDON, J. (1962) *The People of the Abyss*, London, Arco (original publication 1903).
LOVELL, T. (1990) 'Landscapes and Stories in 1960s British Realism', *Screen*, vol. 31, no. 4, pp. 347-76.
MAITLAND, S. (Ed.) (1988) *Very Heaven: Looking Back at the 1960s*, London, Virago.
MOORE-GILBERT, B. and SEED, J. (Eds) (1992) *Cultural Revolution: The Challenge of the Arts in the 1960s*, London, Routledge.
NEUSTATTER, A. (1981) 'The Discreet Charm of Nell Dunn', *The Sunday Times*, 23 August.
STALLYBRASS, P. and WHITE, A. (1986) *The Politics and Poetics of Transgression*, London, Methuen.
WEEKS, J. (1983) *Coming Out: Homosexual Politics in Britain from the Nineteenth Century to the Present*, London, Quartet.
WHEEN, F. (1982) *The Sixties*, London, Century.
WILSON, E. (1980) *Only Halfway to Paradise: Women in Postwar Britain*, London, Methuen.
WILSON, E. (1991) *The Sphinx in the City*, London, Virago.
WOOLF, V. (1967; original publication 1927) 'Street Haunting: A London Adventure', in *Collected Essays*, vol. 4, London, Hogarth Press.

Chapter 8

'Not Happy but Hopeful': Readers of Catherine Cookson in the North-East of England

Sue Thornham, Elaine Brown and Angela Werndly

> Our lives are very different from those of our mothers, and this applies to all women of our generation. For the changes of the last thirty-odd years have made a greater and deeper impression on women than on men. (Heron, 1985)

Introduction

Catherine Cookson is a massively popular writer: Bridget Fowler (1991, p. 73) reports that between January 1983 and July 1985 her novels represented 1 per cent of all adult fiction library loans; in 1987 she had twenty-seven titles in the 100 most loaned titles. Our own local figures are even more startling. In South Shields, where Cookson grew up and where many of the novels are set, the local library service, serving a population of 150,000 and with a collection of some 100,000 books, buys eighty copies of each new book she publishes, and accumulates a waiting list of around 200 before each new publication, rising to some 400 in the weeks immediately preceding publication. (Publication is a bi-annual event: new hardback titles appear at Christmas and on Mother's Day, and they are published as paperbacks exactly a year later.) Almost all of these readers are women. The library aims to clear its reservations within six months by enforcing a short-loan system; of its vast collection (some 2,000) of Cookson novels, it estimates that only between fifteen and twenty copies, in total, will be on the shelves at any one time. Nearby Washington library, with a smaller stock — only sixteen copies of each title — regularly finds itself without any titles on its shelves.

There has been little academic work done on Cookson and her readers. What there is has either placed her firmly within the genre of romantic fiction ('Beyond the anonymous world of romantic fiction, two contemporary romantic novelists have achieved a special pre-eminence: Barbara Cartland and Catherine Cookson', Batsleer *et al.*, 1985, p. 92) or, alternatively, seen her importance in class terms ('Her writing represents both working-class critique of a market-dominanted society and an older element of paternalist thought', Fowler, 1991, p. 96). In the latter study, Cookson and her readers are positioned on a scale of political radicalism, judged in terms of their capacity to 'strip away ideology' (Flower, 1991, p. 90) and envisage social change.

The women in the north-east whom we interviewed for this study, however, on the one hand explicitly *opposed* Cookson's books to those of Cartland ('They're not real, it's not real life. Cookson I think is real' — M; 'I'm not very keen on romantic novels, you know, Barbara Cartland type of thing . . . not realistic enough for me' — K), a finding also of Bridget Fowler's reader survey (Fowler, 1991, p. 174). On the other hand, however, Cookson's books are seen by these women as part of a specifically *female* working-class culture ('I think a lot of Catherine Cookson books are about women, regardless of the men' — Q), a part of their present lives, used by them in much the same way as they use the strong women in soap operas ('I think you do identify with [Cookson's women] and think "I wish I was that way" ' — S; 'I think the soaps give you a goal as well — if she can do that I can do that' — Q).[1] These readers are, then, like Janice Radway's Smithton romance readers, part of a reading community, but this community does not, like that of the Smithton women, function as a substitute for 'older neighbourhood groups' (Radway, 1987, p. 97); rather it functions, no matter how precariously, *within* such a group:

S: . . . family, friends, you pass the books on, then you discuss it when you've finished it.
P: Somebody buys a book and passes it on and then another person buys one and — it's passed round in a circle — so you just discuss it with family and friends. . .

Like Radway's romance readers, the women use the books to blot out the insistent demands of husband and family ('I say I'll read one more chapter, then peel the taties. Then when I finish that chapter, I say I'll read another chapter — I hate housework by the way' — Q). They also use them to assert and maintain a sense of a specifically female history and community.

Sue Thornham, Elaine Brown and Angela Werndly

This chapter investigates the ways in which our sample of nineteen largely working-class women from the north-east of England ('Catherine Cookson Country')[2] uses Cookson's books and the women in them.

Methodology

Between January and July 1993 we interviewed nineteen women who had responded either to a leaflet placed in South Shields library or to a letter in the local paper, the *Northern Echo*. Seven of the respondents came from South Shields, the rest from elsewhere within 'Catherine Cookson Country', an area ranging about thirty miles south and west of the port of South Shields. The research was designed to find out what pleasures Cookson's local readers get from her books, how they see the novels, and how they incorporate them into their own lives. The research method involved both questionnaire and interview. The questionnaire yielded a certain amount of statistical information, but was used mainly as a prompt for discussion, which was then transcribed. Fifteen of the women were interviewed individually, in their own homes; the remaining four, a mother and daughter and two of the daughter's friends, all living within a few streets of each other, met as a group in the home of one of the women and their group discussion was recorded and transcribed. The women's ages ranged from 25 to 70 and they were almost all working-class (see table 8.1). Five worked full-time, six part-time, and the rest were unemployed or retired. Only one described herself as occupied full-time in looking after house and children. Fourteen were married, four separated or divorced, and one widowed. All but one had children.

Findings

'Then' and 'Now'

Asked to name their three favourite Cookson novels, the women came up with twenty-four different titles, with publication dates ranging from 1952 (*The Fifteen Streets*, Cookson's second novel) to 1992 (*The Rag Nymph*, her most recent but one). Despite this apparent range, there was

144

Table 8.1 The Respondents

	Age	Marital Status	Children	Occupation	Husband's Occupation	Class (self-defined)
A	35—44	married	3	p/t nursery nurse	cost accountant	working
B	35—44	married	2	p/t merchandiser	sales manager	working
C	55—64	married	2	retired clerk	p/t insurance rep	middle
D	45—54	married	2	civil servant	sheet metal worker	working
E	35—44	married	2	p/t caterer	sales manager	middle
F	25—34	separated/ divorced	2	p/t bank clerk		working
G	45—54	married	2	p/t school kitchen assistant	electrician	working
H	45—54	separated/ divorced	3	unemployed		middle
I	65+	married	1	retired seamstress	retired factory worker	working
J	55—64	married	2	retired shop assistant	retired miner	working
K	45—54	married	1	electronics (?)	plater	working
L	45—54	married	1	teacher	HGV driver	working
M	55—64	married	4	warden, sheltered housing	retired	working
N	65+	married	3	retired dressmaker	retired	working
O	25—34	separated/ divorced	0	community education development worker		middle
P	65+	widowed	7	retired factory worker		working
Q	25—34	married	2	p/t cleaner	second-hand dealer	working
R	25—34	separated/ divorced	1	unemployed shop worker		working
S	35—44	married	2	home and children	filling station manager	working

no sense of shifting concerns in the novels; instead, in describing the novels, the women clearly identified a Cookson 'world', a world of 'then' not 'now', of 'the way people used to live' (P), 'that feeling of being way back' (S). It is a world seen by them as absolutely authentic ('how people really lived' — P; 'real, real, real' — M), yet as positioned in terms not of the historical detail with which the novels provide us (and on which Fowler concentrates) but, rather, of women's (our *mother's*) lives:

> F: I like reading about what life used to be like ... my nana was in service.

> S: Both my nanas lived in . . . a terraced house . . . like in *The Fifteen Streets*.
>
> K: My granny was in service. . .
>
> J: I've heard of this life, you know. It was the life that my mother had.[3]

What is insisted on by all the women is a 'then' of our mothers and grandmothers against which can be set the 'now' of our own lives.

What, then, can be said to characterize this 'life that my mother had?' Life for women 'then' was 'hard, very hard' (P):

> Q: Like my nana. She was 82 and she never stepped out of that house. Her whole life was housework and children. She never worked from being married and that was her full life. She never had friends she would visit or anything.

It was a life determined, and controlled, by men:

> Q: They thought that they had to marry a man and stop with him — getting bashed up and practically murdered by their men. Now, it's just so easy to split up if your man bashes you up or something. You haven't got to put up with it now. Then, there was nothing else you could do.

Life for women has, the women insisted, changed enormously between 'then' and 'now', and for the better ('Men aren't the bosses they were; women have come up the social ladder. Everything's changed' — J). When asked about changes in *men's* lives, however, the women answered quite differently. Despite the social changes Cookson chronicles in the novels, for men, the women insisted, things are no different:

> Q: Well, they've always had their own minds, haven't they?
>
> S: Yeah: 'I'll do what I want to do' . . .
>
> Q: I don't think it's changed that much because men are still, like, the main breadwinner.

This group discussion was echoed in other interviews:

> M: Most men's attitudes have changed very little.
> H: Men still have that certain attitude that the woman is still to be kept down...

In fact, the women we interviewed were simply not interested in either the working conditions for the men in the novels or the men themselves ('none of them stuck in my mind at all' — Q; 'I haven't filled that one in at all... in most of her books, I think, the woman is the main character' — P). What they did talk about, constantly, was Cookson's women and their lives.

'Then' *as* Now

Although all but one of the women interviewed said that women's lives had changed 'enormously' (68 per cent) or 'a lot' since the 'then' of Cookson's novels, what emerged in discussion was rather different. The improved 'now' could be registered in only the vaguest of terms:

> EB: So what kind of things do you see women doing with the time that they have?
> [noticeable silence]
> S: Well, there's so much choice now, isn't there?
> R: There's activities and all sorts.
> S: We started off with the WOW. It's just recently that they've started doing things for women who have leisure time... That's just recently but it starts you off and you realize there's more you can be doing than just sit in the house. You don't have to stay at home now.

The 'enormous' changes seem to have benefitted *other* women:

> L: Well, there's lots of women going out to work now, that never would in those days... And they've got all the amenities like gadgets and everything... they drive cars...
>
> M: I mean, my daughters are very liberated, one of them doesn't do any ironing, she lets him do it himself.

In contrast, the 'then' of Cookson's women was registered vividly, as experience. And, despite the women's efforts to insist on its distance, it was registered, in fact, as *their own* experience:

S: I know that today there's a lot more money about and that but it's just the same. They have all the tellies and the videos and that but when it comes down to it you are still struggling to keep going. . . . My husband has a lot of old-fashioned values — I gauge it by him and he has got a lot of old-fashioned values, which sometimes makes it a struggle [nervous laughter] but I think it's the same.

K: I was a pitman's daughter, I struggled from the fifteen streets, from that sort of background . . . I mean there is still women today struggling, not in the same sort of way but . . . I don't think things are easy for a lot of women.

This final example exemplifies the struggle, and failure, to register this 'enormous' change:

M: Women's rights, which — many years ago — certainly working-class women — wouldn't have dared stand up to their men 'cause they would have got a damned good hiding most of them. Whereas nowadays, although they still get hit, beaten and abused, they do have a chance to fight back 'cause there's people who will help them fight back.

Tender Men and Real Women

The women were asked to rank the qualities which a Cookson 'hero' and 'heroine' should have. The answers for the 'hero' were very similar to those given by Radway's Smithton romance readers. 'Tenderness' (79 per cent) and 'strength' (63 per cent) were ranked highest, though 47 per cent of respondents required their heroes also to be 'hardworking'. At the same time, however, they clearly recognized that these men belong to the world of 'romance'. One woman, who said she liked the 'romance' in the books, insisted:

Q: I think a lot of Catherine Cookson books are about women, regardless of the men, like because my husband, he... comes from Yorkshire and they're like behind the times anyhow. He would have you pregnant in the summer, barefoot in the winter. I don't know whether that's why I can't see it at all [any similarity between her husband and Cookson's heroes]...

The 'heroines' however, were seen very differently. 'Common sense' (74 per cent), 'kindness' (58 per cent) and 'resilience' (53 per cent) were their most necessary qualities. The women both identified with and admired them (' "I would've done that" or "I wish I could have done that"... "I wish I dare say that" ' — S); they have a 'quality'. They are seen as 'strong' ('it's like an inner strength' — S), but that strength is defined in a quite specific way:

N: The heroine always survives. She's always the strong one, overcomes — everything! No matter what happens to her, she survives, she overcomes...

A: No matter what gets hurled at them they always seem to bounce back.

F: She has to be strong because she always has to fight against everything to overcome the odds.

The following woman slips from characterizing Cookson's women to a more general statement which runs through all the responses:

L: I think you do get stronger women characters in everyday life than you do men. Today, with everyday situations, I mean, I think women are stronger in a way, 'cause I always say they can put up with more pain and everything than a man can.

For this woman it is Cookson herself who provides the bridge between the heroines and their readers: Cookson's own life authenicates the books, is proof that women's 'strength' can make them into not just 'heroines' but 'heroes'. Struggling with the sense that the status she wishes to claim for Cookson is one reserved for men and therefore somehow illegitimate, she nevertheless insists:

Sue Thornham, Elaine Brown and Angela Werndly

L: I read them mainly because I admire her. She's my hero. I know that's male but she is, I'm not just using the word — 'cause she is.

A Community of Women

Janice Radway suggests that, for her respondents, romance reading functions as a substitute for a 'female community capable of rendering the so desperately needed affective support' (1987, p. 96). Despite their affirmation of the 'enormous' changes, changes for the better, in women's lives, it was this kind of community to which the women we interviewed reached out, whose absence they registered as loss:

Q: The poverty and borrowing cups of sugar until payday or whatever — and not ashamed to say 'my debt-man's coming' or something, where now it's 'Come round the back'. Everyone was the same then, and if you lived in the same street, everyone in that street was poor and in the same circumstances, where now they're not.
EB: You're saying there's pressure now to pretend that you don't have those sorts of problems, whereas...
Q: Yes, even if you know everybody's got them, practically everybody, you don't discuss them, sitting in a group like this. Then, you would have.

One woman, who insisted both that 'there has been unbelievable changes to women's lives' *and* that women's strength 'today' lies in our ability to withstand pain, also said, 'I often wish I'd been born in the past... their lives were happier really than people have nowadays I think' (L). In part, this seems a result of the melodramatic structure of the books, in which injustice is individualized and 'they always get their just deserts in the end'. In part, however, it is 'clinging on to your heritage isn't it?' (L). Whether historically real or imagined, this community of women is constantly affirmed. The passing round of the novels, in fact, becomes a part of this affirmation, a means of its continuance into the present:

R: My mam used to buy them all and I used to read them.
Q: I used to borrow them from my nana.

R: They're like passed between generations. A lot of it...
Q: ...it's common ground, you can all talk about...

150

S: I think you forget the generation thing. I haven't heard of a man yet that's read one... There's four girls in our family and my sister started buying them and then you just pass them round. There's always something you can discuss in them with each other.

'Not Happy but Hopeful'

Reading the novels, it is their masochistic structure[4] which is most striking. Katie Mulholland, for example, is beautiful and intelligent: she has that 'quality' of which the women speak. She is raped, beaten, humiliated, imprisoned, her daughter taken from her and her father hanged... the list could go on: her 'quality', and her sexuality, are both affirmed in the novel and constantly punished. For the readers, however, she is simply strong. When asked to describe the typical plot of a Cookson novel, the women divided between those who described a standard romance formula ('Boy meets girl, don't always get on but then meet up again' — H) and those who refused it ('Working-class women try to make life better' — K; 'Strong, realistic, and at times quite shocking' — M). Those who emphasized the romance knew why: 'Well, there's none in my own life' (F). More often, however, the women insisted *both* that a developing relationship between hero and heroine was important in the novels, *and* that the books contain 'exactly what happens in real life — she includes it all' (I). It is as if romance has to be filtered through the structure of female suffering which the women register as reality:

A: I think it must be that [romance] is an integral part of the story, but really the best part isn't about the romance, it's about the struggles.

The endings, therefore, posed some problems of definition. One woman expressed this:

N: No matter what happens to her, she survives, she overcomes, when they get thrown out of the house and things like that, she always manages to come out on top. They're happy endings, usually, aren't they?

151

Another qualified further the idea of a 'happy ending':

> E: [They] always contain sad parts but the endings are — always hopeful, if not happy.

It is this structure of triumph through suffering, triumph *in* suffering, which drove one of our respondents, the only one to see herself as feminist, to expressions of rage. This woman, who had read Cookson's books avidly some years ago, and who still found herself identifying with Cookson's women, now felt betrayed by the books, and by Cookson herself. As she registered her protest, she addressed Cookson directly, personally:

> O: She set us up and told us that, like, it's all right to feel pain for twenty years. I'm sorry, but I disagree with that now. Fuck off. Why should I put up with this? Why don't you tell us that women can be whatever we want to be? And it doesn't have to depend on anybody else's consent.

Cookson's 'Con'

This woman, in fact, both defined and was caught in the contradictory nature of Cookson's appeal:

> O: She uses working-class women, who are dead strong, that was my first insight into them. So it's got to be 'downtrodden, resolute, principled' . . . they take on other people's lives, her women, . . . so they've got to be strong enough to take on the responsibilities of other people. [But] there's never an isolated woman on her own. . .

The supportive community of women seen in the novels is, she feels, 'a con': it never existed. But even in protesting this, she slips between past and present, between 'it's not like that *now*' and 'it was *never* like that':

> O: We want it to be like that, but our communities aren't like that. We stab each other in the back and we nick off one

> another. All of hers was doors left open... I'd *like* to think it was [like that] but you don't know — but that's what I want it to be. That's the con.

In both defining women's strength as the capacity to endure suffering and, simultaneously, convincing us that that was 'then', that things are better 'now', the novels offer a 'con' because they deter us from action:

> O: So you look at a situation in, like, 1893 and look from 1993 and see the choices that are open to you — you think life's better now: 'I would do this'... [So] there's nothing really to challenge — it's safe... she's just conning us — not to make changes for themselves or to change their own condition...

Conclusions

For the women we interviewed, Cookson's books, and Cookson herself, offer evidence of strong women, women who, finding themselves in 'situations not of their own making', discover the 'strength of character' to 'triumph against injustice in the end' (L). In this they are sustained by a working-class community of women, the traces of which are precariously maintained through the communal circulation of the books. For these women, life since the time of Cookson's women has changed 'enormously'; they are sure of that. Women today have more choices; 'women's rights' mean that they are not so downtrodden. It is, however, the world of Cookson's women with which they identify, which structures their fantasy and their sense of identity as working-class women. It is not surprising, and we do not need to invoke notions of 'backlash'[5] to explain it. For even though in one sense men, in these women's responses, 'did not *matter*',[6] they are also profoundly important. Almost all of these women are married, and men, they know, have not changed ('thick as pig-shite, loud, bawdy, full of boast', as O put it). Cookson's 'then' permits the women both to believe that things are better 'now', and to recognize a continuity of experience: 'it was like that, it was like that... it's real... life as it was and life as it still is' (M). This woman went on:

> M: There's my first marriage. I was actually pregnant with my fourth girl when my husband left me. So I had three little girls under school age and I was three months pregnant

when he left me, and I brought them up on my own. I used to think I'd never get through, but reading was my escape, and I sewed and cleaned.

For her, and for many of the others, the books, with their endings 'hopeful if not happy', demonstrate that survival, even an attenuated romance, is possible. In depicting this 'life that my mother had', Cookson herself becomes for some the adoptive mother that so many of her novels feature, the strong woman who, 'fighting against everything', overcomes 'the odds', but whose strength is also a kind of illegitimacy,[7] and is punished as such. In O, the rebellious daughter, this position produces both hate and love:

O: . . . it's this martyr. I hate her for that. . . But I love her for setting [the novels] up here. 'Cause what else have we got? Friggin' Spender.

Notes

1 Much work has been done on the aspect of soap operas, beginning with Dorothy Hobson's (1982) *Crossroads: The Drama of a Soap Opera*. A number of examples of recent work can be found in Seiter *et al.* (1989).
2 'You are entering Catherine Cookson Country' reads a sign as you approach the River Tyne. For comparison, County Durham identifies itself to tourists as 'the Land of the Prince Bishops'.
3 Cf. Barthes (1984, p. 65): history is 'the time when my mother was alive *before me*': 'History is hysterical: it is constituted only if we look at it — and in order to look at it, we must be excluded from it. As a living soul, I am the very contrary of history'.
4 For a discussion of masochistic fantasy as structuring element in another form of popular culture for women, the 'Woman's Film', see Mary Ann Doane (1984). Doane describes the 'perpetual staging of suffering' within these narratives, narratives in which female fantasy is constantly identified with persecution. Whilst Doane's interest is in the way in which these films position their female *spectators*, her account of their narrative structure is nevertheless suggestive in considering Cookson's novels.
5 See Susan Faludi (1991). Faludi sees the contemporary insistence both that the battle 'for women's rights' has been won and that women have 'never been more miserable' (1991, p. 1) as the product of a 1980s backlash against feminism.
6 The phrase comes from Carolyn Steedman's description of the position of her own father in her life: 'A father like mine dictated each day's existence; our lives would have been quite different had he not been there. But he didn't *matter*' (1986, p. 19). Steedman also writes of the attraction Cookson's autobiography, *Our Kate*, had for her: 'what I now see in the book is its fine delineation of the feeling of being on the outside, outside the law; for Catherine Cookson was illegitimate' (p. 9).
7 The theme of illegitimacy runs throughout the novels. On biological mothers, Cookson is frequently very hard. The following, from *Katie Mulholland*, is typical: ' "You know,

Daniel. . . some women shouldn't have sons; they should be taken away from them at birth, they should. I'm telling you. The way that some of them hang on to their daughters is bad enough, but when it's a son, God alive! It's awful. . ." ' (p. 419).

References

BARTHES, ROLAND (1984) *Camera Lucida*, London, Flamingo.
BATSLEER, JANET, DAVIES, TONY, O'ROURKE, REBECCA and WEEDON, CHRIS (1985) *Rewriting English: Cultural Politics of Gender and Class*, London, Methuen.
COOKSON, CATHERINE (1967) *Katie Mulholland*, London, Warner Books.
COOKSON, CATHERINE (1969) *Our Kate*, London, Macdonald.
DOANE, MARY ANN (1984) 'The "Woman's Film": Possession and Address', in DOANE, MARY ANN, MELLENCAMP, PATRICIA and WILLIAMS, LINDA (Eds) *Re-vision*, Los Angeles, The American Film Institute.
FALUDI, SUSAN (1991) *Backlash: The Undeclared War Against Women*, London, Chatto and Windus.
FOWLER, BRIDGET (1991) *The Alienated Reader: Women and Popular Romantic Literature in the Twentieth Century*, London, Harvester Wheatsheaf.
HERON, LIZ (1985) *Truth, Dare or Promise: Girls Growing up in the Fifties*, London, Virago.
HOBSON, DOROTHY (1982) *Crossroads: The Drama of a Soap Opera*, London, Methuen.
RADWAY, JANICE (1987) *Reading the Romance*, London, Verso.
SEITER, ELLEN, BORCHERS, HANS, KREUTZNER, GABRIELE and WARTH, EVA-MARIA (Eds) (1989) *Remote Control: Television, Audiences and Cultural Power*, London, Routledge.
STEEDMAN, CAROLYN (1986) *Landscape for a Good Woman: A Story of Two Lives*, London, Virago.

Chapter 9

Splitting the Difference: Adventures in the Anatomy and Embodiment of Women

Margrit Shildrick and Janet Price

One currently fashionable strand in the philosophy of medicine (Schenck, 1986; Leder, 1990) addresses health in terms of the being-in-the-world of bodies, the sense in which our phenomenological stability is intrinsically tied up with the unified presence of our bodies. In these terms the 'broken' body of sickness has important consequences for our self-perception, so that the loss of a leg or a breast, for example, affects not simply corporeal integrity but also the sense of who we are. At least, that is the theory, but what we want to suggest is that for women there are already a variety of paradoxes in play which problematize the notion of the unity of mind and body. By looking at a linked series of dichotomies which underlie the cultural history of the West, we shall argue that although the bodies of women have figured strongly throughout, they have habitually been conceptualized in a quite different way to those of men. Further, whatever forms the dominant representation has taken, the bodies of women, whether all too present or disconcertingly absent, have served to ground the devaluation of women by men. The 'whole' body of phenomenology is intrinsically masculine, and women, by that token, are never in full existential health.

It is important to mark from the outset that we are concerned not with 'real' bodies, but with the various and seemingly contradictory cultural constructions of them. It is not that we want to deny materiality, but to insist that there is never direct, unmediated access to some 'pure' state. Rather what we take to be the neutral, biological body is itself an effect of language. In short we could always know it, and its biology, in a different way, as indeed a genealogy of the body shows. Our Renaissance forebears who *saw* the female reproductive organs as simply the precise

Adventures in the Anatomy and Embodiment of Women

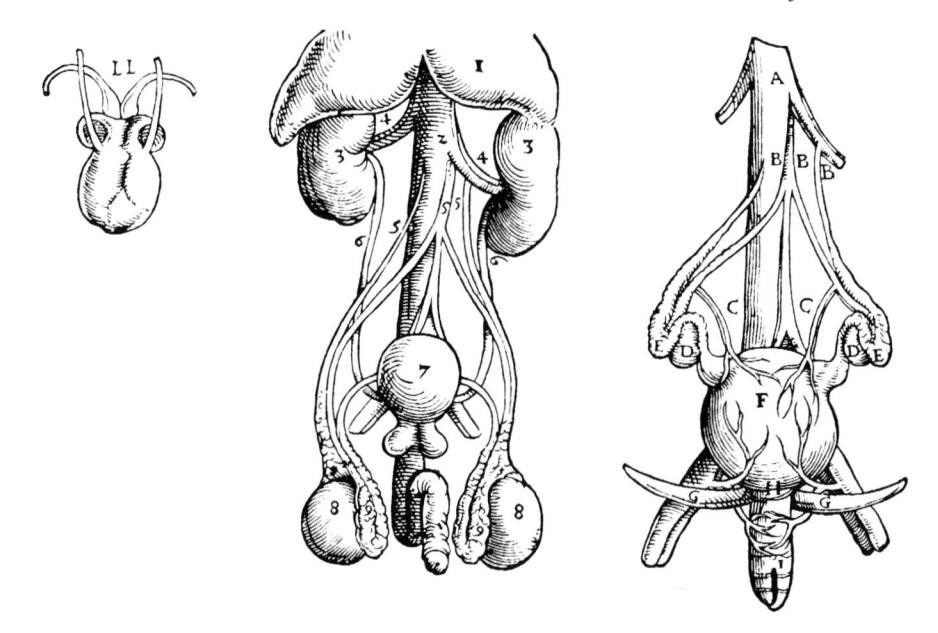

Figure 9.1: Vesalius, Andreas [1514–1564]
Pierre Huard and Marie José Imbault-Huart, André Vésale, iconographie anatomique
... Paris: Roger Dacosta, 1980 plate 87, page 236. male and female gentalia.
Illustrations from Tabulae anatomicae sex, *1538*
Source: The Wellcome Institute Library, London

inverse of male genitalia were not unobservant anatomists or simply bad scientists but were expressing the truth of their age.[1]

In 1538 the anatomist Vesalius published *Tabulae sex,* a set of cheaply printed plates, apparently prepared for medical students and lay readers. It included a representation of the human generative organs (see Figure 9.1). On the left is the male and on the right, the female, disposed to show their anatomical correspondences. It could have been described thus: 'The female matrix or womb, along with its appendages, corresponds in every respect to the male member except that the latter is *outside* the body and the female member, due to woman's coldness of temper, is *inside* the body'. The neck of the womb, or vagina, corresponds to the penis; and the womb itself, with the female testicles and vessels, corresponds to the scrotum. If the female matrix were to be inverted it can be seen that it is clearly homologous with the male scrotum and penis (Aristotle, 1937; Galen, 1968).

The relationship between cultural values and constructions of the body, as part of what Foucault (1980) calls the power/knowledge regime, is a symbiotic one. Though the dominant discourse may dictate certain

157

conceptions of the body, those privileged conceptions are rarely acknowledged as such. What then appears to be reality in turn justifies and perpetuates particular truth claims. What concerns us here is which truths are given to and derived from the female body in a male social order. But though perception and knowledge *are* always mediated, what is done as a result of them has of course real material effects which have direct bearing on our lives as women.

In the discourse of women's health, whatever else goes on, the dominant concern is with women as reproducers, regardless of any individual intention or ability to exercise that capacity. At its simplest, women are simply baby machines; and even when the derogatory valuation of that is put aside, it does seem to express some undeniable truth that the reproductive role is more properly that of the woman than the man. The simple expediency of providing sperm hardly seems to bear comparison with the long process of conception and gestation which is actually internal to women's bodies. Indeed, second-wave feminism, after a sticky start regarding the desirability of motherhood, has made firm efforts to reclaim and revalue maternity and in effect to see it as the source of women's unique power. The reproductive body stands for something essentially female; and to be valorized as a life-giver is to be valorized as a woman. But is this somewhat comforting image really tenable? Consider an image from contemporary medical literature (Figure 9.2).

'So you want to have a baby — that's marvellous . . . It is not really our role as doctors to moralize over your marital status as long as the relationship is seemingly a stable one' (Neuberg, 1992). After all, reproduction is the result of interaction between *two* people, and a *couple* does 'constitute a biological unit' (Kremer, 1977). If you are having trouble conceiving a child, please remember that 'the "problem" is a *joint* one'. Many infertile *couples* have been treated through methods such as surgery to the Fallopian tubes. If as a *couple* you have the problem of azoospermia or severe oligospermia, donor insemination 'may offer the only practical means' for you to have a family. In other cases, IVF might be appropriate — you'll be pleased to hear the success rate is high — a recent count showed that after IVF '107 *couples* were still pregnant' (Ziekenfondsraad, 1989, emphasis added).[2]

What is interesting is that although the recognition of men's biological involvement may be stressed and their social involvement normalized, there is no corresponding shift in the traditional split between masculine mind and feminine body. The underlying subtext of such representations is that women themselves are incomplete without men, and that even their identities as mothers cannot stand alone. Their bodies are after all just bodies, not quite capable of sustaining an

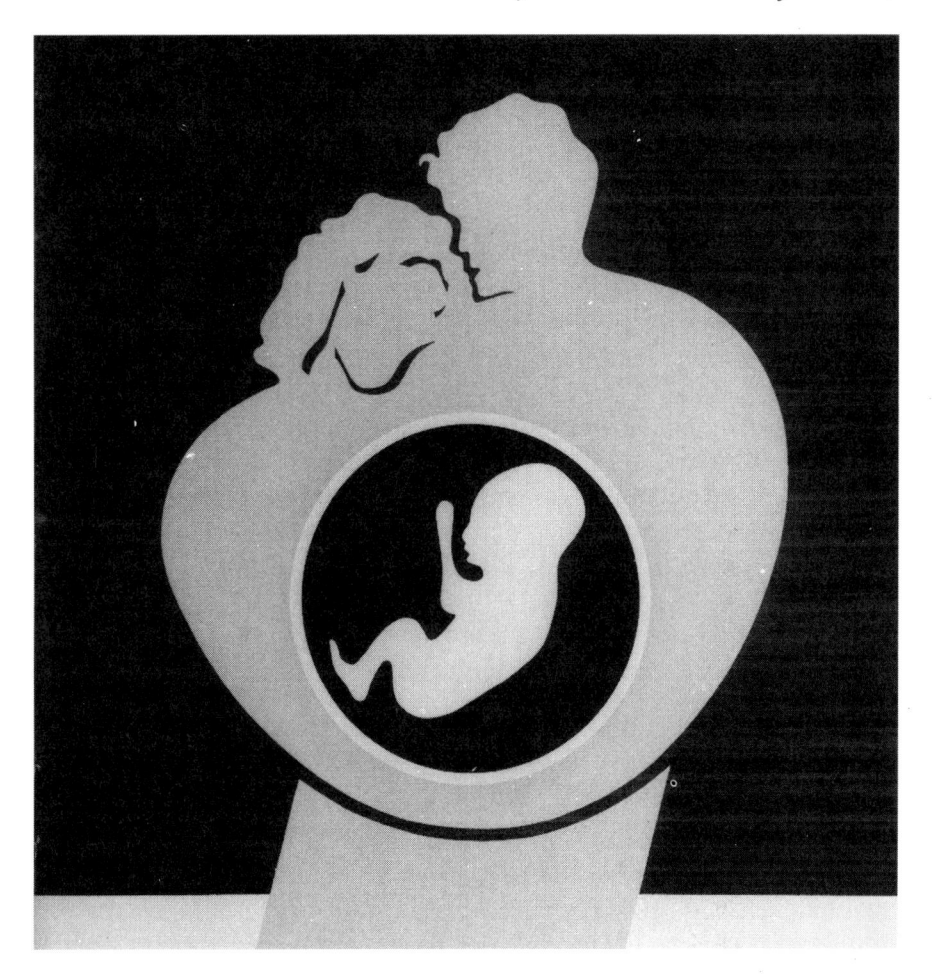

Adventures in the Anatomy and Embodiment of Women

Figure 9.2: Front Cover, So you want to have a baby, Neuberg, R. (1992), *Serono Laboratories UK Ltd.*
Illustration is by Guy Newmountain

independent subjectivity/personhood. Even more alarmingly, the new reproductive technologies of the late twentieth century have increasingly fragmented the female body itself. The wholeness of one's being-in-the-world is undermined in two directions. First, the reproductive organs of women are referred to as discrete entities to be managed. The woman as a person plays little or no part. To achieve success in IVF, the natural menstrual cycle has been shown to be 'inferior to the treated cycle from the standpoint of efficient management', the latter yielding a greater number of oocytes for harvesting. (Hodgen and Van Uem, 1986, p. 36, cited in Kirejczyk and van der Ploeg, 1992, p. 117).

Secondly, the status of the foetus or embryo, even the pre-conceptus at times, is characterized as free-floating, independent, radically other than the mother herself.

> The fetus could not be taken seriously as long as he (*sic*) remained a medical recluse in an opaque womb; and it was not until the last half of this century that the prying eye of the ultrasonogram rendered the once opaque womb transparent, stripping the veil of mystery from the dark inner sanctum, and letting the light of scientific observation fall on the shy and secretive fetus.... The sonographic voyeur, spying on the unwary fetus, finds him or her a surprisingly active little creature, and not at all the passive parasite we had imagined (Harrison, 1982, quoted in Hubbard, 1984).

What these discourses show is a sense in which all women are irrevocably characterized in terms of their biological bodies, but at the same time those bodies express no real sense of personhood. Corporeality and absence are coincidental.

How then can we explain this strange paradox? For a cultural theorist, one starting point might be with the so-called Enlightenment of late-seventeenth-century Europe, when the Cartesian *cogito* 'I think therefore I am' signalled the privileging of mind over body. The self-present, self-authorizing subject became *he* who could successfully transcend his own body to take up a position of pure reason uncontaminated by the untrustworthy experience of the senses. And once the supposedly objective, rational 'view from nowhere' became the new standard for human endeavour, women's pre-existing social disadvantages were philosophically reinforced. Although both sexes clearly do have material bodies, only women, because of their more intimate association with reproduction, were seen as intrinsically unable to transcend them.

There was nothing new of course in this juxtaposition between male and female principles — the ancient Greeks operated similar systems — nor even in the valuation given the male side, but what followed was the growing and by now familiar gap between male/culture and female/nature. Women were simply characterized as less able to rise above uncontrollable natural processes and passions and were therefore disqualified from mature personhood. It is as though bodies could somehow interfere with moral thought, instructing the mind, rather than the other way round as is the case with men. Losing control of oneself is to a large degree synonymous with losing control of, or having no control over, one's body. It is quintessentially a feminine rather than masculine trait so that any man who does experience or manifest the characteristic symptoms of anorexia or hysteria, for example, is somehow deficient in his manhood. For women, of course, losing control is only to be expected whether its cause is the mysterious wandering womb of the ancients or modern hormones, premenstrual tension or menopausal irritability.

'Throughout the childbearing years of a woman's life rhythmic changes concerned with the process of reproduction take place in a monthly cycle' (Clayton *et al.,* 1980, p. 34). A patient may develop premonitory symptoms such as backache, headache, soreness of breasts and general malaise before her period. If the symptoms are sufficient to make her seek medical help, they are referred to as 'pre-menstrual tension syndrome'. This 'is accompanied by varying degrees of irritability, depression and other emotional disturbance... it is said there is a relationship between acts of violence and this condition' (Clayton, 1980, pp. 41, 262). What these specifically feminine maladies justify is paternalistic intervention on the grounds of both medical and moral incompetency. The health care encounter is a paradigmatic site of male power concerned with the control of female irrationality which results not just from the compromised rationality caused by the pain and anxiety of ill-health, but is supposedly rooted in our very natures.

Not surprisingly the post-Enlightenment stress on the differences, focused here on the male mind and female body, extended to the biological differences between bodies themselves. Strange then to find, as Thomas Laqueur has argued, that widespread adoption and acknowledgment of a two-sex model, male and female, for the body was a fairly late feature of medical and more specifically anatomical knowledge. Prior to 1800 what Laqueur refers to as the one-sex model was in operation, a model in which the bodies of women were understood, not just on an abstract level but in material terms too, to be simply inferior versions of the male body (Laqueur, 1990, pp. 25–6).

Figure 9.3 is a diagram of the female generative organs from a plate in Vesalius' *De humani corporis fabrica* (1543a), and is supposedly drawn from life. The female organs are not simply represented to demonstrate their apparent isomorphism with the male, they are directly *seen* as the same. In the absence of a foetus it is difficult to determine the intended sex of the representation. The constructed homologies between male and female extend to an intricate anatomical level, embracing structure, function and response. The labia surrounding the vagina are likened to the prepuce of the penis, guarding its opening.

The vagina or 'neck of the womb' is believed to respond to female desire in the same ways that the penis responds to male desire.

The conventional images of female genitalia as the inverse of the male exposed a medical truth which corresponded to philosophical knowledge. Women were not seen to be radically different and incommensurate with men, but simply imperfectly formed versions of the accepted standard — which was male. They were, in other words, incorporated within the same, judged against a male ideal which they inevitably failed to express, and thereby devalued in their own right. But how could medicine mistake the female body for a version of the male?

In the *Epitome* Vesalius (1543b) produced a series of illustrations which demonstrated the interchangeability of the male and female figure (see Figure 9.4). The male testicles are attached to the penis which can then be overlaid with anatomical precision onto the figure outlined by blood vessels. Alternatively, the female generative organs could be overlain onto this — a shadowy figure that acted as a base for all others. Over this go the organs of the body — and the figure is completed by an overlay of the classical female nude.

There are of course widespread resemblances in very general anatomy, but how could the question of reproduction itself be forced into a universal perspective? For one thing, the practice of post-mortem, as far as it had existed at all, was largely abandoned after Galen (second century AD) in favour of abstract speculation on the body.[3] The teaching of anatomy became a reiteration of classical texts rather than the outcome of the empirical gaze. The guesses, generalizations and plain prejudices of the early medical establishment were reproduced unquestioned and to a certain extent unquestionable. But although human dissection was rarely practised, animals were still occasionally used without that making any apparent impact on the strange, and to our eyes incorrect, mirroring by which the female genitalia were explained. As Laqueur (1990, p. 70) outlines, even after human anatomy was more thoroughly explored in practice, there was an enormous resistance to revising the traditional models.

We must conclude then that the need to uncover a particular truth about women outweighed the evidence of practical anatomy. The point at which that evidence became undeniable, and indeed accepted as the new orthodoxy, was the point at which the mind/body split of the Enlightenment decisively shifted the parameters of subjectivity, of personhood, right away from the body. The *universal* isomorphic truth of the human body was displaced by the oppositional split of mind/body, male/female. Once the body itself was devalued there was no further ideological interest in maintaining the fiction that female bodies

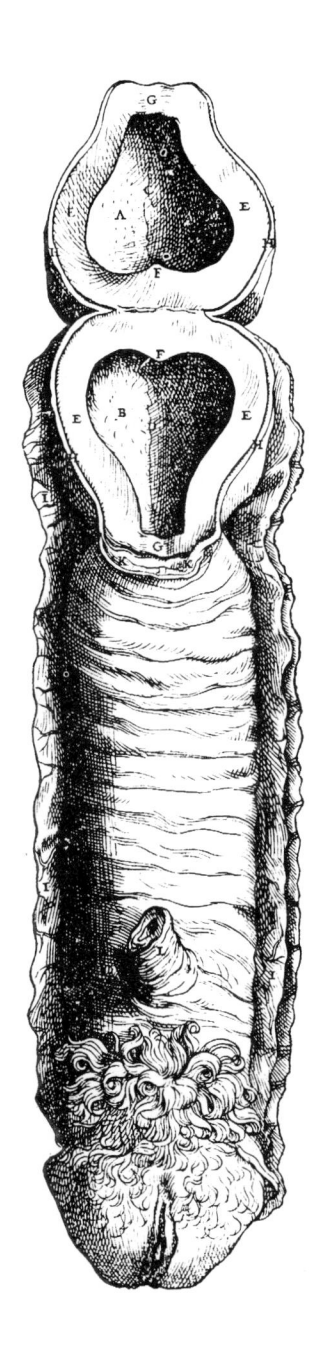

Adventures in the Anatomy and Embodiment of Women

Figure 9.3: Vesalius, Andreas [1514–1564]
A. Vesalius, De humani corporis fabrica, *Basel: oporinus, 1543. Lib. V, illustrating digestive system, etc. p. 381, fig. 27, uterus and vagina*
Source: the Wellcome Institute Library, London

163

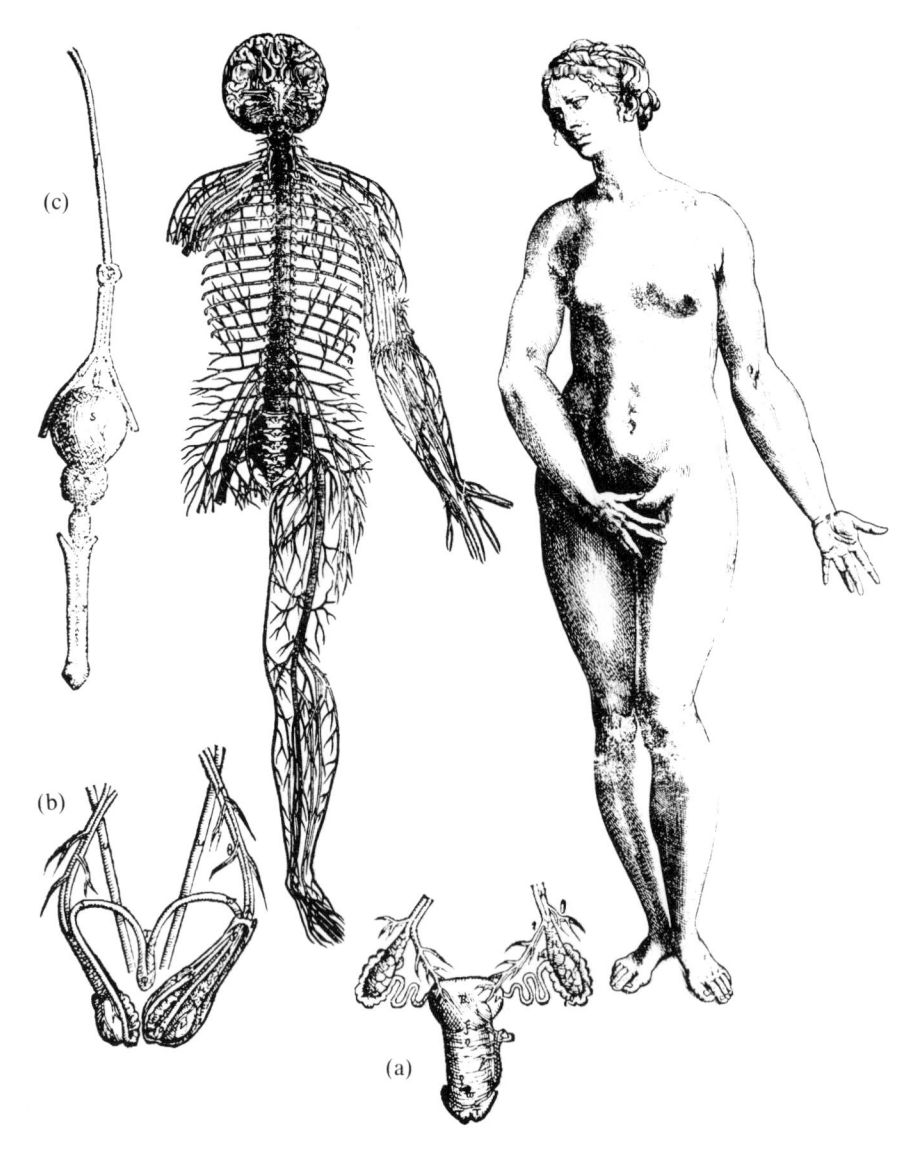

Figure 9.4: Vesalius, Andreas [1514-1564]
A. Vesalius, De humani corporis fabrica, Basel: Oporinus, 1543. lib. IV, pp. 353-4, *final nerve-figure*

A. Vesalius, Suorum de humani corporis fabrica librorum epitome, Basle: J. Oporinus, 1543 Leaf L recto, *standing female nude*

A. Vesalius, De humani corporis fabrica, Basel: Oporinus, 1543. lib. III, p. 314, (a) *uterus and ovaries*

A. Vesalius, De humani corporis fabrica, Basel: Oporinus, 1543. lib. III, p. 313, (b) *testes*, (c) *penis*

Source: The Wellcome Institute Library, London

Adventures in the Anatomy and Embodiment of Women

were imperfectly formed male bodies. The male determined standard of sameness gave way to recognition of what was *other* than the male. In other words, difference was recognized but the hierarchy was maintained.

This changing anatomical knowledge finds an echo in the differential way in which not simply the *organs* of reproduction but the very *process* itself has experienced a radical shift in perception. Just as the one-sex model of the body held sway until the late eighteenth century, so women's specific part in reproduction was obscured by the insistence on the male as the progenitor of life. If women were morphologically inferior, then clearly their role in conception and even gestation could not be given serious credit. That is not to say that the classical authorities were in agreement as to how reproduction worked, but the common thread which links Aristotle to Galen was the determined downgrading of female agency. Aristotle was quite clear that women played no real part in the process, but simply provided the raw material, to which the male sperma alone brought form. The material body was in effect the nutritional container for new life, but played no part in generation itself. This almost complete erasure of active female participation mirrors Aristotle's view that the active spirit was an exclusively male attribute, and finds its analogue in Judaeo-Christian views of the creation. Almost two millenia later, the same move reappeared in the doctrine of spermatic preformation.[4]

In 1694 Nicolaus Hartsoeker illustrated the appearance within the sperm of an animalcule which he believed would be found if one could see through the skin that hides its form (see Figure 9.5). Preformationists held that all living things were created at the beginning, later generations being enclosed within earlier ones. Each sperm in effect contained a perfectly formed homunculus which was simply activated by being implanted in the female womb. There was never new generation in nature but only an increase in size and hardness of parts that were already present (Tuana, 1988, pp. 51–5).

It is worth noting here that even now a similar image of increase appears in at least one major anatomy text, and the imagery employed by anti-abortionists regularly suggests the presence, at all stages post-conception, of a fully formed infant body, as Rosalind Petchesky (1987) has shown in her analysis of the film *The Silent Scream*.

The Embryology section of *Gray's Anatomy* provides us with an illustration of changes in size and bodily proportions of the foetus from the fourth to the tenth lunar month. What is shown, as with the concept of preformation, is simply a lengthening or increase in parts (Warwick and Williams, 1989, p. 264).

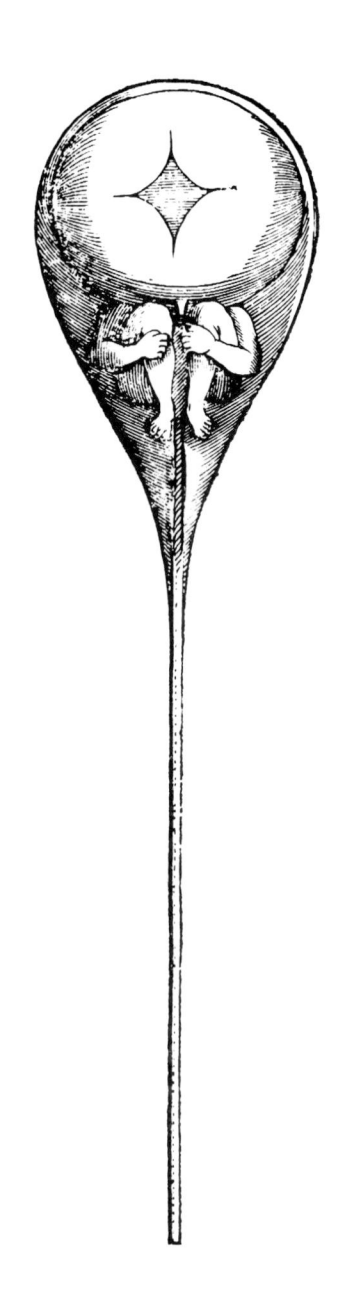

Figure 9.5: Hartsoeker, Nicolaus [1656-1725]
N. Hartsoeker, Essai de diotropique, Paris: J. Anisson, 1694 p. 230 woodcut: spermatozoon
Source: The Wellcome Institute Library, London

Against the Aristotelian view of one-seed gestation, that is of the male as progenitor, the rather more sophisticated explanation associated primarily with Galen allowed that conception involved the fusion of both male and female seed. Nonetheless, the former remained highly influential, and both models perpetuated the same bias. The essential problem with women, and this is an idea which recurs again and again throughout our cultural history, is that they lacked heat and were instead excessively cold and moist. This heat deficiency was the proximate reason why they were unable to produce fertile seed of their own, the reason why their genitalia remained underdeveloped and internal, and the reason, too, why their brains simply did not function at the level of male minds. In monthly menstruation women further dissipated their bodily vigour and their intellectual capacity. In other words, unlike the self-contained and self-containing men, women leaked.[5] Or, as Sartre (1957) put it rather more recently: 'the obscenity of the feminine sex is that of everything that "gapes open" '.

Where Artistotle simply asserted the heat/cold dichotomy as the basis of women's generative and intellectual inferiority, Galen went so far as to provide an anatomical explanation. As he saw it — and remember seeing is always discursively constructed — the male and female embryos were formed in crucially different ways.

The male embryo resulted from the fusion of a seed from the man and one from the right-hand ovary of the woman. The blood supplying the right-hand ovary passed first through the kidney, where it was cleansed, and then into the ovarian vessels. In contrast, the female embryo was in part supplied by a seed from the left-hand ovary which, unlike its pair, was supplied, via the ovarian vessels, with blood which had not yet passed through the kidneys and was therefore impure. The resulting female child was already marked by waste material, lacking pure blood and unable to generate heat (Graaf, 1672, p. 6; see Figure 9.6). This scientific explanation of the day so perfectly served to support cultural expectations that it went on unchallenged well into the Renaissance, even when the wider practice of human dissection might have been expected to reveal that Galen's claims were based on anatomical inaccuracies.

Again, the final abandonment of the old orthodoxy could be linked to the post-Enlightenment downgrading of bodies in general. Once mind became the superior power, and the real mark of human self-consciousness, male dominance shifted its justificatory claims. Far from occupying a secondary position in relation to reproduction, women's bodies and consequently women's identities were now reconstructed as (a) essentially different from men's and (b) focused on the maternal function. This is

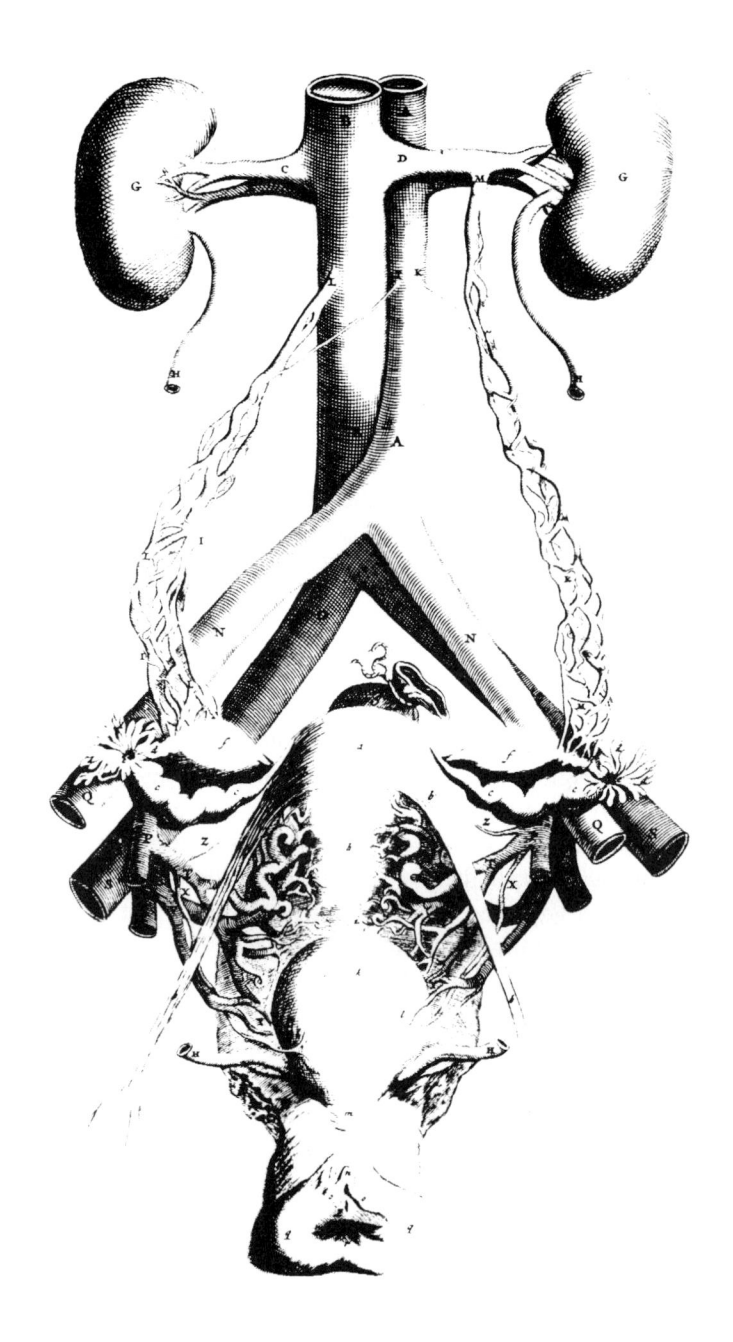

Figure 9.6: Graaf, Regnerus de [1641-1673]
R. De Graaf, De mulierum organis generationi inservientibus tractatus novus, *Leyden: 'Off. Hackiana', 1672. Facing page 6*
Source: The Wellcome Institute Library, London

not to say that men ceded material power over reproduction but that their own subjectivities were expressed elsewhere. Flesh-and-blood bodies, and their particular capacities and problems, were the mark of the feminine.

A contradiction thus exists between feminine immanence, the being-in-the-body that precluded mental maturity, and a certain ongoing insubstantiality about the very things, largely in the field of reproduction, which are the grounds for women's inability to transcend their bodies. This has become increasingly evident in the context of new reproductive technologies, those strange postmodern effects of dispersal on embodied selves; but significantly the paradox of female insubstantiality is suggested even at the time of the renaissance of anatomy between the fifteenth and seventeenth centuries when, as Laqueur claims, the one-sex model was still predominant. There is a sense in which where male bodies are represented in terms of structure and solidity, women's bodies are dematerialized, and seem to be split between smooth surfaces and internal spaces.

In a typical plate from Valverde (1560, after Vesalius), we encounter the solidity of the male (Figure 9.7). The skin has been dissected away from the body to expose the substantiality of the underlying muscle and bone. The starkly delineated structure embodies the very presence of masculine being in the world. The plate of the female torso (Figure 9.8) presents us with a different view of the body. The skin is smooth and flows over the surface of the body and when it is dissected back from the abdomen, it reveals not bone and muscle but space and unsupported emptiness (Valverde, 1560; Vesalius 1543a).

In contrast to the male the female displayed is a matter of interior spaces in which the organs of reproduction are 'suspended'. The female body unveils its inner secrets to the anatomical gaze as something quite apart from surface impressions. The inner and outer body are somehow divided against each other.[6]

Wax anatomical models played an important role in the eighteenth century, both for teaching and for wider popular display (see Figures 9.9 and 9.10). Known as Venuses, the female figures are recumbent, lying on velvet or silk cushions. They have long hair, and often hair in the pubic area too, are adorned with pearl necklaces, and have ectastic expressions. They are soft and feminine and draw attention to their sexual potential. The upper surface of the models can be removed, to display their internal anatomy and reveal their inner spaces to the public gaze. There is a foetus in the uterus, organs and blood, but *no muscle or bone.*[7]

Just as the inner and outer female body is discontinuous, so too in many images the embryo/foetus has no essential connection with the

Figure 9.7: Valverde de Hamusco, Juan [c 16th cent.]
J. *Valverde de Hamusco*, Anatomia del corpo humano, *Rome, A. Salamanca etc., and Venice, N. Bevilacque, 1560. Engravings by N. Beatrizet. p. 64, lib. II, tav. i*
Source: The Wellcome Institute Library, London

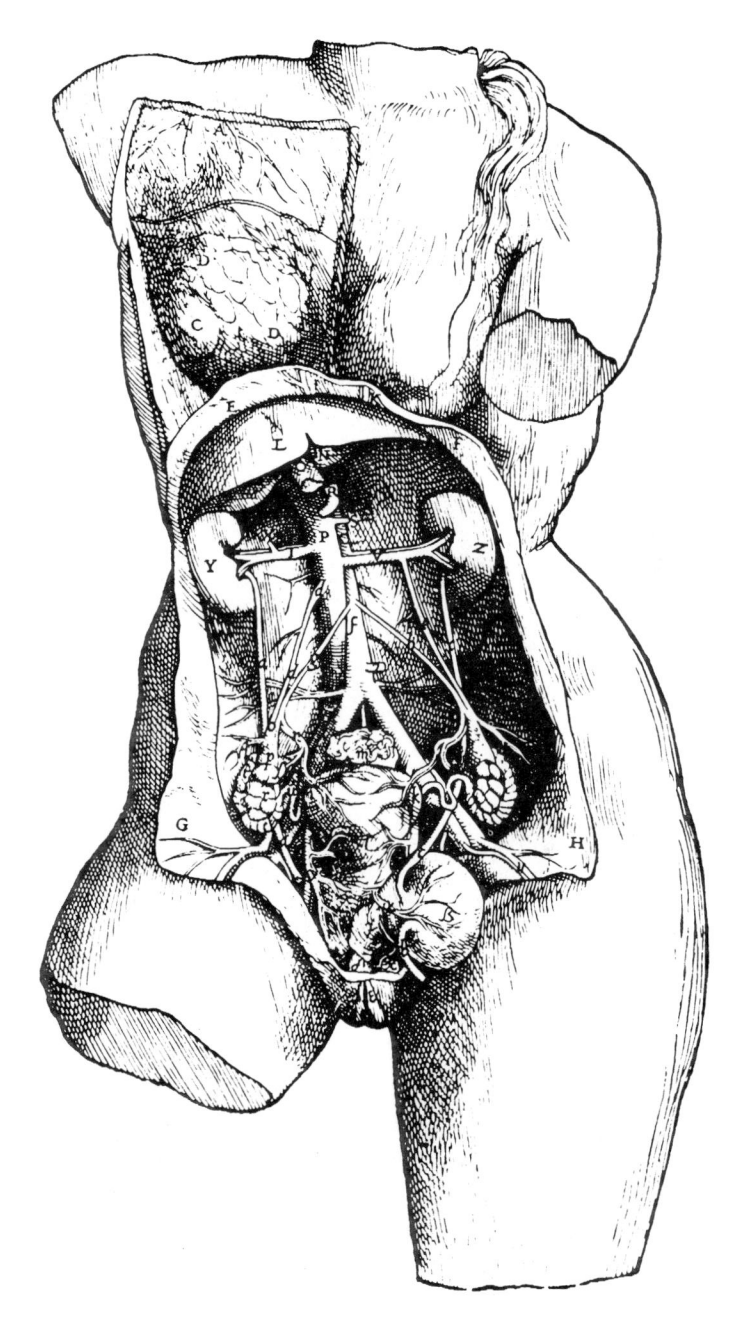

Adventures in the Anatomy and Embodiment of Women

Figure 9.8: Vesalius, Andreas [1514–1564]
Pierre Huard and Marie José Imbault-Huart, André Vésale, iconographie anatomique. . . Paris: Roger Dacosta, 1980 plate 61, page 166. upper female torso. from De humani corporis fabrica, *1543*
Source: The Wellcome Institute Library, London

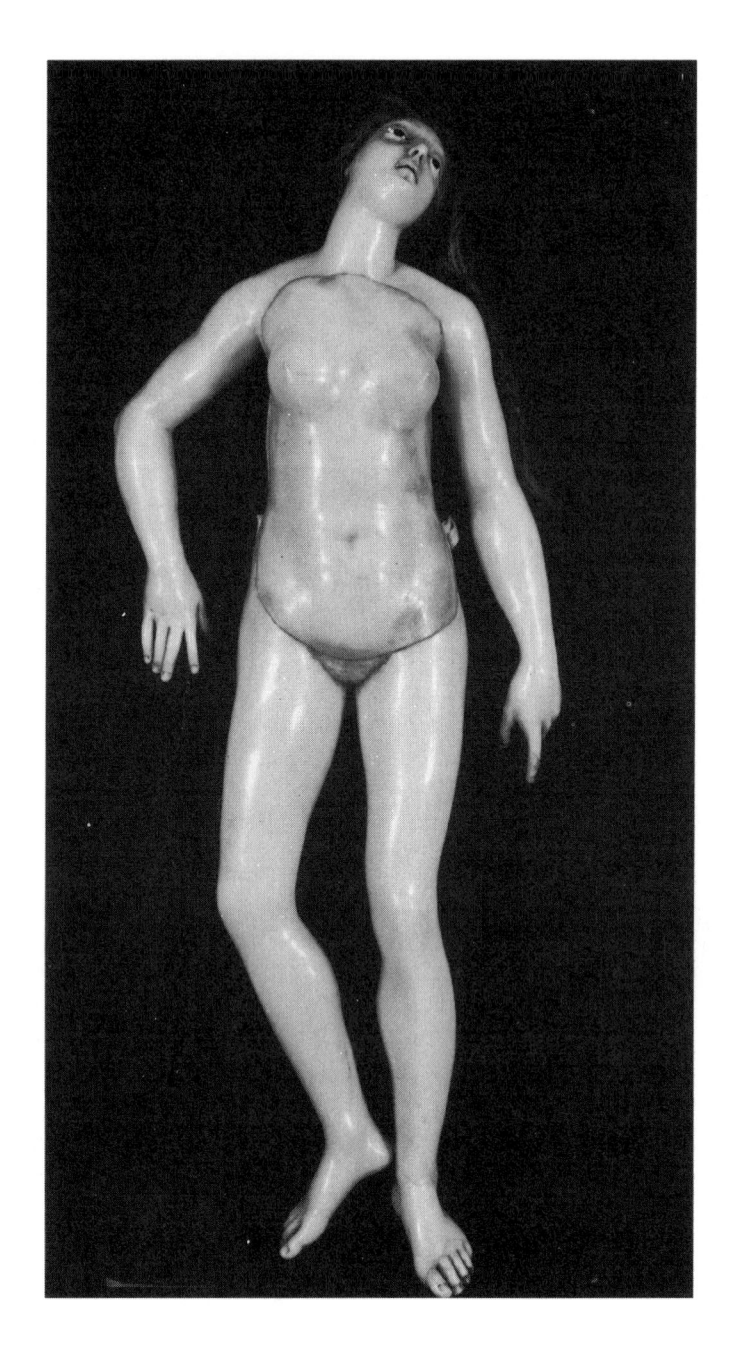

Figure 9.9: Anatomical figures: French, 18th century Wax anatomical teaching figure: female, with removable layers revealing internal anatomy; anon., French, 18th century. whole figure
Source: The Wellcome Institute Library, London

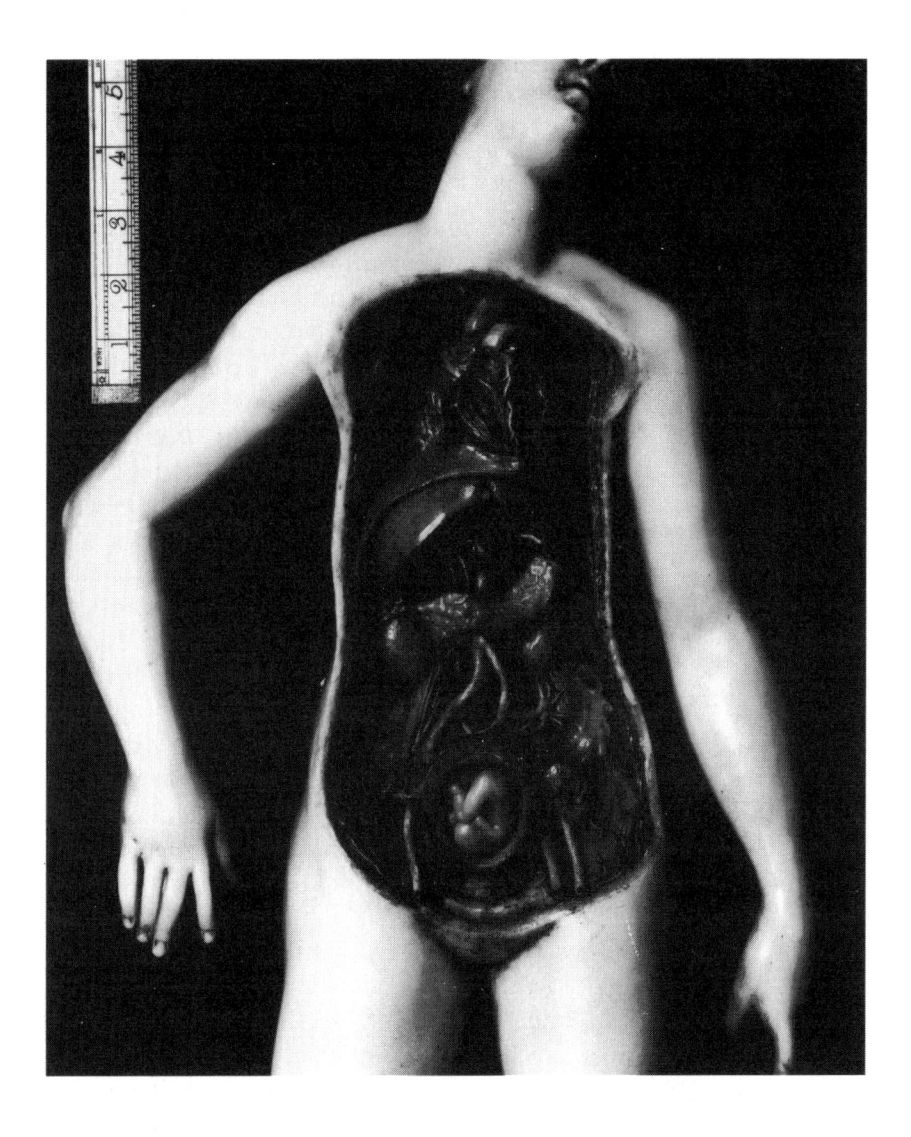

Adventures in the Anatomy and Embodiment of Women

Figure 9.10: Anatomical figures: French, 18th century
Wax anatomical teaching figure: female, with removable layers revealing internal anatomy; anon., French, 18th century
Source: The Wellcome Institute Library, London

maternal body. It is already separate, already autonomous, finding temporary shelter and nurturance rather then connectedness.

In a 1723 illustration of Siegemund's work (Figure 9.11), the foetus is fully formed, moving around in its own space, and the female body is absent in its entirety. The foetus here 'floats' in the disembodied uterus, attached through the umbilical cord only to an *abstract source* of life, and simultaneously, through the hand pushing up from the vagina, to the outside world.

This form of imaging has found its apotheosis in later twentieth-century reproductive technologies where both verbal and visual representation reinforce the dis-integration of women's bodies. It is not simply a radical disjunction between outer and inner, but an effective disappearance of the whole body/whole person as such. There is little sense in current medical literature of the woman as intentional agent, but only of disembodied and discrete reproductive processes. What is given is not a representation of the mother, but a display of fragmentary parts. Even in very early stages of pregnancy, the shadowy images of ultrasound serve to construct the foetus as a separate entity. The rest is space and silence.

A similar sense of emptiness pervades at least one strand of classical medical discourse which remained influential over many centuries. The wandering womb, suggested by Hippocrates and later endorsed by Aretaeus of Cappadocchia, was seen as the cause of a range of symptoms, called in medieval texts *'suffocatio matricis'*, and now known as hysteria. Sometimes the pressures of unexpelled menstrual fluid flooding the brain were held responsible, but often it was the womb itself which rose up to compress breathing (Jacquart and Thomasset, 1988). By using a variety of techniques such as manual stimulation, sexual intercourse, and herbal applications, the aim of the early physicians was to lure the womb back to its rightful place in the body. Late modern medicine is no less concerned with the organs of reproduction as the reductive determinants of feminine behaviour and no more able to treat women's bodies as an integrated whole. Even in the mid twentieth century, though clinical techniques have evolved, the medical gaze remains focused on the traditionally accepted markers of femininity.

In the mid 1950s, Cohen *et al.* carried out a comparative analysis of operations performed on the bodies of fifty women diagnosed as having hysteria, and a control group of fifty healthy women. The 'hysterical' group were diagnosed as such on the basis of criteria which define hysteria as a chronic illness beginning before the age of 30, in women with a dramatic, vague or complicated medical history and a large number of unexplained symptoms, including anxiety attacks, fatigue, sexual indifference, depression and headaches. In the so-called healthy

Adventures in the Anatomy and Embodiment of Women

Figure 9.11: Siegemund, Justine [1648–1705]
J. Siegemund, Die königl. preussische und churbrandenb. Hof-Wehe-Mutter, *Berlin: J. A. Rüdiger, 1723. ch. 4, pl. 5. foetus being removed from the womb*
Source: *The Wellcome Institute Library, London*

175

women, a comparatively small number of operations were recorded, mainly in the neck and pelvic area and around the left knee. In the 'hysterical' women the operations recorded in the pelvic area were greater by a factor of more than five. It appears that the medics looked for their explanations of behavioural markers in the reproductive organs of these women — and that the massed assault is unlikely to have left any of them with uteri or ovaries intact.

The metanymic circulation of specific body parts simply emphasizes the absence of the body itself. And in the discourse of psychoanalysis, which Foucault (1978) characterized as the paradigmatic human science, the material, and by now representational, absence of the penis has been taken as the defining factor of femininity. Women are castrated men, their bodies marked by lack, and what is hidden is just a hole. Where for men, the phallus, real and symbolic, has become the very signifier of presence and of wholeness, women, having no thing, are in consequence nothing. In a scathing critique of Freud's analysis of women, Luce Irigaray attributes to him the view that *'Nothing to be seen is equivalent to having no thing. No being and no truth'* (1985, p. 48, emphasis in original).

These brief snapshots of women's bodies, then, contradictory and often discontinuous as they are, should alert us to the dangers of regarding biology as given. Though we are familiar with the view that holds health to be both a normative and normalizing term, our analysis needs to go further to problematize the corporeal body itself. As women, our being-in-the-world cannot be understood by reference to any fixed or essential bodily core. Ways of seeing and ways of knowing are not predicated on a reality somehow beyond discourse, but are deeply implicated in the construction of bodies and selves. As Foucault (1980) has demonstrated, power and knowledge are indissoluably linked and productive forces; and in patriarchal society the dominant discourses are those which consolidate and extend the male social order. Accordingly, though there is *in reality* no fixed referrent, the male body (in its own various constructions) is posited as the natural standard against which the female body is measured and valued — as inferior, as different, as insubstantial, as absent. We make no claims to a continuous history of the body, but only to a series of relationships which devalue female embodiment. And yet we need not end in pessimism. There are always counter-discourses, moments of resistance which undermine the stability of the naturalized and normalized model. What a feminist project might aim to do is to uncover the mechanisms of construction, flaunt the contradications and insist on a diversity of bodily identifications. The move towards embodied selves need not threaten a new dead end of essentialism; it can speak both to the refusal to split body and mind, and to the refusal to allow ourselves to be fragmented and pathologized. At the same time to stress particularity *and* substantiality for the female body challenges the universalised male standard and opens up for us new possibilities of healthy being-in-the-world.

Acknowledgments

We are grateful to The Wellcome Institute Library, London for help in tracing the sixteenth- to eighteenth-century images, and for permission to reproduce them, and to Serono Laboratories (UK) Ltd for permission to reproduce the cover of the leaflet 'So you want to have a baby' Figure 9.2.

Notes

1 We are indebted to Laqueur (1990), Tuana (1988) and Jacquart and Thomasset (1988) for work on anatomical representations and the notion of the 'one-sex' body, which acted as a stimulus to the ideas developed in this paper.
2 This section draws on extracts from work by Kremer (1977) and Ziekenfondsraad (1989) cited in Kirejczyk and van der Ploeg (1992).
3 For an account of human post-mortem and dissection in the Alexandrian School see Phillips, 1987, pp. 139–60.
4 There was a parallel discourse of ovist preformation, but that was shorter-lived and generated its own problems.
5 For mediaeval views of women's bodies as excessive, permeous and fissured, see Lochrie (1991).
6 In *De humani corporis fabrica* (1543a), Vesalius illustrates the 'administration of an anatomy', the classical formal, sequential dissection of a human body (Saunders and O'Malley, 1950). In Book Five, the male torso is gradually exposed through eight stages of dissection which demonstrate sequential layers of muscle, bone and finally abdominal organs. In contrast, the female torso is shown dissected in only two stages, both of which reveal internal abdominal/pelvic organs and space.
7 This wax image is currently held at the Science Museum in London. Male wax figures, demonstrating muscle and bone, were also constructed. See Stafford 1991, p. 65, Figure 33, *Anatomical Wax Figure, 18th c*. See also Jordanova (1989, pp. 44–8) for further discussion of female wax figures.

References

ARISTOTLE (1937) *The Generation of Animals*, trans. A.L. Peck, London, Loeb Classical Library.
COHEN et al. (1953) 'Excessive Surgery in Hysteria', *Journal of the American Medical Association*, 151, pp. 977-86.
CLAYTON, S.G., LEWIS, T.L.T. and PINKER, G. (Eds) (1980) *Gynaecology by Ten Teachers*, London, Edward Arnold.
FOUCAULT, M. (1978) *History of Sexuality*, Harmondsworth, Penguin.
FOUCAULT, M. (1980) 'Truth and Power', in *Power/Knowledge: Selected Interviews and Other Writings, 1972-77*, ed. Colin Gordon, trans. Colin Gordon et al., Brighton, Harvester Press.
GALEN (1968) *On the Usefulness of the Parts of the Body*, trans. M.T. May, Ithaca, Cornell University Press.
GRAAF, R. DE (1672) *De mulierum organis generationi inservientibus tractatus novus*, Leiden, 'Off. Hackiana'.
HARRISON, M.R. (1982) 'Unborn: Historical Perspective of the Fetus as Patient', *Pharos*, Winter, pp. 19-24.
HARTSOEKER, N. (1694) *Essai de diotropique*, Paris, Anisson.
HODGEN, G.D. and VAN UEM, J.F.H.M. (1986) 'Follicular Growth, Ovulation and the Use of Ovarian Stimulants', in FISHEL, S. and SYMONDS, E.M. (Eds) *In Vitro Fertilisation: Past, Present, Future*, Oxford, IRL Press.
HUBBARD, R. (1984) 'Personal Courage Is Not Enough: Some Hazards of Childbearing in the 1980s', in ARDITTI, R., DUELLI KLEIN, R. and MINDEN, S. (Eds) *Test-Tube Women: What Future for Motherhood?*, London, Pandora.
IRIGARAY, L. (1985) *Speculum of the Other Woman*, New York, Cornell University Press.
JACQUART, D. and THOMASSET, C. (1988) *Sexuality and Medicine in the Middle Ages*, Cambridge, Polity Press.
JORDANOVA, L.J. (1980) 'Natural Facts: A Historical Perspective on Science and Sexuality', in MACCORMACK, C. and STRATHERN, M. (Eds) *Nature, Culture and Gender*, Cambridge, Cambridge University Press.
JORDANOVA, L.J. (1989) *Sexual Visions: Images of Gender in Science and Medicine between the Eighteenth and Twentieth Centuries*, London, Harvester Wheatsheaf.
KIREJCZYK, M. and VAN DER PLOEG, I. (1992) 'Pregnant Couples: Medical Technology and Social Constructions around Fertility and Reproduction', *Issues in Reproductive and Genetic Engineering*, vol. 5, no. 2, pp. 113-25.
KREMER, J. (1977) *Fysiologie en pathologie van de menselijke vruchtbaarheid*, Groningen, Rijksuniversiteit.
LAQUEUR, T. (1990) *Making Sex: Body and Gender from the Greeks to Freud*, Cambridge, MA, Harvard University Press.
LEDER, D. (1990) *The Absent Body*, Chicago, University of Chicago Press.
LOCHRIE, K. (1991) *Margery Kempe and Translations of the Flesh*, Baltimore, University of Pennsylvania Press.
NEUBERG, R. (1992) *So You Want To Have a Baby*, Serono Laboratories (UK) Ltd.
PETCHESKY, R.P. (1987) 'Foetal Images: The Power of Visual Culture in the Politics of Reproduction', in STANWORTH, M. (Ed.) *Reproductive Technologies: Gender, Motherhood and Medicine*, Cambridge, Polity Press.
PHILLIPS, E.D. (1987) *Aspects of Greek Medicine*, Philadelphia, The Charles Press.
SARTRE, J.-P. (1957) 'The Hole', in *Existentialism and Human Emotions*, New York, The Philosphical Library.
SAUNDERS, J.B. DE C.M. and O'MALLEY, C.D. (1950) *The Illustrations from the Works of Andreas Vesalius*, Cleveland, World Publishing Company.

SCHENCK, D. (1986) 'The Texture of Embodiment: Foundation for Medical Ethics', *Human Studies*, 9, pp. 43–54.
SIEGEMUND, J. (1723) *Die konigl. preussische und churbrandenb. Hof-Wehe-Mutter*, Berlin, J.A. Rudiger.
STAFFORD, B.M. (1991) *Body Criticism: Imaging the Unseen in Enlightenment Art and Medicine*, Cambridge, MA, MIT Press.
TUANA, N. (1988) 'The Weaker Seed: The Sexist Bias of Reproductive Theory', *Hypatia*, vol. 3, no. 1, pp. 35–59.
VALVERDE DE HAMUSCO, J. (1560) *Anatomia del corpo humano*, Rome, A. Salamanca/Venice, N. Bevilacque.
VESALIUS, A. (1538) *Tabulae Sex*.
VESALIUS, A. (1543a) Liber V, *De humani corporis fabrica*, Basel, Oporinus.
VESALIUS, A. (1543b) *Suorum de humani corporis fabrica librorum epitome*, Basel, J. Oporinus.
WARWICK, R. and WILLIAMS, P.L. (1989) *Gray's Anatomy*, 37th ed., Edinburgh, Longman.
ZIEKENFONDSRAAD (1989) *Advies inzake in vitro fertilisatie*, Amstelveen, Uitgave van de Ziekenfondsraad.

Section IV

Women's Studies and Feminist Practice

Introduction

There is an unease within the women's movement about the growing strength of Women's Studies as part of academe. The unease is as much about the loosening of bonds of solidarity among women as about the seeming delinking of theory from practice. Activism, participation, consciousness-raising — the words that say so much about the strength of the women's movement — seem to be disappearing from the vocabulary of academic feminists. This is causing increasing anxiety among women's groups who see themselves struggling not only against patriarchy and its political institutions, but also against what seems a growing indifference to political activism in those involved in Women's Studies but not in the women's movement. Academic feminists, on their part, feel under twin pressures too. The academy is hardly a favourable turf for women academics. The battles they have to fight on university committees with men in grey suits, with entrenched and blind prejudice, to promote not only Women's Studies but also equal opportunity practices are fierce, time-consuming, and politically important. The lack of sympathy that they feel from their sisters outside the academy makes them feel misunderstood and undervalued by those who should be more sensitive to the pressures of working women.

This anxiety both within the women's movement and Women's Studies reveals the deep roots of the 'sisterhood mythology'. Having left the discourse of 'sisterhood worldwide' seemingly behind us in a celebration of difference, we still are bounded by an imaging of women and women's movements that seeks to create an ideal world of women in friendship. The three chapters in this section, in different ways, present and confront this mythology. Conflict is difficult to handle, and more so when expectations are high — of sympathy, of listening, of group democracy, of power diffusion, of support. As Hollway writes in her chapter on 'Relations among Women: Using the Group to Unite Theory and Experience', 'The idea that women are good at support is a pervasive and attractive one, but in practice is fraught with difficulties which are not necessarily produced by the failures of actual women to respond in the desired manner, but as much by the fears and fantasies which make it difficult for women to ask for suport'.

Among the reasons for not seeking support from other women are the anxieties that we carry within ourselves around issues of inclusion and exclusion. Lynda Birke writes of the hostile territory of academic science, but she is also aware of the exclusion she experiences within feminist circles because of her inclusion in a male domain: 'I have also to say, unfortunately, that there was also hostile territory within the Women's Liberation Movement, and I remember squirming when I was surrounded by several women who wanted to know how I could possibly be doing research in science because it was so heavily patriarchal'.

The anxiety around inclusion and exclusion is of course underscored by the imbalances of power that we all experience in one or another way. The institutionalization of power imbalances that has taken place historically between the 'East' and the 'West' is the focus of critique in Nora Jung's chapter, 'East European Women with Western Eyes'. Questioning the construction of Eastern European women by Western feminists, Jung is very aware that the ways in which the structuring of power relations take place also involve a collusion born of the anxiety to be included in Western-dominated feminist discourse: ' "Feminism" has more negative connotations in Hungarian than in English. Therefore members of the [Hungarian Women's] Association use "feminism" in English and avoid it in Hungarian in order to win recognition both from the Hungarian women, who are less likely to accept the label "feminist", and from Western women's organizations who would be happy to see feminist consciousness on the rise'.

Issues of identity, ethnicity and representation are thus explored in this section in all the three chapters. The authors, in the best traditions of Women's Studies/the Women's Liberation Movement, do this by situating their own experience within their wider academic and political concerns.

Chapter 10

Interventions in Hostile Territory

Lynda Birke

To decide that you want to become a scientist, and then to work as one, is to enter hostile territory for a woman: the territory becomes a minefield if you are a feminist too. I want to begin charting that minefield by talking a bit about my own passage through it: the personal is political after all. But I think it's a fairly representative story for those of us who have tried to combine working in science with being a feminist. And many of the issues it raises are not unique to doing science: dealing with problems of discrimination, and at the same time trying to think about how to change the way that knowledge is constructed, are issues faced by feminists in other disciplines. But there are two important points to make specifically about science: first, it tends to be thought of as a male preserve and so may be more hostile than some other disciplines; and secondly, it is science that purports to study and define nature — including, of course, gender.

Early on in my life I realized that, however much I wanted to do science, it was not considered a very suitable thing to do. Girls simply were not supposed to excel at things like physics and maths. I did not need any particular social skills as a 17-year-old to read the face of the young man at the school dance on discovering that, no, I was not doing secretarial subjects but something decidedly unfeminine. It was not, of course, only doing science that has put me out on the minefield; I went through my childhood and teenage years being a tomboy who preferred to ride horses and read chemistry books, rather than go out with boys. Fortunately for my sanity, I have remained 'unfeminine'; I retained the interest in science. And I still ride horses.

Like many other women in science, I have encountered problems of discrimination, on grounds of gender, but — important though issues of discrimination are — they do not (to me) pose a terribly interesting set of questions. Partly this is because many other occupations and disciplines are discriminatory (although some less so than science, perhaps). Partly, too, I think it is because I am more interested in the ways in which feminists can ask questions about the content and practice of science — how gender as a construct enters our thinking about science, for example (Keller, 1985, 1993). The trouble with worrying about women in science is that there is a danger that it poses *women* as the problem: we need more women in science to provide a trained workforce, we need everyone to understand science better so that they will support it — so the rhetoric runs. But the feminist critiques emphasize *science*, not women, as the problem: and it is that that is my point of departure (Birke, 1986).

Yet issues of discrimination undoubtedly help to create hostile territories. I remember a conversation with a feminist scientist in the US, in which I commented that it was a pity in some ways that she did not stay in physics; after all, I stressed, we haven't exactly got many feminists working in physics, and it is an area of inquiry that seems to fit in with a kind of macho heroism (see Traweek, 1988). After a long pause, she looked at me levelly, and said, 'listen, I was doing physics, at Harvard, I'm black and a lesbian: something had to go'.[1] That sums it up: important though it may be to find feminists in science, it is also important that each of us retains her integrity and survives. It is just not possible to battle on all those fronts at once.

In my own life, the experience of hostile territory is not so much about being a woman; my disadvantages of gender are, to some extent, offset by the advantages that spring from my being white and middle-class. But I encountered the hostile territory around being a feminist, and perhaps more especially about being a lesbian. It has been around those aspects of myself in my personal life that the battles have been fought. Stroppy dykes are not necessarily welcome in most of academia, but if you question the holy canon of science, then your problems multiply. At the heart of that problem, I think, lies the macho culture of the lab. That culture is rarely spoken about, but you can find its traces in, for example, the way that Rosalind Franklin was treated in Watson and Crick's descriptions of the discovery of the structure of DNA. She was, they stated, 'unfeminine' and prickly. The macho culture, a kind of 'cowboy', gung-ho approach to studying nature, also pervades some descriptions of scientists using animals (for example, Arluke, 1992, described the 'cowboys' working in some primate labs; it is also evident in Lynch's (1985) study of the 'laboratory shop talk' of neuroscientists). Women can sometimes survive that culture by becoming one of the boys (arguably easier for a lesbian?): but they run risks. I have experienced male colleagues not knowing how to respond to me; or rather, I did not respond to the heterosexual flirting. That is not really playing the game. You might be all right in the lab: but what do they do with you at the laboratory party?

I have also to say, unfortunately, that there was also hostile territory within the Women's Liberation Movement, and I remember squirming when I was surrounded by several women who wanted to know how I could possibly be doing research in science because it was so heavily patriarchal. I did wonder at the time and I'm still wondering since why science gets singled out. Can you name one area of the academy that isn't patriarchal? There is still hostility to (or lack of interest in) science in the women's movement, although I think it has changed since those early days. Opposition to science undoubtedly persists (and quite rightly: feminists have found much to criticize about the ways in which it operates), but now there is also a recognition that we might need to get inside it. There are more women in science than there used to be — but a few feminists working inside wouldn't go amiss.

Nonetheless, there remains little interest in science within the women's movement or Women's Studies. Where there is interest, it is usually around specific issues such as women's health. But there are precious few Women's Studies courses or books that explicitly address science and technology. Partly, I think this lack has to do with the fact that most women do not study science, and that Women's Studies has tended to arise out of subjects like sociology. But partly, too, I think it has something to do with the fact that those of us who did become scientists have been so busy criticizing the stuff from our feminist perspectives, that we have forgotten to get across the message that the reason we did science in the first place was that it was *fun*. Messing about in the lab has a quality that few other academic subjects can match. We are as much to blame as the women who are not scientists for the negative images (of difficult, abstract knowledge, or of political abuses, for example) that science has in feminist circles.

Another problem for our critiques is that there is often misunderstanding about just what it is that feminist critics are addressing. Women scientists, after claiming that they have not been particularly discriminated against as women, sometimes object strongly to what they often perceive as feminist claims that 'women would do science differently'. For differently, read inferior: not surprisingly, women want to be seen to be, just as good at doing science as men. I can recall the incredulous, and indignant, woman scientist who followed a talk I gave at the British Association for the Advancement of Science with the outburst that, if we followed my reasoning, 'science wouldn't even *be* science any more!'

Lynda Birke

The person who has written most about the difficulty of dealing with the clash between feminist critiques (which emphasize gender) and those concerned with equity issues (which emphasize sex) has been Evelyn Fox Keller. She has been particularly instrumental in talking about the gender of science. Now by that, what she means is gender as a construct, that science, in its pursuit of distancing and objectivity, is intrinsically masculine. She has had a lot of flak from all kinds of quarters about that:

> 'Despite repeated attempts at clarification, many scientists, (especially, women scientists) persist in misreading the force that feminists attribute to gender ideology as a force being attributed to sex, that is, to the claim that women, for biological reasons, would do a different kind of science. The net effect is that, where some of us see a liberating potential (both for women *and* for science) in exhibiting the historical role of gender in science, these scientists often see only a reactionary potential, fearing its use to support the exclusion of women from science'. (Keller, 1993, p. 20)

And that has generally been a problem for any of us who have been working in and around feminism and science. It can be difficult sometimes to speak to other feminists because of that anti-science feeling; but it's terribly difficult to talk to other women scientists about feminist ideas. You're out on your own; and that can be very hostile territory indeed. But somehow, in spite of all that, I did manage to make it into scientific research, even if I was a scientist with the rather nasty habit of criticizing the stuff from within.

Now at that point I was faced with a problem: how do you do science as a feminist or do you just forget feminism and get into the lab? What would it mean to 'do science as a feminist' (Longino, 1989)? One obvious answer (and one that is not unique to science) is that you could try to answer questions or develop methodologies that are relevant to women's interests. In biology, that might mean, for instance, doing research that had relevance to (say) women's health.

Yet making links in my mind between my feminism and my science posed problems, too. This was partly because a lot of work that I was doing was *also* based on critiques that were in a sense wider than feminism. Apart from feminism, radical critiques of science have come from other sources: the radical science movement, for example, which grew up in the late 1960s and early 1970s has had concerns that have overlapped with feminist critiques. More recently, so too has the environmental movement — the overlap being most obvious in the form of ecofeminism (see, for example, Plant, 1989; and essays in special issue of *Hypatia* on ecological feminism). Alternative accounts of science also come from non-Western sources, as Sandra Harding has emphasized (1986).

Within biology itself, there are critics concerned to move the theory of biology away from the kind of reductionism of which feminists and others have been critical. There are many people who want to question the canons of biology. I suppose we thought of it and still think of it as radical biology. It's rooted in a kind of anti-reductionism, trying to think how on earth you do (and if you can) a biology that is, or moves away from, the reductionism that feminists so often criticize (e.g., the Dialectics of Biology Group, 1982; Rose et al., 1984). These approaches tend to be antagonistic to neo-Darwinian ideas in evolutionary theory, and antagonistic to reducing the processes of development of organisms simply to the acting out of genetic codes. They tend, too, to emphasize holistic understandings and interrelationships between units (be they individual organisms, species, or lineages of cells). There are attempts to retheorize some of that, to emphasize different approaches (e.g., Birke, 1989; Fausto-Sterling, 1992; and essays in Hubbard and Birke, in press).

Trying to develop other ways of thinking about nature, whether or not we label that as feminist, is of course something which challenges biological orthodoxy; if you are trained in biology, you are brought up to believe that Darwin was absolutely right. So, to question Darwin's theory of evolution (at least in its common form of neo-Darwinism; evolutionary theory remains, as it was in the nineteenth century, a highly contested terrain: Ereshevsky, 1992) is actually quite problematic even within the framework of biology.

Nor does trying to develop radical ideas in biology endear you to the media, who always want facts, simplicity. It is much easier to claim that (say) gender differences are rooted in either your hormones or your genes, and anyone who tries to say that it is actually more complicated than that risks being branded as nuts or a feminist! A couple of years ago, I had the misfortune to have reviewed a dreadful book called *BrainSex: The Real Difference between Men and Women* (Moir and Jessell, 1989). It started off with claims that, of course, the real reason you don't know much about these wonderful scientific accounts of brain differences between men and women is because these nasty feminists and woolly-minded liberals have been trying to cover up the evidence. Here, they say, is the real evidence; in it, you discover really important things like the claim that, because of the way that their hormones have organized their brains, women are better than men at loading the dishwasher!

Whatever the problems, many of us have tried to think about what it means to do science as a feminist. We know that we cannot hope to create a 'feminist science' (even supposing we knew what one looked like) in a society that is so clearly anti-feminist (or anti-women). Science is too deeply rooted in the practices and ideology of Western culture for any such change to be possible.

Yet it is, unfortunately, still necessary to do some rather boring stuff reacting to assumptions about biology. Within Women's Studies, for example, there has tended to be a reaction against essentialism. We know we don't like essentialism, particularly in the form of biological determinism. But, at the same time, what that reaction has tended to do is to collapse biology into a kind of notion of fixity: our biology — our bodies, for example — becomes a kind of unchangeable bedrock. In doing so, we have also been guilty of supporting the mind/body duality. For it is only the notion of 'biology' applied to 'the mind'/behaviour to which we object: no one seems to mind the fact that having two X chromosomes has something to do with having ovaries, which has something to do with producing oestrogens. Bodies have biology; minds do not, in this formulation.

Feminist theory has (not surprisingly perhaps) concentrated on ideas such as the social construction of gender, or cultural representations. Important though these are, they effectively leave 'biology' untheorized; yet bodies hurt and bleed, contributing much to our experience of our lives as human, and sometimes as gendered, beings. Leaving 'biology' untheorized in feminist thinking, leaving it as somehow unchangeable (or unchallengeable) ignores not only the body, but also nature, and other kinds of animals. That worries me; as a biologist, I cannot reconcile my view of humans as part of the remit of 'biology' with the view that seems to come from much of the social sciences and feminism, that humans are somehow apart (see Benton, 1993; Plumwood, 1991).

Outside of Women's Studies, that need to go on defending ourselves, to go on critiquing the boring 'it's all in the genes/hormones' kind of line, is remarkably persistent. Some of it, we know, is explicitly in response to feminism (like the *BrainSex* book I mentioned above). Much of it is less explicit about its ideological assumptions. The most recent salvos have centred on the 'biological causes of homosexuality': yet again, we have to deal with the simplistic stuff about brain, hormones, genes, chromosomes or whatever that are said to cause gender or sexual orientation.

Now I suppose I should (as a lesbian) be thankful that scientists are a bit like Queen Victoria, they don't really believe we exist. So, in Simon

LeVay's much vaunted work on 'the homosexual brain', he said he failed to find any lesbian brains. LeVay did, however, find brains that were alleged to be from gay and straight men (and a few — allegedly — heterosexual women). What he was looking for in these brains was a gay/straight difference in the size of a tiny bit of the brain called INAH for short.[2] His search stemmed from an earlier claim that this bit of the brain showed a difference between males and females. Critics were quick to pounce on LeVay's methodology: he had brains from only forty-one people, some had died of AIDS (which might affect brain cells), there was a great deal of overlap in size between different samples, and so on. At the very least, the critics urged a caution that was inevitably ignored by the following media outbursts.

The latest piece of biological determinism to hit the newspapers at the time of writing is that there are genes for homosexuality (in men of course). The scientists claimed first to have found that gay men were more likely than expected to have gay brothers — and that having gay relatives was more common on the mother's side of the family. So, they began to look for the gene on the X chromosome (which men inherit only from their mothers) of pairs of homosexual brothers. And it was there that they claim to have found it, through analyzing the DNA (that comprises the genes) of these men (Hamer *et al.,* 1993).

Again, we can criticize the methodology, or the assumptions that the scientists made about homosexuality (Anne Fausto-Sterling has alread been doing so in the US: see *New Scientist*, 24 July 1993, pp. 4–5). But it is the implications that are particularly worrying for feminists. First of all, locating a specific gene could open up the horrifying possibility of prenatal diagnosis for possession of the alleged gene, followed by offering a pregnant woman a chance to get rid of a 'gay foetus'. Secondly, if you get your X chromosome from your mother, then it could become another way of blaming mothers for their sons' homosexuality. Thirdly, this kind of argument fixes and reifies sexual orientation: behaviour that is as complex as human sexuality must have very complex causes (if its causes are something we deem worth studying — a debatable point, perhaps, especially since the alleged causes of exclusive heterosexuality are rarely studied explicitly).

Those of us who are feminists, biologists and lesbians have to confront this tedious stuff; there is a real resurgence of it at this moment. We need (all of us, not just lesbians or just biologists) to think about why there is a resurgence, and what we can do to challenge it. The politics of it are particularly worrying, especially the extent to which it is being taken up within the gay community: many welcome the notion that it is genetic because this, they feel, 'explains' everything about how they feel.

Lynda Birke

Playwright Jonathan Tolins, writing in *Time* (26 July, 1993, p. 38) claimed, for example, that he 'knew in my bones that my own sexuality was not a decision but a natural part of who I am. . . . To find a biological or genetic basis for this variation of human nature made perfect sense'. I understand the attraction of that kind of thinking; it says that 'I am a natural kind, and you should accept me as such; I can't change'. But the polarization on which it is based — biological base or choice — is a misleading one. And it worries me greatly to find that belief becoming so entrenched in the lesbian and gay community. Comforting thought it may be (to some): but I doubt that it makes homophobia any less of a hostile terrain.

So, although science itself contains some pretty hostile territory for me as a woman/feminist/lesbian, what also needs to be challenged is the ideological power of cultural ideas about what is 'biology', that construct our sense of biology as fixed and somehow more fundamental. Those are issues in which we can all intervene. We should be questioning what is meant by biology. I don't think we have done it enough, not least because feminism has tended to leave science to the boys. That is not likely to make it less hostile.

Notes

1 Conversation with Evelynn Hammonds, Harvard, March 1992.
2 This stands for the Interstitial Nucleus of the Anterior Hypothalamus, a part of the brain lying close to the pituitary gland that controls many of our hormones. The hypothalamus is said to be involved with sexual functions.

References

ARLUKE, A. (1992) 'The Ethical Culture of Primate Labs', talk given at Conference, 'Science and the Human-Animal Relationship', Amsterdam, March.
BENTON, T. (1993) *Natural Relations: Ecology, Animal Rights and Social Justice*, London, Verso.
BIRKE, L. (1986) *Women, Feminism and Biology*, Brighton, Wheatsheaf.
BIRKE, L. (1989) 'How do Gender Differences in Behaviour Develop? A Reanalysis of the Role of Early Experience', in BATESON, P. and KLOPFER, P. (Eds), *Perspectives in Ethology*, vol. 8, New York, Plenum.
DIALECTICS OF BIOLOGY GROUP (Gen. Editor, S. ROSE) (1982) *Towards a Liberatory Biology*, London, Allison and Busby.
ERESHEVSKY, M. (Ed.) (1992) *The Units of Evolution*, Cambridge, MA, and London, MIT Press.

FAUSTO-STERLING, A. (1992) *Myths of Gender*, New York, Basic Books.
HAMER, D. H., HU, S., MAGNUSON, V.L., HU, N. and PATTATUCCI, A.M.L. (1993) 'A Linkage between DNA Markers on the X Chromosome and Male Sexual Orientation', *Science*, 261, pp. 321–7.
HARDING, S. (1986) *The Science Question in Feminism*, Milton Keynes, Open University Press.
HUBBARD, R. and BIRKE, L. (Eds) (in press) *Reinventing Biology*, Bloomington, Indiana University Press.
KELLER, E.F. (1985) *Reflections on Gender and Science*, New Haven, Yale University Press.
KELLER, E.F. (1993) *Secrets of Life, Secrets of Death*, London, Routledge.
LEVAY, S. (1993) *The Sexual Brain*, Cambridge, MA, MIT Press.
LONGINO, H.E. (1989) 'Can There be a Feminist Science?' in TUANA, N. (Ed.) *Feminism and Science*, Bloomington, Indiana University Press.
LYNCH, M. (1985) *Art and Artifact in Laboratory Science*, London, Routledge.
MOIR, A. and JESSELL, D. (1989) *BrainSex: The Real Difference between Men and Women*, London, Michael Joseph.
PLANT, J. (Ed.) (1989) *Healing the Wounds: The Promise of Ecofeminism*, Philadelphia, New Society.
PLUMWOOD, V. (1991) 'Nature, Self and Gender: Feminism, Environmental Philosophy, and the Critique of Rationalism', *Hypatia*, 6, pp. 3–27.
ROSE, S., KAMIN, L.J. and LEWONTIN, R.C. (1984) *Not in Our Genes*, Harmondsworth, Penguin.
TRAWEEK, S. (1988) *Beamtimes and Lifetimes: The World of High Energy Physics*, Cambridge, MA, Harvard University Press.

Chapter 11

Eastern European Women with Western Eyes

Nora Jung

Introduction

In this chapter I discuss the Eastern European approach to the 'woman question' before and after 1989 — using the Hungarian case as an example — and compare it to Western feminist evaluations of the situation of Eastern European women. I should tell you at the beginning that I have problems with this title myself. I have lived in Canada for the past ten years and I am interested in the activities of new women's groups in Hungary. Does this put me in the category of the 'Western eye' gazing at Eastern Europe, even though I was born and raised in Hungary?

I do not suggest that there is a universal perspective that I call the 'Western eye', neither do I see Eastern European women as a homogeneous group. Nevertheless I found that my own views have been profoundly influenced by the fact that I have been exposed to a different political environment in Canada. I also found that many Eastern European scholars who have been living in Western European or North American countries have a different approach to the situation of Eastern European women than Eastern European scholars who have stayed in their home countries. In trying to describe these differences I run into the problem of how I can refer to these people without presenting an essentialist view of 'Eastern' and 'Western'. I found the term 'post-communist' equally if not more problematic to use in the context of my argument.

I have chosen to retain the terms Western and Eastern European, because it helps me to identify historically specific political and economic differences that have had different impacts on women's organizing as well as on theorizing about the situation of women in these two regions. By Eastern and Western I do not simply refer to geographical locations. These terms also denote the historically specific division between capitalist and formerly socialist countries which in turn signify not only different modes of production but also distinct political systems with their concomitant dominant ideologies. Even though there was a competition between liberal ideology in the Western capitalist countries and Marxist ideology in Eastern European socialist countries, neither in the capitalist nor in the socialist countries did dominant ideologies go unchallenged.

The 'Woman Question' in Hungary

Hungary's history shows that the actual political climate of the country had always had a profound impact on changing attitudes towards women's roles and women's liberation. While the conservative reservations regarding women's role in politics were challenged by the ideas of the 1848 revolution, the political climate created by the suppression of the revolution did not favour the emancipation of women. During the short-lived Hungarian Soviet Republic of 1919 the 'woman question' was on the agenda in terms of women's political education and organizing. The era after the collapse of the young Soviet Republic was characterized by anti-communism, anti-semitism and anti-feminism (Szegvari, 1981).

The official policy towards the 'woman question' continued to change after 1945 and can be followed up in the history of Hungarian women's organizations. The first women's organization after World War II was the MNDSZ (Democratic Federation of Hungarian Women). In the first years of its existence this Federation was to a large degree independent from party influence. With the party gaining power the MNDSZ became more and more directly dependent on the party and finally it merged with the Popular Front. The rationale for this move was that since women are organized as workers in their unions, or in their cooperatives, there is no need for organizing them twice.

In the uprising of 1956 women's issues did not play a major role in mobilizing people, but women's dissatisfaction with the regime was addressed to some extent. In 1956 the socialist party regained its power with Soviet help. In spring 1957 the party sanctioned the establishment of the Hungarian Women's Council. However, there remained the pressure to merge the Women's Council with the Popular Front, as before 1956. This pressure led to a drastic reduction of the branches of the Women's Council, especially in the urban areas. This move was the result of a compromise between the party's effort to dissolve the Council and the Council's resistance. This reduced Council became less effective as well as more dependent on the party. The following years led to a gradual decline of the importance of the Council and finally to its dissolution in 1989 (Jung, 1992).

Hungarian Scholarship before 1989

Despite a low tolerance for a counter-discourse during state socialism, the knowledge produced by Eastern European scholars was not monolithic. Already in the 1970s we can find authors who were critical of the regime's achievements regarding women's emancipation (see Markus, 1976). However, the influence of Western feminist theory is typically absent in the works of Hungarian scholars. In her work on the origins of stereotypes about women and men Judit Sas seems to have had access to an impressive amount of literature in various social science disciplines, but she does not include any feminist approaches in her work (Sas, 1984). Women's issues are usually discussed within a Marxist theoretical framework and rarely do authors seriously challenge the official approach to the 'woman question'. The study by Katalin Koncz, on women and work (Koncz, 1982) is an example of this.

Western feminism, if addressed at all, received only critical comments from authors during this period. Zsuzsa Ferge argues that the demands of the women's movement have been included — although formulated differently — in socialist theory from the beginning. She maintains:

> At the same time today these demands are in the same, or even in more extreme forms included in the ideology of Western feminist movements. The problem in the case of feminism is . . . that all men seem to be the enemies of all women in all spheres of life. The 'forgotten' element is the existence of class, or class-like inequalities. . . . Neglecting social conflicts which are independent of gender inequalities. . . leads to an image of society in which all interests of males are common male interests, and all interests of females are common female interests. This is

expressed, among other things, in the slogan of 'sisterhood'.
(Ferge, 1983, p. 245, my translation)

Here Ferge's discussion of feminism is based on a simplified and distorted image of feminism. We can see that 'feminists' are a homogeneous group who are perceived as the 'other' by her. Ferge suggests that knowledge produced by Western feminists about the emancipation of Eastern European women is inadequate, because it lacks class analysis. We have heard similar arguments from socialist feminists in the West. Ferge's argument, however, also implies the superiority of knowledge produced by scholars in Eastern Europe, who actually start from a Marxian analysis.

In Ferge's interpretation the Western feminists/scholars are the 'others', and, similarly to what we have seen in the literature on the process of otherization, the Western authors/scholars are seen as less enlightened (see, for example, Said, 1978). In her discussion Western feminists are depicted as having inferior academic skills, as lacking the necessary tools to analyze the 'woman question' in Eastern Europe, and as people who can learn from something from Ferge and scholars like her. Just as Eastern European women often become 'the others' in the writings of Western feminists, Western feminists became 'the other' in Ferge's writing.

To be sure, Ferge's critique of Western feminism is based on some rather problematic assumptions about feminism. My point, however, is that she does not accept the knowledge created by Western feminists about women's issues as being superior to the knowledge created by Eastern European scholars.

Autonomous Women's Organizations after 1989

In the 1970s groups critical of state socialism became more and more visible in Hungary. By the late 1980s these groups, collectively called dissidents, organized into a few dozen parties ready to run for elections. In 1989 it became obvious that the Hungarian Socialist Workers' Party would sanction a multi-party system (Swain, 1989; Szelenyi and Szelenyi, 1991).

The Women's Council — which was the only official women's organization before 1989 — held its 1989 conference in this political climate. The membership approved the dissolution of the Council and established a new organization which is called the Association of

Hungarian Women. The new Women's Association claimed to be distinctly different from the former Women's Council. However, critics of the Association see too many similarities between the former and the present organization. In trying to prove themselves as a new, independent organization the Association established close links with women's groups from abroad. Being recognized by Western women's organizations seems to be an important factor in this process.

The changing attitudes of the Association towards feminism also deserve some discussion. In 1991 during my first discussions with the members of the Women's Association I found that they avoided being labelled 'feminist'. In 1992 I noticed that when speaking to Western self-declared feminists, members of the Association used the term 'feminist' several times to describe their activities. 'Feminism' has more negative connotations in Hungarian than in English. Therefore members of the Association use 'feminism' in English and avoid it in Hungarian in order to win recognition both from the Hungarian women, who are less likely to accept the label 'feminist', and from Western women's organizations who would be happy to see feminist consciousness on the rise.

In contrast to the Association the other newly emerged women's group calls itself the Feminist Network in Hungarian as well. This organization grew out of a need to break away from the approach practised by the former Women's Council. The members of the group emphasize that they are distinctly different from the Women's Association. They see no difference between the former Women's Council and the new Women's Association; they do not even call it by its new name. In their view the Council/Association is part of the establishment, in contrast to the Network which defines itself as a grassroots movement.

Although few women in Hungary know about the existence of the Network, their 'Declaration of Intent' is available to English-speaking feminists in the 1991 winter issue of *Feminist Review*. Women's emancipation, according to this document, was reduced to the right to work. In order to extend this narrow definition of emancipation the 'Network aims to achieve the recognition of specific female interests and points of view' (Adamik, 1991). These 'specific female interests' are interpreted by the members in a number of ways.

East European Scholarship after 1989

After 1989 authors who depicted Western scholars/feminists as 'others' seem to have withdrawn from publishing on women's issues. I discovered the following tendencies in the works of Hungarian writers who addressed women's issues after 1989:

- they tend to concentrate on the critical evaluation of the past and blame the former regime for women's subordinated role in Hungarian society; and/or

- they tend to address Western feminists as their audience either by introducing Western feminist jargon in their writings, or by writing in Western feminist publications.

For example in 1982 Katalin Koncz discusses women's work within a Marxist theoretical framework, whereas in her 1990 publication she tries to adopt a feminist framework. She talks about 'female culture', 'women's particular values' and 'male dominance'. All these terms were absent from her earlier publications. She blames the former regime for the lack of autonomous women's movements.

While both of Koncz's articles appeared in Hungarian, the following Hungarian authors published their articles in *Gender Politics and Post-Communism* which is a collection aimed at a Western audience.

Eniko Bollobas refers to the socialist approach to the woman question as 'Totalitarian Lib' and blames communism for everything, including dreadful architecture. Bollobas, who as a member of the new governing party worked in the Hungarian Embassy in Washington, DC, in 1990, should know that neither poor architectural design nor pressing social problems are solely produced by communism. The fact that American women are in a subordinated position can hardly be blamed on communism. While Bollobas (1993) has nothing to say about women's situation after 1989, the other Hungarian author, Maria Adamik, has a long list of issues that have effected women's lives after 1989 (Adamik, 1993). However, given that her article is only five and a half pages long these issues remain only listed without elaboration. In this jam-packed article Adamik does not miss the opportunity to discredit the Hungarian Women's Association, which she simply equates with the former Women's Council. The third Hungarian author in Funk's collection, Olga Toth, starts her article with a critical comment on Western feminism (Toth, 1993). As it turns out, her criticism is aimed only at socialist feminists, who naively envied Eastern European women, because they believed that women in Eastern Europe were more emancipated than in the West. Toth also remains focused on the period before 1989.

These writings might be more pleasing to the Western eye than the works of Ferge, or that of Koncz before 1989. It is, however, questionable whether these works are any closer to Hungarian women's reality than those old discredited approaches were.

In applying the term 'post-communist', Nannette Funk, the editor of *Gender Politics and Post-Communism* (1993) does not differentiate between Eastern European women who were born, raised and remained in Eastern Europe and those who left their home countries several years ago. There are, however, some important differences between articles that were written by Westerners, or Western-trained Eastern Europeans and those written by 'home-grown' Eastern Europeans.

Among the Eastern European contributors to this collection, women who remained in Eastern Europe focus more often on showing the failure of the socialist regime to emancipate women. They are more likely to discredit the women's organizations that existed during the previous regime and to blame women's disadvantaged situation on the policies of the former regime. Their critical comments on Western feminism are usually aimed at socialist feminists, who naively gave some credence to women's emancipation in Eastern Europe.

Compared to Eastern European authors, Western or Western-trained authors in the collection usually spend less time on discrediting the former regime and former women's organizations. They are more likely to pose the question 'what did Eastern European women lose with the departure of socialist regimes?' (see for example the sections on Bulgaria or the Czech and Slovak Republics).

Western Scholarship on Women in Eastern Europe

Western Scholarship before 1989

As I mentioned in the introduction, Western discourse on Eastern European women is a polyphonic discourse. I will discuss some aspects of this polyphony before and after 1989. I wil show how some Western scholars tend to focus on achievements of socialist governments in terms of women's emancipation, while other scholars tend to emphasize the failures of these governments to achieve full sexual equality. These are not the only approaches within Western scholarship, but these are the most common ones. I will base my discussion on the 'focus on achievements' and the 'emphasis on failures' approaches on the following works: Barbara Jancar's *Women under COMMUNISM* and Gail Lapidus' *Women in Soviet Society*. Both of these authors published their works in 1978 in the USA.

In her work Barbara Jancar emphasizes that Eastern European governments failed to emancipate women despite their commitment to sexual equality. She compares women's situation in the West and in Eastern Europe without paying any attention to the historical, economical and cultural differences between these countries. Jancar treats Eastern Europe as a homogeneous region. Eastern European scholars are also a monolithic group for her, she simply refers to them as 'communist sources'.

In her scheme Eastern European societies consist of powerful, active regimes and powerless, passive individuals. She perceives these countries as the realization of Marx's ideas, therefore she does not distinguish between her criticism of Marxism and her criticism of existing socialist regimes in Eastern Europe. Jancar rejects Marxism as a possible framework to address the woman question. Sexual equality depends, in her view, on the level of technological advancement. The USA and other industrialized countries are close to the stage where emancipation becomes possible. Eastern Europe is somewhat behind in this evolutionary scheme, but might eventually catch up.

Lapidus talks about Soviet women and she agrees with Jancar that they have not yet achieved full emancipation. However, analyzing women's situation from a historical perspective she points out the achievements in Soviet women's emancipation. She pays more attention to cross-cultural differences than Jancar does; also Soviet social scientists represent a heterogeneous group for her with differing opinions. In her assessment the Soviet regime had not been monolithic and did not have unlimited power either; there is some room for individuals, or for groups to react. Lapidus believes that equality is valued in societies East and West. She sees the Bolshevik revolution as an attempt to establish social equality.

Based on these two works the changes of 1989 can be explained differently as well. Jancar's evolutionary scheme would offer an explanation depicting Eastern Europe as 'catching up' with the West. In her framework there is little room for the various parties that emerged during the 1980s, or for opposing factions within the former governments. In Lapidus' historical framework the Soviet regime as well as Soviet society consist of heterogeneous groups of people with conflicting views. In her framework we can trace the histories of various opposition groups, and we can find the roots of Soviet feminism in the 1980s (see Mamonova, 1989).

Both authors point out the importance of Western feminist organizations. However, their underlying assumptions about how change will occur differ. In Jancar's opinion Eastern European women have nothing to offer to Western feminists. North America is on its way to a better society, which will be secured by its superior technology. Lapidus' scheme is more complex. In comparing the situation of women in the USA and in the Soviet Union she weighs the advantages and disadvantages of both societies. Although she suggests that Soviet women may be inspired by Western feminism, she does not exclude the possibility that Western feminists can learn from the experience of Soviet women as well.

Let me discuss one more piece of Western scholarship before 1989 that focuses on the situation of women in Hungary: Chris Corrin's article 'The Situation of Women in Hungarian Society'.

In her introduction Corrin cautions the 'Western Eye':

> There are obvious dangers here for analysts in imposing Western prescriptions onto different cultures. Feminism is an excellent body of writing from which to make a critique of social policy, but the values of a largely white, Western feminism cannot be neatly transposed into other situations with different historical, economic and cultural backgrounds and a different prioritizing of needs and desires. (Corrin, 1990)

By the 1980s 'Third World' scholars had widely criticized those Western feminist scholars who ignored issues of race, or analyzed the situation of 'Third World' women within a framework of Western norms and values. Corrin is correct in reminding us not to commit the same mistake in studying Eastern European women. However, she failed to recast her caution to fit the Eastern European context.

We can certainly draw parallels between how the terms 'Third World women' and 'Eastern European women' are conceptualized by some Western feminists. According to Chandra Mohanty, Western feminists tend to approach 'Third World women' as 'others' and treat them as a monolithic group (Mohanty, 1991). We have seen that Barbara Jancar did exactly the same with Eastern European women. Eastern European women, however, are not only perceived as white, they often share the prejudice against non-whites. Corrin's advice to avoid white bias refers to perceived racial differences. But in the Eastern European context it would be more appropriate to caution the 'Western eye' to avoid ethnocentrism, which Corrin herself is guilty of as she discusses the hardships Hungarian women have to face:

> Labour-saving equipment is not readily available to the 'average' Hungarian woman. By this I meant that such necessities (certainly in households with young children) as modern, *reliable* washing machines, are expensive and difficult to obtain. Whilst many households have some form of washing machine, it is a commonplace that more time has to be spent trying to fix them or attempting to obtain some sort of part for them. They cannot be viewed in the same light as their counterparts in Western countries. Such equipment as tumble dryers are almost unheard of in most households. In terms of stocking-up on food and other household goods, the norm in many Western countries is of a household shop once a week, or even once a month, with such things as milk, eggs and even yoghurt and fruit juice being delivered by milk deliveries. Such a situation is a long way off for Hungarian shoppers. . . . The other negative feature of this daily shopping requirement is that even in the larger supermarkets it is not always possible to get everything that is required. Sometimes one shop will run out of yoghurt, or another will run out of bread and so on. (Corrin, 1990)

After maintaining that 'There is an obvious danger of imposing Western prescriptions onto different cultures' Corrin seems to come very close to doing exactly that. Based on what I know about the hardships some Canadian poor women have to face it seems to me that Corrin compares the situation of middle-class urban Western women to the 'average' Hungarian woman, who cannot be viewed in the same light as her counterparts in the West, just like the washing machines. In her discussion the 'average' Hungarian woman becomes the stereotyped Eastern European woman who is compared to the Western woman. The division between these two universal categories of 'average' Hungarian and Western woman is based on the availability of goods and services, and at this point the West comes out superior to the East.

Western Scholarship after 1989

A polyphonic discourse remains characteristic of Western feminist literature after 1989. Some authors emphasize that Eastern European women have gained a lot by the changes, other authors focus on what they have lost.

In her article about women's liberation in Poland, Bishop maintains that 'under Communism' there was a 'lack of feminist consciousness' among Eastern European women, while after the 'fall of Communism' we could see a 'mushrooming of feminist movements'. The implication is that the change from a planned economy to a market economy was paralleled by the development from a stage of fighting for women's rights to a more advanced and more desirable stage of feminist politics (Bishop, 1990). Bishop's argument contradicts Lynne Segal's conclusion in her article 'Whose Left? Socialism, Feminism and the Future'. In comparing women's emancipation in Eastern Europe and in the Western world, Segal maintains that 'despite the largest and most influential feminist movement in the world it is the American women who have seen the least overall change in the relative disadvantages of their sex' (Segal, 1991). Other authors like Barbara Einhorn seem to balance between the above positions. She states: 'many demands of Western women's movements during the 1970s were already taken for granted in many Eastern European countries'. On the other hand she points out the limitations of state socialist interpretations of Marxian theories of women's emancipation (Einhorn, 1991).

Let me reflect on two Western contributions to the collection *Gender Politics and Post-Communism* (Funk, 1993). In her article Zillah Eisenstein maintains:

> Although there is little agreement about what exactly feminism is or its appropriate role in creating post patriarchal democracy between women in the Czech and the Slovak Republics, the United Germany, or the former Soviet Union, there are feminist voices to be heard. (Eisenstein, 1993, p. 314)

To the best of my knowledge there is little agreement about 'what exactly feminism is' in North America and Western Europe as well and Eisenstein is well aware of the differences between Western feminists. If she can accept the diversity of feminisms in the West, why does she presuppose that there has to be an agreement about it in Eastern Europe? Most importantly why can she not imagine that feminism in the East could take a new form in these countries? What counts as 'feminist voices' that are heard in Eastern Europe is apparently defined in Western terms. Eisenstein might be willing to give Eastern European women a choice between versions of feminism established in the West but anything else does not count.

Nanette Funk wrote the concluding article to the collection. She starts with a response to Slavenka Drakulic, a writer from Zagreb, who made some critical comments about Western feminists after receiving Nanette Funk's invitation to write about women in former Yugoslavia. Funk feels that these comments are not only against her personally, but against all Western women. As an editor of a collection about and by Eastern European women this is what Funk has to say in defence of Western women:

> First, Slavenka Drakulic's comments reflect the tension arising from the structural power and economic imbalances between Eastern and Western women and the societies of which they are part. In this particular case that imbalance means that publishing in the West potentially brings greater recognition and financial benefits than publishing in the East, and that some Western women will have greater access to that publishing world than most Eastern women. *Paradoxically, the opposite is true in this case; this publishing project gave a voice to post-communist women, and did not speak for them. Nor is it true that Western women generally, even professional women, have such ready access to publishing.* (Funk, 1993, p. 319, emphasis added)

Nevertheless, within a year after Drakulic published her book, Funk finds access to publishing her response in a collection in which Drakulic, a 'post-communist woman', is given a voice. I do not want to deny Funk's right to respond. However, I believe that in this particular case she does not acknowledge her power, neither does she tell her audience her location in terms of her interests and her loyalties.

Many white feminists became active in helping women of colour of 'Third World' women in their struggle against racism. However, only a few are ready to acknowledge, as did Ann Russo, that we benefit from whiteness (Russo, 1991). We can draw some parallels here with some Western feminists' approaches to Eastern Europe. Funk stubbornly takes issue with Drakulic in defence of Western women. Funk is willing to give voice to 'post-communist' women, but she is unwilling to accept that even the fact that she is able to give voice to them and not the other way around is a statement made from the position of power. To be sure, being Western by itself does not guarantee one's privileged position. Similarly, being white by itself does not guarantee privilege unless white signifies privilege within a racist context. The superiority of the West is assured in several ways. For example the dominance of the English language allows English-speakers easier access to resources as well as to publishing.

Looking at my own situation, as an immigrant woman in Canada I belong to an underprivileged group of Canadian society. Nevertheless, I enjoy certain privileges. Part of these privileges are rooted in the education I obtained in my native country which allowed me to go to university. Part of my privileges, however, are related to the fact that I am a student in a major North American metropolis. Let me unpack this statement: as long as I speak only my native tongue, Hungarian, I have access to a much smaller academic community than with English. All major conferences accept English as an official language and even within Hungary native Hungarians make an effort to present their papers in English.

The dominance of English also allows English-speakers greater access to the academic community worldwide. Works of Polish, Czech, or Russian scholars are more likely to be translated into English than into Hungarian. Also if we meet at an international conference we are most likely to communicate in English. Similar advantages arise if one tries to publish an article. Of course the dominance of the English language is intimately linked to the history of imperialism. It does not matter whether I agree or disagree with white supremacist practices, I benefit from the fact that I am white. Similarly no matter how critical I am of colonialism and American imperialism, I benefit from the fact that I speak the language of the rulers.

Funk's reaction to the comments of Drakulic raises the question: to what extent do writers who are less well established than Slavenka Drakulic have access to publication if they have something critical to say about Westerners?

The Non-Western Response to Western Feminism

The events of 1989 fundamentally challenged the dominant discourse of former Eastern European regimes. The shift cannot be compared with what happens in countries in North America or Western Europe after electing a new government. Political and economic institutions which had existed for decades had been abolished and new ones were established to re-orient the whole region from centrally planned economy to market economy. The models for the new institutions came from Western Europe and North America. Would-be politicians, managers, or other professionals, who used to be trained in Eastern European universities, are now flocking to get their education in North America or Western Europe. We have also seen how the name of the city of Leningrad was changed back to St Petersburg, just as streets that were named after communist heroes were changed back to the names of old saints. These two examples also parallel the two main political directions presently existing in Eastern Europe: imitating Western liberal democracies with the economic limitations given in Eastern Europe, or turning to nationalism, possibly to neo-fascism and totalitarianism.

In Hungary the changes occurred in a relatively peaceful manner. In the 1990 election none of the parties had won enough votes to form a majority government. The three parties that built a coalition government holding over 60 per cent of the seats were labelled as 'centrist' in the media. Soon enough ultra-conservative, anti-semitic nationalists emerged from the right wing of the main governing party (MDF). Some commentators interpreted it as a rise of neo-fascism, especially in the light of right-wing racist violence elsewhere in the region. Similarly to other Eastern European countries, there have been demonstrations against right-wing nationalism in Hungary. As a result the right-wing group stamped with the name of Istvan Csurka became isolated and finally in 1993 excluded from the governing party. This, however, does not mean that the threat of neo-fascism is over. Activists and scholars concerned about women's issues have to build their alliances, strategies and their theories within this political environment. Their activities are also determined by the political directions dominating in Hungary. As I maintained earlier, Eastern and Western not only signify geographical locations but also refer to differing political environments within which women can organize and theorize. These political spaces have a controlling effect on what people do within them. Given the alternatives open to women in Eastern Europe we can anticipate that there will be a continuing pressure to accept the hegemony of Western feminist discourses.

I do not argue that feminist theories are useless or should be avoided by Eastern European scholars who try to find new theoretical tools to analyze women's lives in their countries. Some feminist theories helped me a lot to understand more about women's situation in Eastern Europe. Neither do I deny the liberatory potential of feminism. I argue, however, that feminist scholars who perceive knowledge produced in the West to be superior to that produced by non-Westerners should be challenged. For the sake of my argument I will call this type of feminist 'Western supremacists'. We have seen examples of this approach within Western scholarship on Eastern European women. Similarly to Audre Lorde's article 'The Master's Tools Will Never Dismantle the Master's House' (Lorde, 1984) we can argue that it is highly unlikely that 'Western supremacist' feminism will be challenged from within.

Before 1989 there had been little dialogue between Western feminist scholarship and Eastern European scholars analyzing women's issues within their countries. Critical approaches like Ferge's outburst against Western feminism were primarily meant for an Eastern European audience and were hardly ever read by Western feminists. After 1989 Eastern European scholars committed to women's emancipation saw Western feminist theories as the alternative to the old discredited (although I would argue often misinterpreted) Marxist theory about the woman question.

The case is somewhat different in the literature about 'Third World Women'. Scholars such as Chandra Mohanty and Marnia Lazreg are familiar with various feminist approaches and especially with various approaches to analyzing the lives of non-Western women. The discrepancies they discovered between the concepts and categories created by some Western feminists and the real life experiences of many non-Western women have led them to write critical works that I would consider real challenges to 'Western supremacist' feminist theories (Lazreg, 1988; Mohanty 1991).

In Western Europe and North America the collapse of Eastern European state socialism was interpreted as a victory of capitalism, which weakened any attempt from the left to challenge the dominant liberal discourse. Presently challenges to the status quo are more likely to come from feminist, anti-racist, or environmental movements than from the labour movement or left radicals. Western authors writing on Eastern European women continue to be driven by politically diverse motives, but there seems to be little if any real challenge to the notion that knowledge produced in the West — or within Western frameworks — about women's situation in Eastern Europe is superior to whatever is produced from other perspectives.

References

ADAMIK, M. (1991) 'Hungary: A Loss of Rights?', *Feminist Review*, no. 39 (Winter).
ADAMIK, M. (1993) 'Feminism and Hungary', in FUNK, N. (Ed.) *Gender Politics and Post-Communism*, Routledge.
BISHOP, B. (1990) 'From Women's Rights to Feminist Politics: The Developing Struggle of Women's Liberation in Poland', *Monthly Review*, no. 42, November.
BOLLOBAS, E. (1993) ' "Totalitarian Lib": The Legacy of Communism for Hungarian Women', in FUNK, N. (Ed.) *Gender Politics and Post-Communism*, Routledge.
CORRIN, C. (1990) 'The Situation of Women in Hungarian Society', in DEACON, B. and SZALAI, J. (Eds) *Social Policy in the New Eastern Europe*, Avebury, Gower, pp.

179–91 (originally a paper for Social Policy and Socialism Conference, Leeds, April 1988).
EINHORN, B. (1991) 'Where Have All the Women Gone? Women and the Women's Movement in East and Central Europe', *Feminist Review*, no. 39 (Winter).
EISENSTEIN, Z. (1993) 'Eastern European Male Democracies: A Problem of Unequal Equality', in FUNK, N. (Ed.) *Gender Politics and Post-Communism*, Routledge.
FEMINIST NETWORK (1991–1993) *Noszemely* (Hungarian Feminist Newsletter), nos. 1–3.
FERGE, Z. (1983) 'Valtozik-e a nok helyzete?' ('Is the Situation of Women Changing?') in OLAJOS, A. (Ed.) *Tanulmanyok a noi munkarol (Studies about Women's Work)*, Budapest, Kossuth Konyvkiado.
FUNK, N. (Ed.) (1993) *Gender Politics and Post-Communism*, Routledge.
HUNGARIAN WOMEN'S ASSOCIATION (1991) Programme and Activities (unpublished).
HUNGARIAN WOMEN'S ASSOCIATION (1992) *On the Association of Hungarian Women* (pamphlet).
JANCAR, B. (1978) *Woman under COMMUNISM*, Baltimore and London, Johns Hopkins University Press.
JUNG, N. (1992) 'Importing Feminism to Eastern Europe?', paper presented at the 1992 ISSEI Conference in Aalborg, Denmark.
KONCZ, K. (1982) *Nok a munka vilagaban (Women in the World of Work)*, Budapest, Magyar Nok Orszagos Tanacsa Kossuth Kiado.
KONCZ, K. (1990) 'Nok a politika szinpadan' ('Women on the Political Stage'), *Aula*, no. 4, Budapest.
LAPIDUS, G. (1978) *Women in Soviet Society*, Berkeley and Los Angeles, University of California Press.
LAZREG, M. (1988) 'Feminism and Difference: The Perils of Writing as a Woman on Women in Algeria', *Feminist Studies*, 14/1.
LORDE, A. (1984) *Sister Outsider*, The Crossing Press Feminist Series.
MAMONOVA, T. (1989) *Russian Women's Studies*, New York, Pergamon Press.
MARKUS, M. (1976) 'Women and Work', in HEGEDUS, A., HELLER, A., MARKUS, M. and VAJDA, M. *The Humanization of Socialism: Writings of the Budapest School*, London, Allison and Busby.
MOHANTY, C. et al. (Eds) (1991) *Third World Women and Feminism*, Indiana University Press.
MOLYNEUX, M. (1990) 'The Women Question in the Age of Perestroika', *New Left Review*, no. 176, September/October.
OLAJOS, A. (1983) *Tanulmanyok a noi munkarol (Studies about Women's Work)*, Budapest, Kossuth Konyvkiado.
RUSSO, ANN (1991) 'We Cannot Live Without Our Lives', in MOHANTY, C. et al. (Eds) *Third World Women and Feminism*, Indiana University Press.
SAID, E. (1978) *Orientalism*, New York, Random House.
SAS, J. (1984) *Noies nok es ferfias ferfiak (Feminine Women and Masculine Men)*, Budapest, Akademia Kiado.
SEGAL, L. (1991) 'Whose Left? Socialism, Feminism and the Future', *New Left Review*, no. 185, Jan/Feb.
SWAIN, N. (1989) 'Hungary's Socialist Project in Crisis', *New Left Review*, no. 176, July-August.
SZEGVARI, N.K. (1981) *Ut a nok egyenjogusagahoz (The Way to Women's Emancipation)*, Budapest, Kossuth Konyvkiado.
SZELENYI, K. and SZELENYI, S. (1991) 'The Vacuum in Hungarian Politics: Classes and Parties', *New Left Review*, no. 187, May-June.
TOTH, O. (1993) 'No Envy, No Pity' in FUNK, N. (Ed.) *Gender Politics and Post-Communism*, Routledge.

Chapter 12

Relations Among Women: Using the Group to Unite Theory and Experience

Wendy Hollway

Introduction

In the academic year 1992/3 on the Bradford University MA in Women's Studies, an optional course was offered, in addition to the main curriculum, which aimed to help women to learn about women relating together in a group, through understanding the experiences of the course group. The group was scheduled to meet with a facilitator for one and a quarter hours every week for a term. In the event a core of about ten women from the course attended regularly throughout the first term and decided to continue. The group met weekly throughout the academic year, with the same facilitator — myself — attending whenever possible.[1]

The initial idea had surfaced the previous year when, partly as a result of an unusually large intake, many students, when convened in the full group for certain parts of the course, felt ill at ease and inhibited from contributing to the topic. Many women felt that it was difficult to find a place on the course for their relevant experience, as women, and this felt particularly unacceptable given the history of Women's Studies and the aims of the Bradford course, which follow the principle that the personal is political and the traditions of consciousness-raising and deprivatizing women's experiences. Moreover, fears abounded that their own choices and lifestyles would be found unacceptable to women who were 'different': dimensions of difference among the women, based, among other themes, on 'race', class, sexuality, age, marital and motherhood status, were providing channels for anxiety and inhibitions which were operating to silence many women. An experiential group was offered initially as a forum for addressing this issue which also threatened to constrain the kind of learning opportunities which the course could provide.

The group's aims were set out in the first session as:

- to help to create a well-functioning social group for the course which would provide a good context for learning and exploration;

- to provide understanding of social relations amongst a group of women; their similarities and differences, attachments and conflicts; and to help women to learn about their own part in the group;

- to help to integrate personal experience and academic learning.

This paper presents an account of some of the themes raised in the recent, year-long group. It analyzes women's relations among women, based on the process of working with some of the difficult as well as positive feelings which emerged. The paper uses notes kept by the facilitator and incorporates the findings of an evaluation which was conducted as a course project. It concludes by considering the merits of such a provision on Women's Studies courses.

Four Themes

The themes of such a group are difficult to summarize, and those of us who participated would undoubtedly pick out different aspects. Partly because of my distinct role as facilitator, I had a different agenda from the group members who predominantly saw the primary task of the group as one of support. Their purpose complemented my aim to explore and analyze the dynamics of a group of women in order for them — and me — to understand more about wider relations among women and also to function more effectively as a learning group and therefore enhance their experience of the course.

The linked themes of similarities and differences and dealing with conflict were already salient for me, having recently been a member of a group of women training as psychodynamic psychotherapists.[2] Moreover the short previous year's pilot group had impressed upon me how difficult it was for an all-women Women's Studies group to live out the dominant notions of 'sisterhood'. I will always remember one woman's comment at the first group meeting. She said that she had been removing her wedding ring every Wednesday morning because she was afraid of what other women would think of her if they knew she was married.

For me, this comment — and other contributions which followed it and which echoed fears from every quarter about not being accepted by other women — raises fundamental and important issues about 'sisterhood'. Despite the more recent recognition of differences within feminism, notably those of race, sexuality and class, certain ideas run very deep: that women will relate together successfully; will be able to share personal experiences; will empathize, give support and like each other. The notion of sisterhood picked up on pre-feminist ideas about women's interpersonal facility and caring, ideas which were only ever part of the story.

Politically the social divisions of race, class and sexuality have been salient and these themes surfaced in the group. However, in this piece I want to focus on some of the relational psychodynamics which I believe underpin the experience of all social differences, including the ostensibly more minor dimensions of difference among the women on the course: mothers and non-mothers; partnered and single; younger and older; those recently academically qualified and those not; those on the full-time course and those on the part-time course; the MA students and the few PhD students who followed the course; foreign and British students; those whose first language was English and those for whom it was not; those who worked on the Feminist Archive in their spare time and those who did not; those who met up for coffee and those who did not; those who attended the group and those who did not. The desire to be included and the anxiety and resentment about feeling excluded is a common theme that ran through these differences which, particularly at the beginning of the group, surfaced with strong feeling.[3]

The idea that women are good at support is a pervasive and attractive one, but in practice is fraught with difficulties which are not necessarily produced by the failures of actual women to respond in the desired manner, but as much by the fears and fantasies which make it difficult for women to ask for support, to show themselves as needing help rather than to be the helpers, the copers, the 'mothers'. And so the process of turning a notional support group into one that felt really supportive was not a simple matter, but required the negotiation of boundaries, the testing of trust, the experience of difficult differences successfully explored, the containment of distress.[4] One other difficulty was maybe more surprising: the difficulty of sharing good news, of disclosing happiness or success, appeared to be even more threatening than sharing problems. I shall discuss this below in terms of the fears that emerged of other women's envy.

The significance of these themes emerged at certain stages in the history of the group. They did not remain static and there was a striking development of confidence that the group could transform such problems through articulating them, experiencing the difficulties and not only surviving but feeling changed. By the end of the course, the group was working well as a support group.[5] However, it was acknowledged that their investment in its supportive function had made them reluctant to explore any areas of conflict in the group.

I shall explore a further theme, that of power difference and authority in the group, with particular reference to my role as facilitator. This theme is raised in the next section, where I detail what kind of a group this was, and where it derived its principles and structures. The following three sections are organized around the three themes that I have outlined above: inclusion/exclusion; asking for support and fear of envy.

An Experiential Women's Group

For most women on the course, the dominant idea of a group is the consciousness-raising group, with its principles of using women's experience, deprivatizing it through sharing, and making the personal political. From my side, I also applied principles from my earlier experience of facilitating 'T' groups ('T' for training, not for therapy) and my recent experience of being a member of a women's group (see note 2). From the start I imposed a basic structure on the group which derived from these backgrounds and differed from women's consciousness-raising groups. First, the group adhered to a fairly strict time structure. We met for a specific time and at the end of that time, I would get up and go. Second, my role was different from a group member. It involved facilitating others' explorations and understanding of the process, through comment, interpretation and containment of anxiety. It meant not succumbing to the temptation or to the pressures to share my own experience; to become one of them, to camouflage my difference. At the same time, I was not responsible for being a leader in the traditional senses either of controlling or initiating the group's activities.

For example, in the first week, when most women in the group were still unfamiliar with my role as I had described it, anxiety about the size of the group and doubts about my role led to a question whether they could use the time slot for smaller groups instead. My reply was 'if enough of you decide not to come to this group, it won't happen'. In other words I was not going to provide them with a decision, but was reminding them that they had a choice whether to come or to organize something else. At the beginning of a session therefore I did not start off the discussion but sat quietly and only contributed when I had something relevant to say which was consistent with my role; that is about the process and significance of the group's interactions. This was not a popular position to adopt. Many group members wanted me to be either a teacher in the usual way[6] or to join in as one of them. This would have been consistent with the democratic and egalitarian principles of consciousness-raising groups, but in doing so would have camouflaged my difference — as a teacher/tutor, rather than a student, on the course and as someone with expertise in group processes — and would have undermined my capacity to comment on and interpret the group processes. This clear and consistent definition of a different role was the first difference presented to the group and it is not surprising that there was some resistance to it.

Women's consciousness-raising groups are structured along egalitarian lines in order to change and challenge hierarchies which are seen as disempowering some women. The aims of this group included exploring difference when it arose as a barrier to effective group relating. This meant learning about feelings about difference and how to deal with them. My institutional position meant that inevitably I had power of a different kind from the students. Since the institutional reality cannot be changed, it was appropriate that in the group we could work with their feelings about the power and authority of another woman and get to a point where that difference can be used constructively. I wanted to be a model of the capacity to relate as women across a significant difference, recognized as power, in a way which did not involve diluting my authority and expertise, disempowering them, or disempowering me.

Isobel Conlon, writing about the experience of being a woman facilitator in a mixed therapy group, argues that, in the early stages of an experiental therapy group, where the facilitator's authority is a primary dynamic, defences against either or both parts of the dual nature of the mother's power (frustrating and satisfying, 'good' and 'bad' in the infant's fantasy world) can result in denial of her authority, or transference of ideas of nurturance to the group. Either way she is left depleted:

> The female therapist needs to be viewed by the group as individuating successfully; as someone who can be competent

without pretending she is not, who can survive hostile attacks and who does not feel guilty about having something for herself. (Conlon, 1991, pp. 196–7).

The idea of a facilitator who comments and interprets, especially one who does not say anything at the beginning of the session, conjures up notions of a judgmental and off-putting authority figure.[7] There is extra pressure on a woman authority figure to be a caring mother figure whose capacity to say anything challenging or uncomfortable is therefore undermined. Conlon concludes that 'the denial of women's power and of their ability to abuse it has meant that women have been ascribed restrictive roles, causing some aspects of them to be hidden away or projected on to men' (1991, p. 187).

A further reason for keeping to a clear-cut definition of a facilitator's role is to do with the anxieties which this kind of work tends to provoke, at least initially. This was not a therapy group. However, an experiential group invariably raises the spectre of personal disclosures of distress. By their wish to provide support for individual women to bring problems of a personal nature, women were expressing a need for a group which could tolerate and contain difficulties. Of course this provoked anxiety. The difference in my role enabled the group to feel safer than if I had been one of them. This took some time to establish and obviously depended on how I actually handled difficult feelings in the group. After a while, however, it was generally agreed that they could venture into deeper waters when I was present because of the shared feeling that I would 'contain' the distress and anxiety; would not panic, nor let it get out of hand; would know what to do.[8] In fact their increasing confidence in handling distress led to the group functioning very successfully as a support group in my absence.

Like the role difference, the notion of interpretation is also a problematic one given the culture of the women's movement where 'women's experience' is a cornerstone both theoretically and methodologically. For democratic reasons — to avoid exploitation of experience — and maybe also to avoid conflicts about who has the power to frame it, women's experience has often been treated reverentially. I have argued elsewhere that 'experience' generally needs to be seen in the perspective of unconscious processes which will mean avoidances, denials and displacements and the conformity of accounts to acceptable themes (Hollway, 1989, pp. 42–6). Interpretation, for me, is premised on the concept of unconscious defence mechanisms through which unacceptable or uncomfortable feelings, ideas or impulses are kept at bay. When interpretations touch on such feelings, however lightly, there is bound to be resistance and there may be denial. This does not mean that the interpretation is wrong (though it is important to bear in mind that it could be). The group, or individuals within it, will use what interpretations are useful to it at the time. Timing and evidence are important in being able to use and not abuse interpretation. Examples of interpretation and comment will be contained in the following sections. When interpretation works, it can illuminate the processes in depth. As one group member wrote at the end: 'thank you very much for... how you enabled us so often to look at what was *really* going on'.

Inclusion and Exclusion

Early on, one group member (who was a PhD student) announced that she was organizing an informal, open, weekly seminar. She took care to give information in such a way that the arrangement could be seen to include anyone who wanted to participate. In fact, however, because of the timing, it automatically excluded part-timers and there was the additional problem of the desirable size of such a group. Her initial handling of the announcement seemed to demonstrate that she was uneasy about the potential exclusivity of such a group. Rather than acknowledge this, she became involved in a contradiction, between an entirely open group and one which kept numbers down. Later, when I had pointed out the apparent difficulty with which she was faced, and in the context of other preceding examples which meant that the group was aware of the issues about being included or excluded, women were able to express their feelings about this small seminar group: wanting to belong, feeling intellectually inadequate; feeling excluded (despite the invitation); feeling envious of those who were obviously 'in'; feeling resentful. The topic developed to acknowledge the wishes of many women to make friends on the course and how to create those opportunities. For some women, the result of the exploration was to make it easier to establish links with others. When a group has survived the expression of such feelings, it becomes easier subsequently for the issue of difference not to be suffused with issues of exclusion and the fear of conflict. When a similar issue arises, some group members are able to be aware of their feelings and their articulation feels less unsafe. Other women identify with these and become more in touch with their reactions on subsequent occasions.

Support

During one period in the group, one member was frequently distressed and crying. She had been the first to cry in the group and she was admired for her emotional openness. She also elicited protective, warm, maternal feelings from other women, particularly some of the older ones. Although this was not experienced as a problem, after a while I felt that it indicated a group dynamic: was she really the only one experiencing distress or wanting support? If not, what consequences did it have — for her and others — that she was the only one (at that time) to be positioned in that way? In my view, there was a splitting going on, between distress, needing support and vulnerability on the one hand, and caring, mothering and coping on the other. This approach assumes that any set of feelings do not simply belong to an individual, though they are experienced as such, but are part of a relational dynamic.[9] Those doing the support in this instance may be projecting their own distress on to the one woman, where they can relate to it at a safe distance. The evidence for such an interpretation only suggests itself if that position in the group becomes recurrent and no one else takes it up, and also if the distress begins to appear as if it is over and above the real circumstances of the distressed woman.

Later, there was some evidence for my supposition. The woman in question did not turn up to the group, having been in tears in the coffee bar. Several women were worried about her, and spent some time considering if she was alright and what should be done. I pointed out that they were talking about distress that was 'out there', after which another woman talked about her own feelings: what a mess her life sometimes appeared to be in, how she talked about it calmly, as if she was fine, and kept her needy feelings at a distance by support to others. Yet she wanted to be able to cry openly like that other woman. After that several other women talked about their own distressed feelings in terms of their worry that if they started letting it out, they felt they'd never stop. To look after those feelings in someone else therefore kept their own at bay and in control. This tendency was heavily reinforced by the caring roles that most of these women occupied in their lives, notably as mothers, but also in paid employment. After this, expressions of needs for support in the group became more fluid. Towards the end it was possible even for those stalwarts who seemed to have calm and uncomplicated lives to ask for a share.

Fear of Envy

Some difficult issues regarding women friends' envy first came up through comments about the group members' outside friends. For example, when one woman was under strain at home because her husband was being made redundant, one friend — one she felt she had supported loyally over the years — responded in terms of 'I've got too many problems of my own to have time for yours'. In the group, her response to being asked how she felt about this was 'I don't know'. I commented that I found myself feeling angry on her behalf. She then acknowledged that she had felt angry, but had not wanted to risk the friendship. We explored the inequalities of support in friendship. One woman was reminded of a friend who was very supportive when she was having a hard time and cannot handle the relationship now that she is happy. It felt to her as if the friend was envious of her happiness. That account reminded another woman of how she had not been able to talk about her degree education with a friend of hers, who was unqualified. She felt that the friend envied her educational success; to the point that when the friend knew that the degree results were due, she did not ask her about them. This woman too felt resentful, but could not express it for fear of risking the friendship. So they remain 'best friends' but talk about the friend's life. She cannot share a large chunk of hers. In the group we talked about these issues in terms of envy, avoidance of conflict and the difficulty of expressing neediness.

The fear of something similar happening had also surfaced in the group. In the context of how much pressure she was feeling in her job, one woman mentioned that she had felt unable to feel happy about some good news she had received during the week. Her cautious mention of good news looked as if it was not going to be picked up and so I commented that good news seemed not to be able to be shared as easily as difficulties. Given that opening, she hesitantly said that she had got her degree result, that it was a good degree, an upper second. She was still not displaying any feelings about this success, but with further positive comment from me and recognition from the group, for the first time since receiving the news, she acknowledged its importance to her. This enabled her to get in touch with the history of her struggle to become qualified and to relate it in such a way that the whole group was engaged and moved. It was a privilege to hear an open, heartfelt account of this kind; open because it was safe to express powerful feelings in the group. The effect of such an account is generally, I think, to dissolve any anxieties or fantasies about difference, based for example on race, class or sexuality, which feed on lack of knowledge about someone. An account spoken with feeling makes it possible to identify, despite differences in experience. Such moments reflect the best traditions of women's consciousness-raising groups.

Towards the end of the third term the group provided a striking contrast to dynamics fed by difference and fear of envy. The woman who had often been distressed (or, to put it another way, had for a time provided a location for the distressed feelings of the group) arrived looking radiantly happy. With apparently no inhibitions, and at considerable length (previously in the group there had often been worries about taking up too much 'air time'), she told the group how she had ended her relationship and met someone else. There was little need for comment by the others: the atmosphere of the group was one in which her happiness could be shared quietly and generously despite the different positions that many other woman were in.

Conclusions

An experiential group can help women to understand the difficult as well as positive dynamics involved in relations among women and by doing so become more effective as a learning group, as a support group and more generally in their ability to live out notions of sisterhood in a real rather than an idealized way.

The idealization of women as supportive, caring and empathic has been possible partly through the process of locating the negative sides of these qualities in men. In an all-women group which has to work together over a sustained period, as on the MA, it is difficult to recognize the negative qualities and even more difficult to know how to deal with their effects. Yet the unconscious dynamics among women affect everything women do collaboratively. Women's Studies courses, and of course academic courses in general, have no tradition of engaging with this arena of practice. It follows that feminist academics do not necessarily have the skills to facilitate such learning. By paying considerable attention to the importance of structure and role definition, I hope that I have made clear that to facilitate such a group requires care and preferably training and experience of a psychodynamic nature. Even then it takes a while to establish its validity and some women will find it too anxiety-provoking and unfamiliar.

It may seem surprising that the group is experienced as so powerful:

powerfully threatening before it has established itself as trustworthy; powerfully nurturing when it is functioning well as a support; powerfully challenging when risks are taken to explore difficulties in the group's relations. Others' experiences act as a kind of amplification as group members identify with an aspect of what is said and memories and feelings are triggered. The group also acts as a powerful witness, such that, as one woman said:

> The group felt so powerful for me last week. The validation and acceptance were amazing — I just felt understood and recognized. In one way it might appear no different from talking to a friend about what's going on in your life, but it wasn't like that.

Notes

1 I would like to thank all the women who participated, and particularly those who kept on coming and continued to risk difficult feelings for the sake of learning more about themselves and their ways of relating.
2 The Leeds Women's Counselling and Therapy Service organized a one-year part-time Introduction to Psychotherapy course for women. Each week the course group would convene with one of the therapists as facilitator to explore the group's dynamics and our roles, as group members, in these dynamics.
3 It became apparent at the end of the year that many of those women who had chosen not to remain in the group felt very strongly about it. From their perspective it looked like a wonderful supportive group from which they had been excluded and their feelings of envy were only made the more difficult by the fact that it had been their choice not to remain. The decision whether such a group should be optional or compulsory is not clear-cut.
4 For much of the early sessions, for example, the group concentrated on confidentiality issues and whether latecomers should be allowed in, in case they interrupted something important. As one group member pointed out in the discussion of a draft of this paper, at the beginning a constant membership and group commitment were seen as essential. By the end the group easily accommodated a lot of comings and goings. While the group did not feel exclusive to its members, many of those who had chosen not to participate did feel that it became an exclusive, even an elite, group on the course.
5 Such was the value of the support group by this time that it was agreed to continue meeting after the end of the course, even though this would involve long journeys for some women.
6 There were requests after the first session that I should teach about group processes in the traditional way, through introducing relevant published material and concepts, guiding a conceptual discussion etc. My response was that I did not think that would be successful in addressing the main aim of the group.
7 I believe from my experience as a group member myself, backed by the testimony of others, that this is partly due to the projections which get applied to group facilitators.
8 The idea of containment comes from the psychotherapeutic literature, specifically Bion's idea of the carer as 'container'. In Kleinian theory, infants' overpowering and

potentially destructive feelings can be made safe if the mother (or caring figure) can hold these: that is, not be made so anxious that she rejects them and throws them back.
9 I have explored the dynamics of splitting between women and men at length in Hollway (1989).

References

CONLON, I. (1991) 'The Effect of Gender on the Role of the Female Group Conductor', *Group Analysis,* 24, pp. 187–200.
HOLLWAY, W. (1989) *Subjectivity and Method in Psychology: Gender, Meaning and Science,* London, Sage.

Notes on Contributors

Lynda Birke is a biologist in the Department of Continuing Education at the University of Warwick, where she teaches both science and Women's Studies. Her publications include *Women, Feminism and Biology* (Wheatsheaf, 1986) and, with S. Himmelweit and G. Vines, *Tomorrow's Child: Reproductive Technologies in the 90s* (Virago, 1990).

Elaine Brown is a mature student currently completing the MA in Cultural and Textual Studies at the University of Sunderland. She is about to embark on a PhD which will examine contemporary self-development manuals for women.

Kim Clancy lectures in Women's Studies and Cultural Studies at the University of Sussex. She is currently researching cultural constructions of female sexuality in Britain, in the 1960s.

Angelika Czekay is a PhD student in the Department of Theatre and Drama at the University of Wisconsin, Madison. She is currently writing her dissertation on 'Producing History/Subverting Authority — Contemporary Plays by Women in the US, Great Britain and Germany'. Her article 'Distance and Empathy: Constructing the Spectator of Annie Sprinkle's Post Porn Modernist' has recently appeared in the *Journal of Dramatic Theory and Criticism*.

Gabriele Griffin is Reader in Women's Studies at Nene College, Northampton. Together with Elaine Aston she has edited two volumes of plays by women entitled *Herstory* (Sheffield Academic Press, 1991). She is author of *Heavenly Love? Lesbian Images in Twentieth-Century*

Notes on Contributors

Women's Writing (Manchester University Press, 1993) and has edited *Outwrite: Lesbianism and Popular Culture* (Pluto, 1993), and *Difference in View: Women and Modernism* (Taylor and Francis, 1994).

Marianne Hester is a Lecturer at the University of Bristol where she teaches Social Work and Women's Studies. As an activist and academic she is concerned with the links between feminist theory, political action and women's experience. She has written about the eroticization of male dominance and violence against women; femicide and the witch-hunts in the sixteenth and seventeenth centuries, and violence against social services staff. Her publications include *Lewd Women and Wicked Witches: A Study of the Dynamics of Male Domination* (Routledge, 1992).

Wendy Hollway is a Senior Lecturer in Women's Studies in the Department of Applied Social Studies at the University of Bradford. She originally trained in psychology and did her PhD on identity and gender difference in adult couple relations. She is author of *Subjectivity and Method in Psychology: Gender, Meaning and Science* (Sage, 1990), *Work Psychology and Organisational Behaviour: Managing the Individual at Work* (Sage, 1991) and co-author of *Changing the Subject: Psychology, Social Regulation and Subjectivity* (Methuen, 1994).

Nora Jung left her native country, Hungary, in 1992 for Canada where she lives at present. She is a graduate student in the Department of Sociology of York University in Toronto. She is completing her dissertation, which focuses on Hungarian women's organizations. She has been involved with immigrant women's organizations and with shelters for abused women.

Celia Kitzinger teaches Social Psychology and Women's Studies at Loughborough University. Her books include *The Social Construction of Lesbianism* (Sage, 1987), *Heterosexuality: A* 'Feminism and Psychology' *Reader* (Sage, 1993, with Sue Wilkinson), and *Changing Our Minds: Lesbian Feminism and Psychology* (Onlywomen Press and New York University Press, 1993, with Rachel Perkins).

Jennifer Marchbank is a girls' development worker and part-time lecturer based in Central Scotland. Her interests lie in the provision of services by and for women, hence her current research on policy-making and women at the University of Strathclyde, from which her article comes.

Notes on Contributors

Janet Price lives in Liverpool where she has recently stopped working at the Liverpool School of Tropical Medicine, due to ill-health. She trained as a medical doctor, but has never practised as one. Her current interests are in disciplinary practices — both as the subject of them in relation to her illness and as they apply to her work towards a PhD on colonialism and women's health. She retains her mental sanity by writing occasional papers with Margrit Shildrick.

Jill Radford is a feminist activist, campaigner and researcher currently working at Rights of Women, a feminist legal project. She also teaches Women's Studies and Criminology for the Open University and at the University of Westminster. She has published widely in the area of sexual violence, and was co-editor, with Diana Russell, of *Femicide: The Politics of Woman-Killing* (1992). She was founding member of the British Sociological Association women's caucus Violence Against Women Study Group, and has remained an active member.

Shirin Rai teaches Politics and Women's Studies at the University of Warwick. She is author of *Resistance and Reaction: University Politics in Post-Mao China* (Harvester Wheatsheaf, 1991) and co-editor (with Hilary Pilkington and Annie Phizacklea) of *Women in the Face of Change: The Soviet Union, Eastern Europe and China* (Routledge, 1992). At present she is working on a project on 'Women and the State in the Third World'.

Becky Rosa is a 24-year-old, white, working-class lesbian. She is no longer involved in academia but works in a housing office in East London and is active in various lesbian projects. Her chapter is a lesbianized version of an undergraduate dissertation, arrived at through endless conversations with many lesbians/feminists whose ideas, enthusiasm and encouragement enabled her to finish it.

Sasha Roseneil has been a Lecturer in Sociology at the University of Leeds since 1991, and teaches courses on the sociology of gender and feminist thought. She has been involved in the establishment of a new undergraduate degree in Women's Studies at Leeds, and is a member of the Executive Committee of the Women's Studies Network (UK) Association. Her doctoral research on feminist political action at Greenham is to be published in 1994 by the Open University Press under the title *Disarming Patriarchy: The Greenham Common Women's Peace Camp*. Her current research interests include feminist politics and movements, lesbian and gay theory, and male violence in its various forms.

Notes on Contributors

Margrit Shildrick is optimistically engaged with postmodern feminist philosophy in the belief that a workable ethics can be extracted from it. She is currently completing a doctorate at the Centre for the Study of Women and Gender, University of Warwick. Around the edges she teaches medical ethics in the Department of General Practice, University of Liverpool, and moral philosophy for the Open University. She has published several articles in the field of feminism and health care/ethics, and collaborates with Janet Price whenever possible.

Ailbhe Smyth is a joint Irish/UK Editor of *Women's Studies International Forum* and Director of the Women's Education, Research and Resource Centre (WERRC) at University College, Dublin. She writes about Irish feminism (among other topics) and her publications include (as editor): *Feminism in Ireland* (1988), *Wildish Things: An Anthology of New Irish Women's Writing* (Attic Press, 1989), *The Abortion Papers: Ireland* (Attic Press, 1992), and *The Irish Women's Studies Reader* (Attic Press, 1993).

Sue Thornham has taught in schools and colleges and now lectures in Media and Cultural Studies at the University of Sunderland. She teaches courses on feminist theory and popular culture both at undergraduate and at postgraduate level, and is continuing work on Catherine Cookson and her readers, begun in the chapter for this book.

Angela Werndly is a mature student current completing the MA in Cultural and Textual Studies at the University of Sunderland.

Sue Wilkinson is Senior Lecturer in Health Studies Research at the University of Hull, and editor of *Feminism and Psychology: An International Journal,* and of the book series *Gender and Psychology: Feminist and Critical Perspectives* (Sage). Her books include *Feminist Social Psychology* (Open University Press, 1986) and *Heterosexuality: A Feminism and Psychology Reader* (Sage, 1993, with Celia Kitzinger).

Index

abortion 47, 62, 165
  of gay foetus 191
  Ireland 21, 26, 30
  Up the Junction 138-9
academe 2, 4, 5, 24, 187
  Rights of Women 56-7
  Women's Studies 41-3, 183
activism 3-5, 11-12, 423, 183
  Ireland 11, 30
  Rights of Women 53, 56-7
  Women's Liberation Movement 43, 46, 47, 49
age 3, 14, 44-5, 50, 211
agency of women 3, 5, 124-5
  in performance 74, 96-7, 98, 102
Ahluwahlia, Kiranjit 55
anatomy 124, 156-77
Aristotle 165, 167
Association of Hungarian Women 198-9, 200

Barstow, Stan 128, 129
biology 124-5
  anatomy 156-77
  gender identity 189-92
  women's health 158, 161, 177, 188
bisexuals 82, 84
black women 41, 44
  see also race and racism
bookshop 47
Bornstein, Kate 74, 94, 100-1, 102
Boy George 85
brains 189-91
branding with negative symbols 61, 66-7
British National Party 41, 48

bureaucratic culture 65

Campaign for Access to Donor Insemination (CADI) 55
capitalism 51, 196, 209
Cartland, Barbara 143
celibacy 80, 81
child benefit 3, 4, 50
childcare 12, 52, 61-7
childminders 63
child sex abuse 52, 75, 109
chromosomes 190-1
class 11, 82, 110
  Hungary 197-8, 204
  Ireland 28
  Up the Junction 127-40
  Rights of Women 50, 51, 54, 55
  virgin heterosexuality 81
  Women's Liberation Movement 43, 44
  Women's Studies group 211, 213, 219
  see also middle class; working class
CLAWS (Clause 28) 55
colonialism 11, 24-5, 33, 207
communism 200, 202, 205, 208
consciousness-raising 51, 183
  Women's Liberation Movement 44-6, 48-9
  Women's Studies group 211, 214-15, 220
Cookson, Catherine 124, 142-54
cross-dressing 92-3
  see also transvestites
Cruise 48
custody of children 47, 49, 51, 118
  lesbians 49, 51, 118

227

Index

Czech and Slovak Republics 201

Dail Eireann 30
Delaney, Shelagh 127, 128
delaying tactics 61, 64–5
delegitimization 66–7
Democratic Federation of Hungarian Women (MNDSZ) 196
deprivation issue 62, 64
Derry Women's Aid 19
difference 5–6, 11–12, 23, 24, 76, 183
   Rights of Women 52, 55
   Up the Junction 123–4, 131–40
   Women's Liberation Movement 44–6
   Women's Studies group 211–21
   see also power difference
disability 5, 45, 81
   Rights of Women 51, 54, 55
discrimination 51, 185–8
   lesbians 50
distress 213, 216, 218, 220
divorce 49
domination by men 200
   heterosexuality 73, 76, 82, 86, 88
Drabble, Margaret 127
Duffy, Maureen 127
Dunn, Nell *Up the Junction* 123, 127–40

Eastern European women 6, 184, 195–209
ecofeminists 48, 188–9
education 4, 50, 53–4, 62, 64, 115
   Eastern Europe 207
   Ireland 30
   see also Women's Studies
emancipation of women 196–202, 205
employment of women 50, 52
   see also working women
English language 206–7
Enlightenment 2, 160, 161, 167
environmental concerns 40
   see also ecofeminists
envy 214, 219, 220
equality 52, 59, 62, 64–5, 201–2
eroticization of subordination 56, 82
ethnicity 5, 11, 23, 28
   see also race and racism
evolutionary theory 189
exclusion 22, 42, 184, 213, 214, 217

family 1, 2, 4, 18, 21, 47
   gay 114, 118
   love 108–12
fascism 40, 48, 208
fears 184
   middle class 123, 130, 140
   violence 16–18, 20

Women's Studies group 211, 213–14, 217, 219, 220
femicide 40, 41, 49
Feminist Network (Hungary) 199
femocrat in local authority 61–7
fertility control 47, 55, 158
   see also reproduction; reproductive techniques
fetishization 74, 86, 94
films 127–9, 131, 132, 136, 138
first-wave feminism 75, 77
Fowler, Bridget 143
friendship, female 45, 74, 108–9, 111–19, 184
   Cookson novels 150–1, 152, 153
   lesbian 115–16
   love 109, 111–12
   Up the Junction 132
   Women's Studies 217, 219
fucking with gender 73, 83, 84–5, 86
funding 42, 52, 53–4, 63

Galen 162, 165, 167
gay men 54, 95, 100
   biology 190–2
   families 114, 118
   marriage 114–15
   power differences 82
   queer heterosexuality 84, 85, 86–7
   see also homosexuality
gender-bending 85
gender identity 73
   biology 189–92
   heterosexuality 83–5, 6
   performance 74, 92–103
genes 190–1
Gingerbread 63
good news 213–14, 219–20

hermaphrodites 85, 100–1
heterosexuality 22, 44–5
   abusive 75–7, 79, 88
   compulsory 75–7, 79, 81, 85, 88, 107–19
   critique 5, 73, 75–7, 87–9
   domination by men 73, 76, 82, 86, 88
   institutionalized 4, 75
   oppression of women 49, 73, 74, 76, 78–80, 82
   power differences 76, 81–2
   queer 73–4, 77, 82–7, 88
   Up the Junction 127–40
   virgin 73, 77–82, 83, 87–88
Hoggart, Richard
   the Uses of Literacy 128, 130
homophobia 40, 54, 56, 192

228

Index

love and friendship 109, 114, 118
Up the Junction 137
homosexuality 55, 129, 190–1
see also gay men; lesbians
hormones 161, 189, 190
housing 3, 79
Hungary 184, 195–209
hysteria 161, 174

imperialism 24–5
Incest Survivors 47
inclusion 184, 213, 214, 217
International Women's Day 22
internment 18, 19
Ireland 11, 12, 17–34
issue suppression 12, 62–4

Jellicoe, Ann 128

Kerwick, Lavinia (raped) 32
Kilkenny case 27

lack of sympathy (WIIs) 65–6
Lassell, Margaret 130–1
law 46, 50–1
 rape judgment 32
Lennox, Annie 85
lesbians 5, 6, 41, 73–4, 108, 133
 biology 190–2
 challenge to heterosexuality 107, 110, 117–19
 child custody 49, 51, 118
 donor insemination 55
 feminist scientist 185–92
 friendship 115–16
 gender identity 100–1
 heterosexuality critique 75, 77, 88
 Ireland 21–2
 love 110–13
 monogamy 74, 113–15
 power differences 82
 queer heterosexuality 84, 85–7
 Rights of Women 50, 52, 54–5
 virgin heterosexuality 78, 81
 Women's Liberation Movement 43, 44–5
Lessing, Doris 128, 130
local authority 11–12, 53–4
 childcare 61–7
London, Jack 130, 136
love 108–13

Madonna 85
marginalization of women's issues 4, 59–67
marriage 44, 81, 158, 211, 213
 Cookson novels 146

gay 114–115
love 108, 110
rape 50, 75
Up the Junction 128–9, 132, 135
see also monogamy
Marxism 196–8, 200, 202, 205
masturbation 95, 97
memory-bearing women 40, 41, 42, 50
menstrual cycle 159, 161, 167, 174
middle class 14, 44–5, 110
 Ireland 20, 24
 Up the Junction 123, 127, 130–1, 140
 see also class; working class
monogamy 5, 74, 107–19
 lesbian 74, 113–15
 Up the Junction 128, 132

National Childminding Association 63
National Front 48
nationalism 4, 11, 208
 Ireland 11, 17, 22–3, 29–31, 33
neo-fascism 208
 see also fascism
networking 47, 48, 50

O'Brien, Edna 127, 131
oppression of women 11, 108, 109
 heterosexuality 49, 73, 74, 76, 78–80, 82
 Ireland 24, 29, 34
 lesbians 117, 118
 Rights of Women 51, 54–7
 Women's Liberation Movement 40, 45, 46, 48
Osborne, John 128, 131

paramilitaries 18–21
Partition 24, 28
patriarchy 1–2, 4–5, 15, 176, 183
 academe 187
 gender identity 92
 heterosexuality 77, 78–80, 89
 Ireland 18, 22, 24, 30
 marginalization of WIIs 59, 61, 64, 67
 monogamy 118
 Rights of Women 51, 54, 56
 science 187
 Women's Liberation Movement 40, 41, 49
performance arts 5, 74, 91–103
Perry, Janice 74, 94, 97–100, 102
Popular Front (Hungary) 196–7
pornography 85–7, 94–7
 Ireland 20
post-communism 195, 201, 206
postmodernism 73–44, 82–5, 87
post-mortem examinations 162

229

Index

poststructuralism 46, 73, 92–4
poverty 15, 41, 81
   Ireland 18, 22, 28
power
   difference 12, 16, 48, 74, 76, 81–2
   Eastern Europe and West 184, 206
   heterosexuality 76, 81–2
   knowledge 157, 176
   nondecision-making 60, 67
   Rights of Women 51, 54
   Women's Liberation Movement 44–6, 49
   Women's Studies group 214, 215–16, 220–1
pregnancy *see* reproduction
premenstrual tension 161
prostitution 55, 129, 130
psychodynamics 212, 213, 220

queer heterosexuality 73–4, 77, 82–7, 88
queer theory 74, 81–7

race and racism 5–6, 11, 14, 23, 40–1 81
   equal opportunities 64–5
   Ireland 25–8
   power difference in heterosex 76, 82
   Rights of Women 50–2, 54–6
   Up the Junction 127, 131, 137–8, 140
   Western feminists 203, 206, 207, 209
   Women's Liberation Movement 40, 43–5, 49
   Women's Studies group 211, 213, 219
Radway, Janice
   Smithton romances 143, 148, 150
rape 1–2, 14, 40, 52, 86
   condemnation of judgment 32
   Cookson novels 151
   Ireland 30, 31, 32
   within families 111
   within marriage 50, 75
Rape Crisis 47
reproduction 3, 55, 158–60, 165–9, 174–5
reproductive techniques 47, 55, 158–9, 169
Rights of Women 43, 50–7
Royal Commission 53

sadomasochism 15, 82, 85–7, 117
science 6, 184, 185–92
Scotland 11, 61–7
Scottish Council for Single Parents 63
second-wave feminism 43, 77
sexism 51, 52, 59
   equal opportunities 64–5
sexual abuse 27, 30, 31, 40
   children 52, 75, 109
   see also violence

sexuality 4–5, 11, 16, 22, 28
   biology 190–2
   Women's Liberation Movement 43, 44
   Women's Studies group 211, 213, 220
silence about violence 19–23, 27–8, 30
Sillitoe, Alan 128
single parents 1, 2, 41, 54, 55, 56, 63
   Up the Junction 138
Sinn Fein 21
sisterhood 6, 48–9, 55, 183, 198, 213, 220
slums 130, 136
soap operas 128, 143
Somalia 40, 56
Southall Black Sisters 55
Sprinkle, Annie 74, 94–7, 98–100, 102
subordination of women 48, 200
   eroticization 56, 82
   heterosexuality 73, 76, 82, 86, 88
support for women 1, 6, 51, 108, 184
   Women's Liberation Movement 43, 45–6
   Women's Studies group 212–14, 216, 218–21

therapy groups 215–16
Third World women 203, 206, 209
transsexuals 83, 85, 95, 100–2
transvestites 82, 85, 92–3

unemployment 18, 29
unions 52, 196
upper-class 110

violence 4–5, 13–34, 108, 110
   Cookson novels 124, 148, 151
   domestic 19, 32, 49, 50, 52
   Ireland 17–34
   queer heterosexuality 85
   racial 41
   Rights of Women 50, 51, 52
   sexual 1, 41, 46, 50, 52
   silence 19–23, 27–8, 30
   Women's Liberation Movement 46–7, 49
   see also rape; sexual abuse
virgin heterosexuality 73, 77–82, 83, 87–8

war 14–15, 81
   Ireland 11, 17–23, 28–9, 33
   Somalia 40
   former Yugoslavia 1–2, 40
wax anatomical models 169, 172–3
welfare issues 62, 64, 65
Western feminists 6, 184, 195–209
Western supremacists 208–9
Winchester 11–12, 41, 43–50

230

Index

white feminists 14, 43, 45
  see also race and racism
Women's Aid 47
Women's centres 46
Women's Council (Hungary) 196-7, 198-9, 200
women's health 3, 4, 30, 187, 188
  anatomy 158, 161, 177
Women's Interest Issues (WIIs) 59-67, 68-9
Women's Liberation Movement 2, 3, 40-57, 59
  Rights of Women 50-7
  science 184, 187
  Winchester 11-12, 41, 43-50
  Women's Studies 413, 47, 184
women's movements 183, 216
  Eastern Europe 197-200, 205
  Hungary 196, 197-200
  Ireland 21-3, 28, 29
  see also Women's Liberation Movement
women's refuges 3, 4

Women's Royal Voluntary Service (WRVS) 63
Women's Studies 2-4, 6, 11-12, 13, 47, 123
  academe 41-3, 183
  biology 190
  group work 211-21
  Rights of Women 56-7
  science 187
  Women's Liberation Movement 41-3, 47, 184
Woolf, Virginia 135
Workers' Education Association (WEA) 47
working class 44
  Cookson novels 124, 143-5, 148, 151-3
  Ireland 18, 20, 24
  Up the Junction 123-4, 128-31, 134-40
  see also class; middle class
working women 31, 44, 50, 52, 62-5
workplace nurseries 64

Yugoslavia (former) 1-2, 40, 56, 206

231